Debra J. Rasmussen
Diagnostics Quality Assurance

TOTAL QUALITY

HANDBOOK

THE
EXECUTIVE
GUIDE TO
THE NEW
WAY OF
DOING
BUSINESS

Compiled by
George Dixon
and Julie Swiler

Lakewood Books
50 S. Ninth Street
Minneapolis, MN 55402
(612) 333-0471

Editorial Coordinator: Julie Swiler
Production Editor: Helen Gillespie
Production Director: Pat Grawert

Third Printing

Lakewood Publications Inc. is a subsidiary of Maclean Hunter Publishing Company. Lakewood publishes TRAINING Magazine, the Training Directors' Forum Newsletter, Creative Training Techniques Newsletter, The Service Edge Newsletter, Total Quality Newsletter, Potentials In Marketing Magazine, Recreation Resources Magazine, and other business periodicals and books. James P. Secord, president, Mary Hanson, Philip G. Jones, Linda Klemstein, Michael C. Miller, Jerry C. Noack, vice presidents.

ISBN 0-943210-13-5

TABLE OF CONTENTS

INTRODUCTION

"In the new quality paradigm, we will shift our focus from seeing quality as something 'out there' to understanding it as something 'in here.' Quality will begin not as conformance to specifications, fitness for use, or even customer satisfaction. Quality will begin internally as a vision, as an awareness of a creative impulse to express values and ideals.... Quality will become the manifestation of human intellect and ability in its myriad forms. And we will know the quality product or service for what it truly is—the visible and tangible expression of human excellence."—C. Philip Alexander

We call this volume a handbook, but that perhaps is misleading. What we've done instead is compile some worthy recent articles that explore all the many facets of life in a quality-focused organization and group them into broad and logical categories. We hope the material will give you pause to ponder your own role in the quality phenomena and perhaps draw conclusions about how best to make quality happen—or keep it happening—in your organization. That's the same approach, by the way, we take in the *Total Quality Newsletter.*

Here's a a blow-by-blow description of what you can expect to find in this book:

Setting the Stage for Total Quality
What exactly is total quality? Here's one view. When Masaaki Imai was a young man in the 1950s, he worked for the Japan Productivity Center in Washington, D.C. His principal responsibility was escorting Japanese businessmen through U.S. manufacturing facilities to study "the secrets of American productivity."

For a lot of Americans, the tables, of course, have turned. What is the secret of Japan's world-beating success at producing innovative low cost, high quality products? As Imai explains, *kaizen,* or the all-embracing philosophy of continuous quality improvement, differs profoundly from many U.S. management and production practices. It reflects a "process-oriented" way of thinking, rather than the U.S. results-oriented approach. It accounts, Imai says, for the strengths of many Japanese organizations, and it's outlined here in a sometimes provocative and very compelling fashion.

Quality and People
C. Philip Alexander writes of a new wind blowing through the quality

profession, a wind bringing messages that may be hard to reconcile with our traditional understanding of quality. One of those messages we've already cited: "Quality...is the visible and tangible expression of human excellence."

If you take that message seriously, you may need to understand the distinctions between two types of quality assurance methodologies: The "hard" technologies of quality and the "soft" technologies.

Hard (meaning precise, analytical, measurable) technologies include the essential statistical and managerial control methods that underlie any functioning quality control system. After generations of being applied and refined, their benefits are fairly well understood, even if they haven't been universally adopted.

On the other hand, most organizations lag in their understanding of the soft (meaning emotional, subjective, variable) technologies of quality. Meanwhile, many observers are beginning to feel that the soft technologies of quality are really the ones that matter most. Alexander does a masterful job of showing how the hard and soft technologies of quality are intertwined, how both support the other, and how neglect of one reduces if not eliminates your chances for making meaningful quality improvements.

The theme is further explored by Roland Dumas, a well-known consultant associated with the Kaizen Institute. Dumas approaches quality from a human resources perspective and argues that human resources professionals are often the last to be consulted when quality is the issue, when instead they should be among the first. To Dumas, many organizations devote 80 percent of their quality-improvement efforts to perhaps 20 percent of the problem. This crippling misapplication stems from a failure to see what drives quality in the first place— managing and leading people with vision, intelligence, and a commitment to giving them the tools and support they need to make behavioral changes.

Ideas and Issues

Genichi Taguchi has become one of the most influential thinkers in Japan on quality due to ideas such as the one he outlines here. Quality losses result mainly from product failure after the sale, Taguchi says. Customers could care less about whether your company lived up to its "zero defects" creed and the product now in their possession left the factory in conformance to a narrow range of specifications. What matters to customers is if a product goes above and beyond what you've promised—how well it performs after it's been used, overused and even abused. That capability is expressed by Tauguchi's term "robust quality," which is a step beyond zero defects theory (if by that you mean parts, subcomponents and products are allowed to vary within set limits from a target ideal, which is what most U.S. companies shoot for). Trivial defects in the various parts of a product that in themselves may be in conformance to specifications have a way of interacting with each other in the field, says Taguchi. There they "stack up" to become major and expensive problems.

Taguchi's arguments may tax those of you with little involvement in factory production, but they represent a cutting-edge Japanese approach to quality that holds many valuable lessons for U.S. managers—and may show a few American managers how far they have to go before they catch up.

While Taguchi offers one very major reason why total quality fails, Lawrence Holpp, a senior consultant for Development Dimensions International, the Pittsburgh-based human resources and training consulting firm, offers ten of them. Both men approach the same issue from different perspectives—Taguchi's from the shop floor; Holpp's a bird's eye view of the entire organization. Holpp's culprits include self-serving, career-obsessed managers, turf-protecting work units, faddish training departments and the statistically aversive, who are found everywhere. While Taguchi is involved and fond of Zen-like paradoxes, Holpp is short and to the point. Both offer fairly unique commentary on the perils of thinking traditionally when it comes to quality.

Finally, an overview of the three men who have had perhaps the greatest impact on U.S. quality and their messages. If Deming, Juran and Crosby "are all trying to slay the same dragon, why split hairs over their differences?", asks writer Joe Oberle, a staff editor for *TRAINING* magazine. As he shows in discussions of companies that have fallen into the orbits of these three masters, the best method may be to match the guru with the needs of your organization—a careful process that requires a good deal of self-analysis.

Selected Systems

Motorola has become one of the most aggressive advocates of total quality on the U.S. corporate scene. And we do mean aggressive. The winner of the Malcolm Baldrige National Quality Award (see appendix), Motorola has told its suppliers that they, too, must apply for the award if they want to continue doing business with the giant electronics and telecommunications firm. The Baldrige application process is so rigorous that it's not something most companies can take lightly, and Motorola fully expects to drop a substantial number of companies from its acceptable supplier list.

Motorola isn't doing this out of arrogance. The company realizes that in order for it to meets its own quality goals, which are among the most ambitious in the world, it has to be absolutely assured that its suppliers measure up to the same standards it applies to itself.

U.S. automakers put similar pressure on their suppliers for much of the last decade. For example, the unlikely 1988 winner of the Malcolm Baldrige National Quality Award in the small business category, Globe Metallurgical, began its dramatic turnaround when it realized it was about to be dropped from Ford Motor's preferred vendor list. In a period of only three years, Globe went from a rather Dickensian foundry operation that was shut down by strikes almost as often as it was open to perhaps the best-run small industrial company in the nation. The same thing happened to Velcro, which you'll read about in the chapter on case studies.

But first, you'll read a few comments from quality professionals, including a quality engineer at Motorola, on how to set up smooth running supplier relationships. You'll also find some insights into a second major concern for most bigger organizations—managing staff functions to take their rightful role in a quality-focused environment. In this case, author Barbara J. Young argues for looking at staff functions as small businesses and adopting a similar marketplace perspective. She outlines a different and insightful way of thinking about internal operations, and says that since many staff functions face eroding "market share," it may be time to adopt such a view.

Case Studies

Finally, we end this whirlwind tour through some of the issues and ideas that compose today's total quality scene with visits to four companies that have actually put into practice what most U.S. companies are unfortunately still only preaching. When it comes to products, Florida Power and Light, Velcro USA, Motorola and Tennant Corporation have little in common. That is, except for one major factor—their products are best in their class, world class, in fact, and no matter what the vicissitudes of their respective markets, these companies will probably always be at the head of the pack in terms of profitability on return on investment.

Their unassailable positions didn't come about through luck and they weren't built over night. For all of these companies, the achievements came over a long haul, with numerous setbacks and surprises along the way. Their stories are told here, and there is much to learn from them. Most of the readers of this book will find themselves on similar paths at some point, or contemplating whether or not to take that big step. Here are some of the lessons America's most successful companies have learned about making the journey.

Maybe the biggest lesson, says Velcro's K. Theodor Krantz, is this: "In the search for quality, there's no such thing as good enough. There's never a finish line." There is, however, a starting line, and that's what this volume is all about.

THE RIGHT TOOLS FOR TOTAL QUALITY

ROBERT SCHWARZ

Total Quality has put together this volume to suggest ways to help you find the path to total quality for your organization. It won't be easy. Let's look at some of the reasons.

It has been my experience as a consultant to different organizations that total quality above all depends on the empowerment of employees. You must create an environment that is enjoyable and even fun to work in. People must receive continuous job satisfaction. They must feel that what they do matters. The ultimate aim of empowerment: creating an organization in which everyone strives to do things right the first time and everyone participates in problem solving and problem prevention.

A simple enough objective, but how do you accomplish it? Most organizations should start by looking at three basic areas: A Supporting Culture; Training; Rewards and Recognition.

Culture: Steal One if You Can

The philosophy that animates an organization is critical to success in a total quality environment. Total quality means that everyone works together to accomplish understood and accepted goals. Culture is the vehicle for conveying and reinforcing that spirit.

Acceptance of an organization's goals are fundamental. If employees don't accept those goals, if ownership is lacking, quality improvements simply won't happen. "No one ever washes a rented car," says writer Nancy Austin. Simple but apt: if employees do not believe or support goals and objectives, chances are they'll just ignore them.

Creating a culture that empowers employees doesn't have to be hard. All it really takes is a willingness to plagiarize the ideas of many (giving credit, of course, when credit is due). In fact, most organizations that have successfully defined and communicated a culture that supports total quality have drawn their ideas from all over the map.

Not surprisingly, many organizations develop mission statements or guidelines that incorporate the golden rules of recognized quality gurus—Deming's 14 points, Juran's 10 steps, Crosby's 14 steps and six absolutes, Conway's six tools, and so on. While some of these gentlemen may disagree on principles and procedures, their ideas, when distilled down to their essence, have a similar elegance and simplicity that fits in beautifully with developing a total quality culture. You sometimes may hear organizations tarred as "Deming lemmings" or "Crosby clowns," but those same organizations usually have a clear and directly communicated purpose, thanks to their willingness to latch on tenaciously to ideas that seem to make sense. Above all, they succeed largely because they are able to customize "off-the-shelf" ideas in ways that are uniquely meaningful and effective.

It has also become obvious to many that creating a culture that empowers employees requires an intensive team approach. In your planning stages for total quality initiatives, include teams with representatives from different levels and job functions in the organization. Union representatives, too, must be included in unionized environments. If substantially new and different types of behaviors are required, including those whose behavior must change in the strategic planning and goal-setting process is often essential. And make sure you give them the tools they need to thrive in a new total quality environment.

Carry the Right Tools, Speak the Right Language

It's hard to know which poses the greater challenge—selecting the right type of training or actually delivering it. In my experience, when management selects training without employee involvement, it's often perceived as just another announcement of yet another new training initiative. Management is frequently too remote from the real needs of employees to effectively choose training. Employees are rarely asked what they want or need, or how best they'd like to learn. Without employee involvement in the process, training tools may be selected that are ill-suited to begin with, poorly used and inadequately reinforced. The result is disappointment for both employees and management.

Luckily, many of the tools used in total quality involve precise methodologies for approaching solutions to quality problems. The benefits are obvious to everyone. Moreover, using total quality tools creates a communication process—a common language—that allows team members to effectively share their knowledge with others. This results in a synergistic approach to problem solving that often is the only way to achieve results. If management shares the same total quality language, problems and solutions are understood by all and action is facilitated.

One of the most powerful ways total quality tools enhance communication is through graphical representations of problems and proposed solutions. With SPC, work flow analysis, value analysis, cause and effect diagrams and so on, you can see problems and solutions, not just talk about them.

Maybe most important, and this is an area that is often misunderstood, total quality tools are not just limited to manufacturing environments. Increasingly, the tools of total quality, many of which derive from industrial engineering and the shop floor, are being adapted by service organizations to guarantee both internal and external customer satisfaction. Thus, it's important for professionals in all types of organizations to recognize their stake in understanding the principles of total quality. Most of all, many professionals in the decade ahead will discover a need to speak the language of total quality. That is, if they want to communicate with others in their organizations who seem to making things happen.

Love and Money
The final leg of empowering people to strive for total quality is also one of the most controversial. Some experts and consultants insist that employees should make the effort to achieve better quality, which often goes far beyond what they've been traditionally asked to do, without added compensation. Others feel cash rewards, sometimes substantial, are proper and effective. All agree some type of recognition system is needed.

One suggestion: Take a look at the pay structure in your organization. When salaries of some senior executives are typically 20 times greater than those of the lowest paid employee, you've obviously got a culture in which monetary rewards are expected. It's difficult to expect that a thank you will suffice for an idea or extra effort that may serve to expand the gap in salaries even further.

Handing out cash may be easy, but recognition is sometimes difficult for traditional American organizations. Recognition implies that top officials take the time to show appreciation for individual effort. But far too few top executives budget the time to regularly recognize and celebrate exemplary performers. That, however, is one of the easiest things to change as organization's re-orient themselves in total quality's direction.

Above all, the keys to reward and recognition systems are perceived fairness and fun. Few will take on the additional tasks that getting on and staying on the total quality path involves without some form of tangible and emotional payoff. Eventually, however, the increased job satisfaction and the excitement of being part of a total quality organization proves reward enough for many. The challenge is getting there.

Robert Schwarz is president of Total Quality Systems, a Twin Cities consulting and training firm. Much of this section on tools and techniques is adapted from materials for his Tools For A Quality Organization workshop, and from his book Midland City, Recovering Prosperity Through Quality *(Milwaukee, ASQC Quality Press, 1989).*

For more information contact: Total Quality Systems, 465 West Eagle Lake Drive, Maple Grove, MN 55369 (612) 591-0818, (612) 424-2260.

EAST MEETS WEST: A HIGHLY SELECTIVE GLOSSARY OF U.S. AND JAPANESE TOTAL QUALITY TOOLS, TERMS AND TECHNIQUES

CAUSE-AND-EFFECT DIAGRAM AND CARDS (CEDAC) Sometimes called an Ishikawa diagram, after Kaoru Ishikawa, a Japanese quality control guru; most often called a fishbone diagram due to its shape. First used in Japan in the 1940s, it provides simple and easily created pictorial relationships between the many possible causes of a given effect or problem. The diagram is part of a process that involves group brainstorming to create a consensus on causes and the urgency and methods of pursuing solutions.

In recent years Ryuji Fukuda has developed an effective adaptation of the cause-effect diagram. First, a team develops a diagram identifying all causes they can think of regarding a problem they share. The resulting diagram is placed in the work area and team members (or passersby) are encouraged to use cards to add more possible causes to the diagram. They date and sign cards as they are added. The team meets weekly, reviews additions, and reestablishes its action plan for analysis, collection of data, or other tasks leading to a decision on corrective action.

The benefit of CEDAC is that it remains a living and growing process. CEDAC also encourages input from persons not on the team and stimulates team members to keep working on the problem until it is solved.

See *Guide to Quality Control,* Kaoru Ishikawa (Tokyo: Asian Productivity Organization, 1976). *The Principles of Managerial Engineering,* Ryuji Fukuda (Cambridge MA: Productivity Press).

CHECK POINTS AND CONTROL POINTS In many Japanese total quality control management systems, a series of benchmarks are used in measuring quality improvement efforts across managerial levels. Check points are "process-oriented" criteria (see chapters by Masaaki Imai in this book). Control points represent "results-oriented" criteria. The check point to one manager becomes the control point to the manager one step up the corporate hierarchy. The set-up is used in total quality policy deployment, or the process of implementing a clear and structured total quality program directly through line managers and supervisors and indirectly through cross-functional links within the organization.

WILLIAM E. CONWAY Sometimes called a "Deming Disciple," Conway was president of Nashua Corporation, a computer diskette maker, when he hired W. Edwards Deming to help improve the company's quality in 1979. That led to a long-term relationship, and in 1983 Conway founded his own company, Conway Quality, Inc., to promote his own interpretation of the Deming philosophy. Conway declines to define the meaning of quality and instead speaks of quality management, which he calls the "development, manufacturing, administration, and distribution of consistent low cost products and services that customers want and/or need."

To achieve quality management, Conway says organizations should focus on six tools:

1. *Human relation skills*—the responsibility of management to create at every level, among all employees, the motivation and training to make the necessary improvements in the organization.

2. *Statistical surveys*—the gathering of data about external and internal customers, employees, technology and equipment, to be used as a measure for future progress and to identify immediate quality improvement needs.

3. *Simple statistical techniques*—clear charts and diagrams that help identify problems, track work flow, gauge progress and indicate solutions.

4. *Statistical process control* (see below).

5. *"Imagineering"*—a key concept in problem solving that involves the visualization of a process, procedure or operation with all waste eliminated.

6. *Industrial engineering*—common techniques of pacing, work simplification, methods analysis, plant layout and material handling to achieve improvements.

Contact: Conway Quality, Inc., 15 Trafalgar Square, Nashua, NH 03063 (800) 359-0099.

COST OF QUALITY One definition comes from Philip Crosby in *Quality Is Free*. He defines it as the total of expenditures devoted to preventing errors and correcting errors.

Preventing errors includes inspection of products, checking manuscripts, auditing accounts and taking inventories. Correcting errors includes costs of redoing a task, scrap, salvage, returning products to a supplier, the wrong merchandise for a sale and many others.

A lot of data indicates that most businesses, whether service or manufacturing, incur costs for prevention and correction of errors in excess of 20 percent of sales. A cost of errors of 40 percent of sales is not unusual. Since quality initiatives can substantially reduce those percentages and the costs of quality initiatives are dwarfed by resulting savings, Crosby concludes, in effect, that "quality is free."

To further expand on Crosby's and similar arguments, all work done by an organization can be attributed to three areas: prevention, failure or the work done in conducting normal business.

The cost of quality can be computed by estimating how work done by individuals and work units is divided into those three categories. The objective is to eliminate costs of failure by spending more on prevention. This usually requires a heavy up front cost for training and facilities. As the organization matures, the prevention costs diminish, but a significant rise in the costs of doing business may result. But in the next step, accounting systems are changed to reflect the real costs of quality (or, if you prefer, the cost of non-quality). Much of what is lumped under general and administrative overhead then is seen as the cost of errors and the cost of prevention.

PHILIP B. CROSBY Philip Crosby was the first to speak in terms of zero defects while at Martin Corporation in the 1960s, where he was in charge of quality assurance for the Pershing missile project. Later he became director of quality at ITT, and in 1979, established Philip Crosby Associates to promote his ideas. While perhaps not as dogmatic as other quality gurus, he has strong, appealingly simple ideas, one being a definition of quality as conformance to requirements. The cost of quality, Crosby says, can only be measured by the cost of non-conformance, a figure that most organizations must compute before they can understand the economic and marketplace impact of quality.

Crosby's 1979 book, *Quality is Free,* has sold over a million copies and was influential at numerous American companies during the 1980s. In addition Crosby's "Quality College," one of many programs offered by his firm, has become a popular method of initiating quality improvement efforts and is a favorite of many CEOs and senior executives. In *Quality is Free,* Crosby identifies an agenda of 14 action points that have become indelibly linked with his philosophy.

1. Make it clear that management is committed to quality.

2. Form quality improvement teams with representatives from each department.

3. Determine where current and potential quality problems lie.

4. Evaluate the cost of quality and explain its use as a management tool.

5. Raise the quality awareness and personal concern of all employees.

6. Take actions to correct problems identified through previous steps.

7. Establish an ad hoc committee for the zero defects program.

8. Train supervisors to actively carry out their part of the quality improvement program.

9. Hold a "Zero Defects" day to let all employees realize there has

been a change.

10. Encourage individuals to establish improvement goals for themselves and their groups.

11. Encourage employees to communicate to management the obstacles they face in attaining their improvement goals.

12. Recognize and appreciate those who participate.

13. Establish quality councils to communicate on a regular basis.

14. Do it all over again to emphasize that the quality improvement program never ends.

Contact: Philip Crosby Associates, Inc., 807 W. Morse Blvd., Winter Park, FL 32790 (407) 645-1733.

CROSS-FUNCTIONAL MANAGEMENT In the Japanese management sense, the interdepartmental coordination required to realize the policy goals of a total quality control system. After corporate strategic plans are determined, senior managers set objectives for cross-functional efforts that cut laterally throughout the organization. Cross-functional management is considered a major organizational tool for realizing total quality improvements, and in Japan at least it is a highly articulated system. It bears many similarities to Western management techniques, but is often distinguished by an intensive focus on tracking of goals and measures and extensive follow-through. See *Kaizen.*

W. EDWARDS DEMING A pioneer in modern applications of statistical process control and almost a cult figure at many U.S. and Japanese organizations. He is perhaps best known for lighting a fire beneath the Japanese manufacturing sector in the 1950s, when he lectured on statistical process control to Japanese business leaders and told them they could take over the world if they followed his advice. For the most part they did, although most Japanese companies have advanced far beyond Deming's original ideas. The Deming Prize is perhaps the most prestigious Japanese business award.

Deming's basic philosophy is that quality doesn't necessarily mean high quality. It means a consistent and predictable uniformity (assured through statistical process control), at a low cost, that meets whatever particular needs and wants customers have. Hence quality must be defined in customer terms and it requires continual customer research.

Unlike other quality gurus, Deming has not surrounded himself with an organization, although several organized groups fervently promote his ideas. His philosophy is encapsulated in a famous series of 14 points for management:

1. Create constancy of purpose toward improvement of product and service.

2. Adopt the new philosophy. We can no longer live with

commonly accepted levels of delays, mistakes, defective materials and defective workmanship.

3. Cease dependence on mass inspection. Require, instead, statistical evidence that quality is built in.

4. End the practice of awarding business on the basis of a price tag.

5. Find problems. It is management's job to continually work on the system.

6. Institute modern methods of training on the job.

7. Institute modern methods of supervision of production workers. The responsibility of foremen must be changed from numbers to quality.

8. Drive out fear, so that everyone may work for the company.

9. Break down barriers between departments.

10. Eliminate numerical goals, posters, and slogans asking for new levels of productivity without providing methods.

11. Eliminate work standards that prescribe numerical quotas.

12. Remove barriers that stand between the hourly worker and his right to pride of workmanship.

13. Institute a vigorous program of education and retraining.

14. Create a structure in top management that will push every day on the above 13 points.

DESIGN OF EXPERIMENTS A term for a complex group problem solving tool. Also called fractional factorial statistics. Experimental design originated in agricultural research in England as a method to reduce the number of growing seasons needed to select desirable combinations of seed characteristics. It has been adapted for industrial use to provide a statistical method of problem solving that reduces the need to prototype products with combinations of variables under different conditions, which, without experimental design, could involve sometimes thousands of trial runs.

GAIN SHARING A process that shares some portion of the savings created by a change or improvement in how business is conducted. Suggestion systems can be a form of gain sharing when individuals or teams are rewarded for savings they instigate. Gain-sharing formulas, however, are usually more liberal than suggestion system awards.

HAWTHORNE EFFECT Draws its name from the Hawthorne Works of Western Electric Company in Cicero, Illinois, where between 1927 and 1932 Harvard Business School professor Elton Mayo conducted a series of experiments to determine the impact of various physical conditions, such as lighting and humidity, on productivity. With some worker groups, Mayo made frequent changes in conditions and always discussed and explained the changes in advance with them. Mayo found that productivity temporarily increased virtually whenever changes were made and that it appeared to be independent of the changes themselves. He attributed the rise to the increased attention workers felt was being paid to them and their feelings of involvement in decisions about their roles and job satisfaction.

Today, the Hawthorne Effect is generally used to describe the increase in performance that follows any change, especially performance increases that prove temporary. We included it here because it can sometimes accompany poorly-planned quality initiatives, which often achieve early but only temporary successes due to the lack of provisions for continual reinforcement and support.

IMPROVEMENT TEAMS In a broad sense, an improvement team is any group-based approach to attacking specific opportunities for improvement. Teams may be established on an ongoing basis or on a periodic, project-related basis. Common forms of teams include:

Work-Unit Teams—A group within a given work unit.

Cross-Functional Teams—With various departments or functions represented.

Business Unit Teams—Organized around product lines or markets, these groups deal with marketplace or product-specific issues.

Horizon Teams—These groups address long-term planning issues.

Typical terms used for variations of improvement teams include quality circles, productivity teams, cost-reduction teams, Deming teams, Juran teams, zero defect teams, process control/management teams, task teams, value engineering teams, quality teams, corrective action teams and numerous others.

Many organizations do not label their improvement teams. Other organizations choose unique titles that usually form memorable acronyms—PACE (People Achieving Excellence), PRIDE (Professional Results In Daily Efforts), IMPACT (Innovative Minds Pursuing Active Challenges Together) and countless others.

INPUT/OUTPUT ANALYSIS A process for evaluating the performance of a function. The process allows review of each department or group in an organization by collecting and identifying all of the inputs to the department or group along with outputs and their destinations. A team composed of representatives of all departments can then determine where duplication or voids exist.

JOSEPH M. JURAN Deming's rival for title of America's most influential total quality expert, and like Deming, a hugely respected figure in Japan. Studied electrical engineering and law. Was chief of the inspection control division of Western Electric before joining the faculty of New York University. In the 1940s, Juran was one of the first to argue that the technical aspects of quality were well-established and easy to understand; most companies, however, did not know how to manage for quality and did not understand or appreciate the human factors involved. At the time, he argued that 80 percent of most quality problems were due to management. Lectured in Japan in 1954 and help revolutionize Japanese manufacturing.

Today, Juran advocates quality training for everyone (from the CEO on down), quality circles and statistical tools (as long as they don't lead to a "tool-oriented" approach). He does not believe that "quality is free." Rather, there is an optimum point for quality, beyond which further efforts are more costly than any value obtained. Juran also believes that quality improvements are better approached on a project basis rather than an overall organizational basis.

According to Juran, there are two kinds of quality: "fitness for use" and "conformance to specifications," which sometimes conflict. (A product can confirm to specifications but not be fit for use.) His philosophy is encapsulated in a famous series of 10 steps to quality improvement.

1. Build awareness of the need and opportunity for improvement.
2. Set goals for improvement.
3. Organize to reach the goals (establish a quality council, identify problems, select projects, appoint teams, designated facilitators).
4. Provide training.
5. Carry out projects to solve problems.
6. Report progress.
7. Give recognition.
8. Communicate results.
9. Keep score.
10. Maintain momentum by making annual improvement part of the regular systems and processes of the company.

In 1979, he founded the Juran Institute, which teaches a project-by-project, problem-solving, team-method approach to quality in which upper management is involved. The Institute sponsors numerous public seminars and publishes prolifically. Contact: Juran Institute, Inc., 11 River Road, Wilton, CT 06897-0811. (800) 338-7726.

JUST-IN-TIME (JIT) A process or concept of manufacturing developed by Toyota. All materials arrive at a production site just in time for use. Stockpiles and large inventories are eliminated.

JIT requires significant changes in many aspects of production. Suppliers must be certified to perform in a just-in-time environment; their products must be acceptable for use without inspection and delivered at precise times. Machinery must be set up so small lots can be manufactured flexibly, even when changeover time is dramatically reduced. Employees must be trained in statistical process control and must assume responsibility for achieving specified quality levels for any part or service they provide internal "customers."

The benefits of JIT are significant and it became firmly entrenched among many American companies during the 1980s. Benefits include:
- Reduced work in progress.
- Reduced salvage or scrap when a fault is identified.
- Quick identification of faulty product at the next operation in the manufacturing process, often within minutes.
- Reduced inventory costs.
- Shorter changeover times.

Moreover, JIT implies an "attitude" that seems to be a natural part of total quality environments. It forces individuals to think in terms of high quality and maximum efficiency. It affects not only products, but many internal services as well. There are several important other processes that attend JIT, most pioneered by Japanese companies. When JIT has proven a failure in American companies, it has often been because it was attempted in isolation as a panacea and not as one component of an integrated system.

See *Kanban: Just in Time at Toyota,* Japan Management Association (Cambridge, MA: Productivity Press, 1986); *Japanese Manufacturing Techniques,* Richard J. Schornberger. New York: Free Press, 1982).

KAIZEN Japanese term frequently used to express the systematic approach to continual quality improvement successfully practiced by many Japanese companies. (See the first two chapters in this book.)

KAMBAN (or Kanban) An essential element in the visible management techniques necessary to such advanced total quality concepts as just-in-time manufacturing and inventory control. One of many such techniques developed by Taiichi Ohno for Toyota. A kamban is a signboard attached to specific parts in the production line signifying the delivery of a given quantity. When the parts have all been used, the kamban is returned to its origin, where it becomes an order for more parts. One of a number of elements in a fully integrated total quality control system that cannot be used in isolation.

MALCOLM BALDRIGE NATIONAL QUALITY AWARD Created by Public Law 100-107 passed by the U.S. Congress in 1987, the award is given annually to U.S. companies that excel in quality achievement and quality management. It has quickly become perhaps the most prestigious and sought-after mark of recognition in corporate America, similar to the effects of the Deming Prize on Japanese companies. Among the findings in Public Law 100-107 that provided impetus for the award:

"Strategic planning for quality and quality improvement programs, through a commitment to excellence in manufacturing and service, is becoming more and more essential to the well-being of our Nation's economy and our ability to compete effectively in the global economy."

One Baldrige (a former U.S. Secretary of Commerce) award is supposed to be given in each of three categories—manufacturing companies or subsidiaries, service companies or subsidiaries and small businesses—although in the first two years of the program no award was given to a service organization. The award is administered by the National Institute of Standards and Technology of the U.S. Department of Commerce, and managed by The Malcolm Baldrige National Quality Award Consortium, Inc. Approximately 150 quality experts from business, professional and trade organizations, accrediting bodies, universities and government are selected through an application process to review submissions. Winners during 1988 and 1989 included Motorola, Inc. (1988), the Commercial Nuclear Fuel Division of Westinghouse Electric Corporation (1988), Globe Metallurgical, Inc. (1988), Milliken & Company (1989) and Xerox Corporation's Business Products and Systems (1989).

The significance of the program is not the award itself, but the effects it has had on quality improvement efforts in the U.S. In fact, judging criteria are so strict and require so much evidence of measurable and long-term, organization-wide commitments to quality improvements that few U.S. companies currently stand a chance of winning the award. While 77,000 copies of the examination guidelines (which include over 150 items) were requested by U.S. companies in 1988 and 1989, for example, only 106 companies felt advanced enough to apply. And several winners spent many hundreds of thousands of dollars gathering supporting material to augment their submissions.

Instead, the Baldrige award has become so prominent in American quality efforts because it produced for the first time what many feel is a working and realistic definition of total quality management from a uniquely American perspective. Baldrige guidelines quickly met with a consensus approval from a broad cross-section of businesses. Moreover, the examination guidelines themselves have been adopted by hundreds of companies as a way to benchmark their efforts against objective standards, and have provided a starting point for many companies embarking on total quality initiatives. Also, one winner (Motorola) has begun to require suppliers to apply for the award as a condition of continued business. Other companies have announced similar intentions. For those reasons, the influence of the award is expected to grow dramatically during the 1990s.

See Appendix for Malcolm Baldrige National Quality Award examination criteria.

Contact for information or guidelines: Malcolm Baldrige National Quality Award Office, National Institute of Standards and Technology, Gaithersburg, MD 20899. (301) 975-2036.

NOMINAL GROUP TECHNIQUES Refers to various group problem-solving processes, or structured forms of brainstorming, with several unique features. Everyone in the group is part of the discussion and decisions. Everyone in the group is equal from the standpoint of sharing their ideas. The results when applied to quality problems often stand a high chance of being successful. Nominal group techniques work especially well with task teams and quality circles. See *Group Techniques for Program Planning: A Guide to Nominal and Delphi Processes,* Delbecq Van DeVan (Glenview, IL: Scott, Foresman and Co., 1975).

PARTICIPATIVE GOAL SETTING Participative goal setting occurs when employees and managers jointly set employee performance goals and regularly monitor progress toward attaining them. Because the employee participates in setting these goals and is in agreement with them, he or she usually feels added responsibility for achieving the objectives and is generally more self-motivated.

Theoretically, performance should improve because the employee has an emotional investment in the process and feels some control over his or her situation. Participative goal setting is often part of a management by objective (MBO) system.

PERFORMANCE MANAGEMENT Term used by Aubrey Daniels for a process of employee management by reward and recognition. Daniels feels that management must create positive and predictable behavior and consequence relationships. Employees must be able to anticipate consequences.

POKA-YOKE A process often fundamental to successful JIT systems, long advocated by Shingo Shiego, who taught production engineering to a generation of Toyota engineers. Poka-yoke, a Japanese term meaning "mistake proofing" is a philosophy that encourages the use of low-cost, in-process quality control mechanisms and routines that essentially incorporate 100 percent inspection at the source of quality problems. Many poka-yoke ideas are familiar and simple and in effect build the function of a checklist into an operation. Shingo believed that systems rather than human operators were usually responsible for errors. Poka-yoke mechanisms are related to jidohka, or autonoma-tion—the concept of low cost "smart" machines that stop automatically when a process is completed or an error occurs. Developed cooperatively by engineers and shop floor employees, Poka-yoke mechanisms are one of the fruits of the Japanese mania for suggestion systems and represent a cornerstone of Japanese success in continuous production improvements.

See *Zero Quality Control: Source Inspection and the Poka-Yoke System,* Shiego Shingo (Cambridge, MA: Productivity Press, 1986).

QUALITY There are numerous definitions of quality: conformance to specifications; fitness for use; meeting customer expectations. In Japan, quality often means "anything that can be improved," a seeming paradox that underlies the quest for continuous quality improvement. See Organization-Wide Quality Problems in this book for a discussion of placing operational definitions of quality on a hierarchy that ranges from "extra features" (a product is defined as having quality if it has enough extra features to differentiate it from competing products) to product or service quality that develops customers by educating them and exposing them to features and services that enhance the value of the product to them. In an organization sense, recent definitions of quality have dealt with systems and people as well as product and services; here quality assumes an internal dimension that ultimately produces marketplace differentiation.

QUALITY CONTROL Once it meant inspecting finished products for defects. Now it has a broader meaning that runs through all aspects of producing products and services, from conceptualization and design to manufacturing and delivery, to management and administration. Quality control is also now a major concern in vendor and supplier relationships. With just-in-time techniques becoming more popular, many companies must now take an active role in the quality control efforts of those whose products and services they buy. This is leading to dramatically different business-to-business relationships in many industries.

In Japan, while QC is almost synonymous with kaizen, it's focused on applying well-defined tools, such as the "seven statistical tools" and the "seven new tools" to producing products and services. Officially, or at least according to Japanese Industrial Standards, quality control is a "system of means to economically produce goods or services that satisfy customer requirements."

QUALITY DEPLOYMENT A new frontier of quality which is expected to become very important in the 1990s. Widely practice in Japan. This description is from Kaizen: "A technique to deploy customer requirements (known as 'true quality characteristics') into design characteristics (known as 'counterpart characteristics') and deploy them into such systems as components, parts, and production process." Quality deployment is regarded as one of the most significant developments to come out of the TQC (Total Quality Control) movement in Japan in recent decades.

QUALITY OF WORK LIFE (QWL) Increasingly, the emotional, physical and financial satisfaction organizations provide employees is seen as a key contributor to the quality of its products and services. Quality of work life (QWL) refers to those organized and informal elements that motivate human resources to support organizational goals and in turn lead to quality performance. Commonly recognized elements in organizations with a high QWL include: 1. Autonomy, flexibility, and control; 2. Recognition and visibility; 3. Membership and belonging.

QWL does not imply that employees have complete control, nor does it necessarily mean having a voice in decisions remote from daily activities. There are many ways of thinking about QWL. Jerome M. Rosow of the Work in America Institute has compiled numerous elements that are thought to affect QWL into a ten-part framework:

1. *Adequate and fair pay.* Pay is linked to responsibilities. Pay is consistent between occupations and across organizational lines and is competitive with the external labor market of the community and the industry.

2. *Benefits.* A firm provides an adequate employee benefit package that reflects prevailing practice. The employee and the employee's family are protected against the effects of illness, accidents, old age, and death in conjunction with benefits provided by state and federal law. In addition, employees receive time for rest and renewal through holidays, vacations, and opportunities for educational leave.

3. *A safe and healthy environment.* Employees work in conditions that are reasonably safe and that do not unduly endanger the health and safety of the workers or the workers' families. This environment should meet minimum national standards and, in addition, minimize risk to individual workers in regard to its own unique condition.

4. *Job security.* Employment should provide for continuity so that the employee is reasonably secure about the future. The company should recognize past service and performance and have formal rules and policies regarding layoffs, retention, and removal. These policies should not place the entire burden and cost of change on the worker. The company should provide opportunities for retraining, reassignment, and transfer in lieu of separations, and an early warning system should be in place to alert workers of economic changes in the organization.

5. *Free collective bargaining.* Employees should have the right to organize in unions, professional associations, or any other organizations that represent employees as a group. The employee should also have the right to refrain from such memberships.

6. *Growth and development.* Personnel systems should recognize

individual employees as growing, developing human assets, and companies should provide opportunities for employees to compete for training, development, recognition, and promotion. Clear career paths should provide for upward mobility, professional growth, and advancement, and programs that prevent career obsolescence should help employees keep pace with the organization.

7. *Social integration.* The work place should encourage openness, a sense of community, freedom from prejudice, and personal equality.

8. *Participation.* Employee participation should be linked to the organization's productive goals.

9. *Democracy at work.* The organization is a total society in microcosm, and employees deserve rights and privileges compatible with their voluntary membership in the organization. These rights include free speech, privacy, dissent, fair and equitable treatment, and due process.

10. *Total life space.* The work place should be a positive force for itself and for the other people and institutions affected by it. Work should be a balanced part of the entire lifestyle; work schedules, travel demands, and career pressures should balance reasonably well with the needs and responsibilities for family, leisure, recreation, and self-renewal.

SEVEN STATISTICAL TOOLS In Japan, the basic statistical tools used in problem solving by quality circles and other small groups as well as by engineers and managers. Also widely used by U.S. companies in a process more likely to be called "brainstorming." They are pareto diagrams, cause-and-effect diagrams, histograms, control charts, scatter diagrams, graphs and checksheets.

SEVEN NEW TOOLS A newer set of problem-solving tools designed to bring the same rigorous approach to more complex problem-solving situations encountered in quality deployment and other broad quality efforts. In these cases, data may not be available, may be subjective or may be expressed in informal language and not statistical or mathematical form. Also, in collaborative efforts involving several departments, not all participants may be speak the same "language." In Japan, applications for the seven new tools range from research and development to new product development to sales management. According to Masaaki Imai in *Kaizen,* the seven new tools go beyond the analytical approach of the original seven and represent a "design approach" to problem solving.

Some feel the new seven allow managers to plan wide-ranging and detailed total quality objectives for entire organizations. The seven new tools are relations diagrams, affinity diagrams, tree diagrams, matrix diagrams, matrix data-analysis diagrams, PDPC (Process Decision Program Chart) and arrow diagrams (often used PERT [Program Evaluation and Review Technique] and CPM [Critical Path Method]).

See *Management for Quality Improvement: The 7 New QC Tools,* Mizuna Shigeru, ed. (Cambridge, MA: Productivity Press, Inc.)

SINGLE MINUTE EXCHANGE OF "DIES" (SMED) A concept fundamental to successful JIT-style production. Dies refers to its original use as a method of quickly reconfiguring machine tools to produce different products, but the method now has wide industrial applications. It was pioneered by Shiego Shingo for Toyota and saves as much as 90 percent of the time traditionally spent during the changeover period from one product to another. Rapid changeovers make production of small product runs possible and support the concept of stockless production.

See *A Revolution in Manufacturing, the SMED System,* Shigeo Shingo (Cambridge, MA: Productivity Press, 1985).

STATISTICAL PROCESS CONTROL (SPC) The use of statistical methods to track process variance (changes) in products, parts or subcomponents to predict the capability of a process to meet specifications. Methods range from simple to complex. Most organizations can effect quality improvements using simple techniques, and thousands in the U.S. have. The objective of SPC is to check and control the quality of products at various stages in the production path. SPC helps eliminate the need for inspection and makes actual producers responsible for quality. The motto of most SPC advocates: "Get it right the first time."

The following description comes from *TRAINING* magazine:

"A simple explanation for statistical process control.... First, you have to understand that in every process there is random variation from the ideal—and you can never eliminate all the variation to achieve constant perfection. But if a process is stable and under control, that variation will occur within certain narrow limits. In each process, variations usually will be functions of three factors: materials, operators and machinery.

"So when an engineer is designing a process, he will examine each step of it and establish mathematical limits of good performance for each step. The limits are designed to eliminate as much variation as is mechanically and humanly possible. The product is allowed to vary within those limits. For instance, say a piece of paper ideally should measure eight by ten inches. A technician checks a representative piece and finds that it actually measures 7.99 inches by 10.09 inches. Each time the process is measured, the technician places a dot along a chart that contains the upper and lower limits of variation you've decided to tolerate. Whenever the dots form a pattern that indicates the variation is moving out of control, the process needs to be adjusted.... If a dot falls outside the range, the process should be shut down until it's tinkered back into control."

SPC has long been a staple of U.S. industrial engineering and a vital part of war material manufacture in the '40s. One of its biggest advocates, Deming, introduced it to the Japanese in the 1950s where it was enthusiastically embraced as a way out of a chronic poor product quality morass. Many feel SPC can be applied not just to production and assembly process, but to any process that involves set routines and tolerances—from typing letters to processing insurance claims.

There may be hundreds of SPC vendors in the U.S. Personal computers and computer work stations are increasingly used as a way to track SPC applications, and SPC software applications have proliferated. Thousands of employees receive SPC training each year. See *Quality, Quality Progress* and other quality publications for sources of SPC training and information.

TOTAL QUALITY CONTROL A concept that causes all employees to be involved in creating a quality product. Product is defined as what you produce and pass to another person (whether it be a thing or a service). This means everyone within an organization monitors the quality of what they produce and actively attempts to achieve zero defects (memos, designs, parts, etc.).

The process makes everyone responsible for the quality of their work. Contrasting processes, most losing credibility, use a quality control function to find errors (detection) and help identify methods for prevention. In a total quality system, the need for such a function is drastically reduced and often eliminated. Total quality control, while simple enough in theory, requires a major change in the attitudes, responsibilities and ownership of all employees. Results include large reductions in errors and major savings in labor and material. Ultimately, total quality control is assumed to lead to increased customer satisfaction.

See *Japanese Manufacturing Techniques,* Richard J. Schoenberger (New York: Free Press, 1882); and *What Is Total Quality Control?*, Kaoru Ishikawa, translated by David J. Lu (Englewood Cliffs, N.J.: Prentice Hall, Inc., 1985).

VISIBLE MANAGEMENT An element of Japanese production management becoming increasingly popular in the U.S. Refers to a variety of often simple methods to provide information about production processes and job requirements in a clearly visible manner. (See Kamban.) The objective is to maximize productivity and minimize production delays due to quality problems, which are identified and fixed quickly in a visible management system.

I

SETTING THE STAGE FOR TOTAL QUALITY

KAIZEN, THE CONCEPT

From *Kaizen, The Key to Japan's Competitive Success*

MASAAKI IMAI

KAIZEN VALUES

Back in the 1950s, I was working with the Japan Productivity Center in Washington, D.C. My job mainly consisted of escorting groups of Japanese businessmen who were visiting American companies to study "the secret of American industrial productivity."

Toshiro Yamada, now Professor Emeritus of the Faculty of Engineering at Kyoto University, was a member of one such study team visiting the United States to study the industrial-vehicle industry. Recently, the members of his team gathered to celebrate the silver anniversary of their trip.

At the banquet table, Yamada said he had recently been back to the United States in a "sentimental journey" to some of the plants he had visited, among them the River Rouge steelworks in Dearborn, Michigan. Shaking his head in disbelief, he said, "You know, the plant was exactly the same as it had been 25 years ago."

He also spoke of his recent visit to Europe, where he had led a group of businessmen on a study of European tile-manufacturing plants. As they roamed from one plant to another, the group members became increasingly restless and dismayed at the "archaic" facilities.

The group was surprised to find that these plants were still using belt conveyors, and that not only the workers but even visitors had to walk over or under them, indicating a general lack of safety precautions. One member said, "There is no management if they don't care about the workers' safety." It is rather rare to see belt conveyors in modern Japan. Even if they are still used, they are designed so that people do not have to walk over or under them.

In spite of these observations, Yamada also noted that he had found the facilities at Western universities and research institutions far more advanced, and Western research projects rich in originality and creativity.

I was recently traveling in the United States with Fujio Umibe, chief specialist at Toshiba's Research and Development Center. Umibe told me of a recent encounter with a co-worker from one of Toshiba's outlying plants in Japan. Upon hearing that Umibe had not set foot in the plant for over ten years, the man chided him: "You really should come out and see the plant. You won't recognize it today!" By way of substantiation, I have been told that a quarter of the production lines at one Toshiba plant were changed while the plant was shut down for the week-long summer holiday in 1984.

These conversations set me to thinking about the great differences in the ways Japanese and Western managers approach their work. It is inconceivable that a Japanese plant would remain virtually unchanged for over a quarter of a century.

I had long been looking for a key concept to explain these two very different management approaches, one that might also help explain why many Japanese companies have come to gain their increasingly conspicuous competitive edge. For instance, how do we explain the fact that while most new ideas come from the West and some of the most advanced plants, institutions, and technologies are found there, there are also many plants there that have changed little since the 1950s?

Change is something which everybody takes for granted. Recently, an American executive at a large multinational firm told me his company chairman had said at the start of an executive committee meeting: "Gentlemen, our job is to manage change. If we fail, we must change management." The executive smiled and said, "We all got the message!"

In Japan, change is a way of life, too. But are we talking about the same change when we talk about managing change or else changing management? It dawned on me that there might be different kinds of change: gradual and abrupt. While we can easily observe both gradual and abrupt changes in Japan, gradual change is not so obvious a part of the Western way of life. How are we to explain this difference?

This question led me to consider the question of values. Could it be that differences between the value systems in Japan and the West account for their different attitudes toward gradual change and abrupt change? Abrupt changes are easily grasped by everyone concerned, and people are usually elated to see them. This is generally true in both Japan and the West. Yet what about the gradual changes? My earlier statement that it is inconceivable that a Japanese plant would remain unchanged for years refers to gradual change as well as abrupt change.

Thinking all this over, I came to the conclusion that the key difference between how change is understood in Japan and how it is viewed in the West lies in the Kaizen concept—a concept that is so natural and obvious to many Japanese managers that they often do not even realize that they possess it! The Kaizen concept explains why companies cannot remain the same for long in Japan. Moreover, after many years of studying Western business practices, I have reached the conclusion that this Kaizen concept is nonexistent, or at least very weak, in most Western companies today. Worse yet, they reject it without knowing what it really entails. It's the old "not invented here" syndrome. And this lack of Kaizen helps explain why an American or European factory can remain exactly the same for a quarter of a century.

The essence of Kaizen is simple and straightforward: Kaizen means improvement. Moreover, Kaizen means ongoing improvement involving everyone, including both managers and workers. The Kaizen philosophy assumes that our way of life be it our working life, our social life, or our home life deserves to be constantly improved.

In trying to understand Japan's postwar "economic miracle," scholars, journalists, and businesspeople alike have dutifully studied such factors as the productivity movement, total quality control (TQC), small-group activities, the suggestion system, automation, industrial robots, and labor relations. They have given much attention to some of Japan's unique management practices, among them the lifetime employment system, seniority-based wages, and enterprise unions. Yet I feel they have failed to grasp the very simple truth that lies behind the many myths concerning Japanese management.

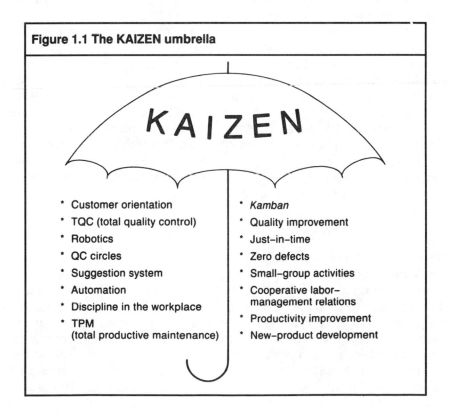

Figure 1.1 The KAIZEN umbrella

KAIZEN

* Customer orientation
* TQC (total quality control)
* Robotics
* QC circles
* Suggestion system
* Automation
* Discipline in the workplace
* TPM (total productive maintenance)

* *Kamban*
* Quality improvement
* Just–in–time
* Zero defects
* Small–group activities
* Cooperative labor-management relations
* Productivity improvement
* New–product development

The essence of most "uniquely Japanese" management practices—be they productivity improvement, TQC (Total Quality Control) activities, QC (Quality Control) circles, or labor relations can be reduced to one word: Kaizen. Using the term Kaizen in place of such words as productivity, TQC, ZD (Zero Defects), Kamban,[1] and the suggestion system paints a far clearer picture of what has been going on in Japanese industry. Kaizen is an umbrella concept covering most of those "uniquely Japanese" practices that have recently achieved such worldwide fame. (See Figure 1.1.)

The implications of TQC or CWQC (Company-Wide Quality Control) in Japan have been that these concepts have helped Japanese companies generate a *process-oriented* way of thinking and develop strategies that assure continuous improvement involving people at all levels of the organizational hierarchy. The message of the Kaizen strategy is that not a day should go by without some kind of improvement being made somewhere in the company.

The belief that there should be unending improvement is deeply ingrained in the Japanese mentality. As the old Japanese saying goes, "If a man has not been seen for three days, his friends should take a good look at him to see what changes have befallen him." The implication is that he must have changed in three days, so his friends should be attentive enough to notice the changes.

After World War II, most Japanese companies had to start literally from the ground up. Every day brought new challenges to managers and workers alike, and every day meant progress. Simply staying in business required unending progress, and Kaizen has become a way of life. It was also fortunate that the various tools that helped elevate this Kaizen concept to new heights were introduced to Japan in the late 1950s and early 1960s by such experts as W.E. Deming and J.M. Juran. However, most new concepts, systems, and tools that are widely used in Japan today have subsequently been developed in Japan and represent qualitative improvements upon the statistical quality control and total quality control of the 1960s.

KAIZEN AND MANAGEMENT

Figure 1.2 shows how job functions are perceived in Japan. As indicated, management has two major components: maintenance and improvement. Maintenance refers to activities directed toward maintaining current technological, managerial, and operating standards; improvement refers to those directed toward improving current standards. Under its maintenance functions, management performs its assigned tasks so that everybody in the company can follow the established SOP (Standard Operating Procedure). This means that management must first establish policies, rules, directives, and proce-

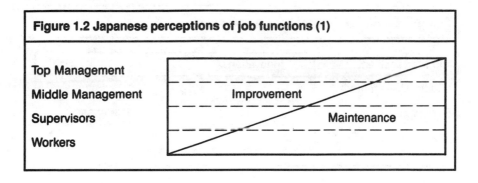

Figure 1.2 Japanese perceptions of job functions (1)

Top Management

Middle Management

Supervisors

Workers

Improvement

Maintenance

dures for all major operations and then see to it that everybody follows SOP. If people are able to follow the standard but do not, management must introduce discipline. If people are unable to follow the standard, management must either provide training or review and revise the standard so that people can follow it.

In any business, an employee's work is based on existing standards, either explicit or implicit, imposed by management. Maintenance refers to maintaining such standards through training and discipline. By contrast, improvement refers to improving the standards. The Japanese perception of management boils down to one precept: maintain and improve standards.

The higher up the manager is, the more he is concerned with improvement. At the bottom level, an unskilled worker working at a machine may spend all his time following instructions. However, as hc becomes more proficient at his work, he begins to think about improvement. He begins to contribute to improvements in the way his work is done, either through individual suggestions or through group suggestions.

Ask any manager at a successful Japanese company what top management is pressing for, and the answer will be, "Kaizen" (improvement).

Improving standards means establishing higher standards. Once this is done, it becomes management's maintenance job to see that the new standards are observed. Lasting improvement is achieved only when people work to higher standards. Maintenance and improvement have thus become inseparable for most Japanese managers.

What is improvement? Improvement can be broken down between Kaizen and innovation. Kaizen signifies small improvements made in the status quo as a result of ongoing efforts. Innovation involves a drastic improvement in the status quo as a result of a large investment in new technology and/or equipment. Figure 1.3 shows the breakdown among maintenance, Kaizen, and innovation as perceived by Japanese management.

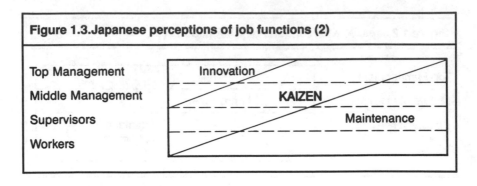

Figure 1.3.Japanese perceptions of job functions (2)

Top Management

Middle Management

Supervisors

Workers

Innovation

KAIZEN

Maintenance

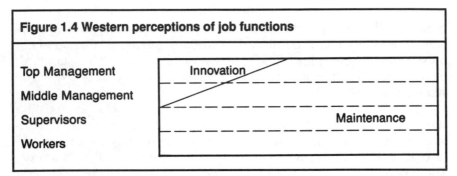

Figure 1.4 Western perceptions of job functions

Top Management

Middle Management

Supervisors

Workers

Innovation

Maintenance

On the other hand, most Western managers' perceptions of job functions are as shown in Figure 1.4. There is little room in Western management for the Kaizen concept.

Sometimes, another type of management is found in the high-technology industries as shown in Figure 1.5. These are the companies that are born running, grow rapidly, and then disappear just as rapidly when their initial success wanes or markets change.

The worst companies are those which do nothing but maintenance, meaning there is no internal drive for Kaizen or innovation, change is forced on management by market conditions and competition, and management does not know where it wants to go.

Since Kaizen is an ongoing process and involves everyone in the

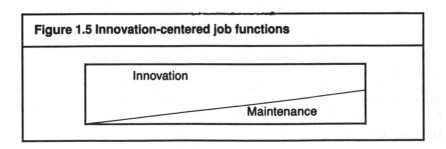

Figure 1.5 Innovation-centered job functions

Innovation

Maintenance

Figure 1.6 Hierarchy of KAIZEN involvement

Top Management	Middle Management and Staff	Supervisors	Workers
Be determined to introduce KAIZEN as a corporate strategy	Deploy and implement KAIZEN goals as directed by top management through policy deployment and cross-functional management	Use KAIZEN in functional roles	Engage in KAIZEN through the suggestion system and small-group activities
Provide support and direction for KAIZEN by allocating resources		Formulate plans for KAIZEN and provide guidance to workers	
Establish policy for KAIZEN and cross-functional goals	Use KAIZEN in functional capabilities	Improve communication with workers and sustain high morale	Practice discipline in the workshop
Realize KAIZEN goals through policy deployment and audits	Establish, maintain, and upgrade standards	Support small-group activities (such as quality circles) and the individual suggestion system	Engage in continuous self-development to become better problem solvers
Build systems, procedures, and structures conducive to KAIZEN	Make employees KAIZEN-conscious through intensive training programs	Introduce discipline in the workshop	Enhance skills and job-performance expertise with cross-education
	Help employees develop skills and tools for problem solving	Provide KAIZEN suggestions	

organization, everyone in the management hierarchy is involved in some aspects of Kaizen, as shown in Figure 1.6.

IMPLICATIONS OF QC FOR KAIZEN

While management is usually concerned with such issues as productivity and quality, the thrust of this book is to look at the other side of the picture—at Kaizen.

Any serious discussion of quality, for instance, soon finds itself entangled in such issues as how to define quality, how to measure it, and how to relate it to benefits. There are as many definitions of quality as there are people defining it, and there is no agreement on what quality is or should be. The same is true of productivity.

Productivity means different things to different people. Perceptions of productivity are miles apart, and management and labor are often at odds over this very issue.

Yet no matter what the substance of quality and productivity, the other side of the coin has always been Kaizen. Thus, the moment we start talking about Kaizen, the whole issue becomes breathtakingly simple. First of all, nobody can dispute the value of improvement, since it is generic and good in its own right. It is good by definition. Whenever and wherever improvements are made in business, these improvements are eventually going to lead to improvements in such areas as quality and productivity.

The starting point for improvement is to recognize the need. This comes from recognition of a problem. If no problem is recognized, there is no recognition of the need for improvement. Complacency is the archenemy of Kaizen. Therefore, Kaizen emphasizes problem-awareness and provides clues for identifying problems.

Once identified, problems must be solved. Thus Kaizen is also a problem-solving process. In fact, Kaizen requires the use of various problem-solving tools. Improvement reaches new heights with every problem that is solved. In order to consolidate the new level, however, the improvement must be standardized. Thus Kaizen also requires standardization.

Such terms as QC (Quality Control), SQC (Statistical Quality Control), QC circles, and TQC (or CWQC) often appear in connection with Kaizen. To avoid unnecessary confusion, it may be helpful to clarify these terms here.

As already mentioned, the word *quality* has been interpreted in many different ways, and there is no agreement on what actually constitutes quality. In its broadest sense, quality is anything that can be improved. In this context, quality is associated not only with products and services but also with the way people work, the way machines are operated, and the way systems and procedures are dealt with. It includes all aspects of human behavior. This is why it is more useful to talk about Kaizen than about quality or productivity.

The English term *improvement* as used in the Western context more often than not means improvement in equipment, thus excluding the human elements. By contrast, Kaizen is generic and can be applied to every aspect of everybody's activities. This said, however, it must be admitted that such terms as quality and quality control have played a vital role in the development of Kaizen in Japan.

In the years immediately following Japan's wartime defeat, Hajime Karatsu, Technical Advisor to Matsushita Electric Industrial, was working with NTT (Nippon Telegraph and Telephone Public Corp.) as a young QC engineer. NTT had problems. "Whenever I tried to call somebody up, I invariably got a wrong number," recalls Karatsu. Seeing the terrible state of affairs at NTT, General MacArthur's staff invited some American quality control experts from Western Electric to help NTT. The American experts told NTT management that the only solution was to apply quality control. Says Karatsu, "In our pride, we told them that we were applying quality control at NTT the Japanese way. But when they asked to see our control charts, we didn't even know what a control chart was!"

It was from such humble beginnings that efforts were begun to improve Japanese quality-control practices in the late 1940s. An example was the establishment of the quality-control subcommittee at the Union of Japanese Scientists and Engineers (JUSE). At about the same time, the Japanese Standards Association started organizing seminars on statistical quality control.

In March 1950, JUSE started publishing its magazine *Statistical Quality Control*. In July of the same year, W. E. Deming was invited to Japan to teach statistical quality control at an eight-day seminar organized by JUSE. Deming visited Japan several times in the 1950s, and it was during one of those visits that he made his famous prediction that Japan would soon be flooding the world market with quality products.

Deming also introduced the "Deming cycle," one of the crucial QC tools for assuring continuous improvement, to Japan. The Deming cycle is also called the Deming wheel or the PDCA (Plan-Do-Check-Action) cycle. (See Figure 1.7.) Deming stressed the importance of constant interaction among research, design, production, and sales in order for a company to arrive at better quality that satisfies customers. He taught that this wheel should be rotated on the ground of quality-first perceptions and quality-first responsibility. With this process, he argued, the company could win consumer confidence and acceptance

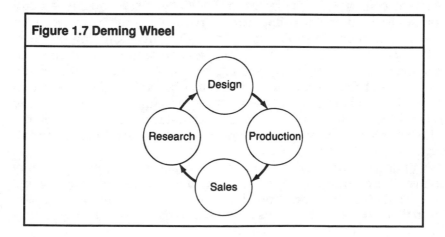

Figure 1.7 Deming Wheel

and prosper.

In July 1954, J. M. Juran was invited to Japan to conduct a JUSE seminar on quality-control management. This was the first time QC was dealt with from the overall management perspective.

In 1956, Japan Shortwave Radio included a course on quality control as part of its educational programming. In November 1960, the first national quality month was inaugurated. It was also in 1960 that Q-marks and Q-flags were formally adopted. Then in April 1962 the magazine *Quality Control for the Foreman* was launched by JUSE, and the first QC circle was started that same year.

A QC circle is defined as a small group that *voluntarily* performs quality-control activities within the shop. The small group carries out its work continuously as part of a company-wide program of quality control, self-development, mutual education, and flow-control and improvement within the workshop. The QC circle is only part of a company-wide program; it is never the whole of TQC or CWQC.

Those who have followed QC circles in Japan know that they often focus on such areas as cost, safety, and productivity, and that their activities sometimes relate only indirectly to product-quality improvement. For the most part, these activities are aimed at making improvements in the workshop.

There is no doubt that QC circles have played an important part in improving product quality and productivity in Japan. However, their role has often been blown out of proportion by overseas observers who believe that QC circles are the mainstay of TQC activities in Japan. Nothing could be further from the truth, especially when it comes to Japanese management. Efforts related to QC circles generally account for only 10 percent to 30 percent of the overall TQC effort in Japanese companies.

What is less visible behind these developments is the transformation of the term quality control, or QC, in Japan. As is the case in many Western companies, quality control initially meant quality control applied to the manufacturing process, particularly the inspections for rejecting defective incoming material or defective outgoing products at the end of the production line. But very soon the realization set in that inspection alone does nothing to improve the quality of the product, and that product quality should be built at the production stage. "Build quality into the process" was (and still is) a popular phrase in Japanese quality control. It is at this stage that control charts and the other tools for statistical quality control were introduced after Deming's lectures.

Juran's lectures in 1954 opened up another aspect of quality control: the managerial approach to quality control. This was the first time the term QC was positioned as a vital management tool in Japan. From then on, the term QC has been used to mean both quality control and the tools for overall improvement in managerial performance.

Initially, QC was applied in heavy industries such as the steel industry. Since these industries required instrumentation control, the application of SQC tools was vital for maintaining quality. As QC spread to the machinery and automobile industries, where controlling the process was essential in building quality into the product, the need for SQC became even greater.

At a later stage, other industries started to introduce QC for such products as consumer durables and home appliances. In these industries, the interest was in building quality in at the design stage to meet changing and increasingly stringent customer requirements. Today, management has gone beyond the design stage and has begun to stress the importance of quality product development, which means taking customer-related information and market research into account from the very start.

All this while, QC has grown into a full-fledged management tool involving everyone in the company. Such companywide activities are often referred to as TQC (Total Quality Control) or CWQC (Company-Wide Quality Control). No matter which name is used, TQC and CWQC mean company-wide Kaizen activities involving everyone in the company, managers and workers alike. Over the years, QC has been elevated to SQC and then to TQC or CWQC, improving managerial performance at every level. Thus it is that such words as QC and TQC have come to be almost synonymous with Kaizen. This is also why I constantly refer to QC, TQC, and CWQC in explaining Kaizen.

On the other hand, the function of quality control in its original sense remains valid. Quality assurance remains a vital part of management, and most companies have a QA (Quality Assurance) department for this. To confuse matters, TQC or CWQC activities are sometimes administered by the QA department and sometimes by a separate TQC office. Thus it is important that these QC-related words be understood in the context in which they appear.

KAIZEN AND TQC

Considering the TQC movement in Japan as part of the Kaizen movement gives us a clearer perspective on the Japanese approach. First of all, it should be pointed out that TQC activities in Japan are not concerned solely with quality control. People have been fooled by the term "quality control" and have often construed it within the narrow discipline of product-quality control. In the West, the term QC is mostly associated with inspection of finished products, and when QC is brought up in discussion, top managers, who generally assume they have very little to do with quality control, lose interest immediately.

It is unfortunate that in the West TQC has been dealt with mainly in technical journals when it is more properly the focus of management journals. Japan has developed an elaborate system of Kaizen strategies as management tools within the TQC movement. These rank among this century's most outstanding management achievements. Yet because of the limited way in which QC is understood in the West, most Western students of Japanese QC activities have failed to grasp their real significance and challenge. At the same time, new TQC methods and tools are constantly being studied and tested.

TQC undergoes perpetual change and improvement, and it is never quite the same from one day to the next. For instance, the so-called Seven Statistical Tools have been indispensable and have been widely used by QC circles, engineers, and management. Recently, the original seven have been supplemented by a "New Seven" used to solve more sophisticated problems such as new-product development, facility improvement, quality improvement, and cost reduction. New applications are being developed almost daily.

TQC in Japan is a movement centered on the improvement of managerial performance at all levels. As such, it has typically dealt with:
1. Quality assurance
2. Cost reduction
3. Meeting production quotas
4. Meeting delivery schedules
5. Safety
6. New-product development
7. Productivity improvement
8. Supplier management

More recently, TQC has come to include marketing, sales, and service as well. Furthermore, TQC has dealt with such crucial management concerns as organizational development, cross-functional management, policy deployment, and quality deployment. In other words, management has been using TQC as a tool for improving overall performance.

Those who have closely followed QC circles in Japan know that their activities are often focused on such areas as cost, safety, and productivity, and that their activities may only indirectly relate to product-quality improvement. For the most part, these activities are aimed at making improvements in the workplace.

Management efforts for TQC have been directed mostly at such areas as education, systems development, policy deployment, cross-functional management, and, more recently, quality deployment.

KAIZEN AND THE SUGGESTION SYSTEM

Japanese management makes a concerted effort to involve employees in Kaizen through suggestions. Thus, the suggestion system is an integral part of the established management system, and the number of workers' suggestions is regarded as an important criterion in reviewing the performance of these workers' supervisor. The manager of the supervisors is in turn expected to assist them so that they can help workers generate more suggestions.

Most Japanese companies active in Kaizen programs have a quality-control system and a suggestion system working in concert. The role of QC circles may be better understood if we regard them collectively as a group-oriented suggestion system for making improvements.

One of the outstanding features of Japanese management is that it generates a great number of suggestions from workers and that management works hard to consider these suggestions, often incorporating them into the overall Kaizen strategy. It is not uncommon for top management of a leading Japanese company to spend a whole day listening to presentations of activities by QC circles, and giving awards based on predetermined criteria. Management is willing to give recognition to employees' efforts for improvements and makes its concern visible wherever possible. Often, the number of suggestions is posted individually on the wall of the workplace in order to encourage competition among workers and among groups.

Another important aspect of the suggestion system is that each suggestion, once implemented, leads to a revised standard. For instance, when a special foolproof device has been installed on a machine at a worker's suggestion, this may require the worker to work differently and, at times, more attentively.

However, inasmuch as the new standard has been set up by the worker's own volition, he takes pride in the new standard and is willing to follow it. If, on the contrary, he is told to follow a standard imposed by management, he may not be as willing to follow it.

Thus, through suggestions, employees can participate in Kaizen in the workplace and play a vital role in upgrading standards. In a recent interview, Toyota Motor chairman Eiji Toyoda said, "One of the features of the Japanese workers is that they use their brains as well as their hands. Our workers provide 1.5 million suggestions a year, and 95 percent of them are put to practical use. There is an almost tangible concern for improvement in the air at Toyota."

KAIZEN AND COMPETITION

Western managers who have had some business experience in Japan invariably remark on the intense competition among Japanese companies. This intense domestic competition is thought to have been the driving force for Japanese companies in the overseas markets as well. Japanese companies compete for larger market shares through the introduction of new and more competitive products and by using and improving the latest technologies.

Normally, the driving forces for competition are price, quality, and service. In Japan, however, it is safe to say that the ultimate cause of competition has often been competition itself. Japanese companies are now even competing in introducing better and faster Kaizen programs!

Where profit is the most important criterion for business success, it is conceivable that a company could remain unchanged for more than a quarter of a century. Where companies are vying with each other on the strength of Kaizen, however, improvement must be an ongoing process. Kaizen ensures that there will be continuous improvement for improvement's sake. Once the Kaizen movement has been started, there is no way to reverse the trend.

PROCESS-ORIENTED MANAGEMENT VS. RESULT-ORIENTED MANAGEMENT

Kaizen generates process-oriented thinking, since processes must be improved before we get improved results. Further, Kaizen is people-oriented and is directed at people's efforts. This contrasts sharply with the result-oriented thinking of most Western managers.

According to Mayumi Otsubo, manager for tournaments and special-event promotion at Bridgestone Tire Co., Japan is a process-oriented society while the United States is a result-oriented society. For instance, in reviewing the performance of employees, Japanese management tends to emphasize attitudinal factors. When the sales manager evaluates a salesperson's performance, that evaluation must include such process-oriented criteria as the amount of the salesperson's time spent calling on new customers, time spent on outside customer calls versus time devoted to clerical work at the office, and the percentage of new inquiries successfully closed.

By paying attention to these indices, the sales manager hopes to encourage the salesperson to produce improved results sooner or later. In other words, the process is considered just as important as the obviously intended result—sales!

Japan's national sport is sumo. At each sumo tournament, there are three awards besides the tournament championship: an outstanding performance award, a skill award, and a fighting-spirit award. The fighting-spirit award is given to the wrestler who has fought exceptionally hard throughout the 15-day tournament, even if his won/lost record leaves something to be desired. None of these three awards is based solely on results, that is, how many bouts the wrestler wins. This is a good example of Japan's process-oriented thinking.

This is not to say, however, that winning does not count in sumo. In reality, each wrestler's monthly income is based largely on his record. It is just that winning is neither everything nor the only thing.

Japanese temples and shrines are often built in the mountains, and the most sacred altar is usually in the highest sanctuary. A worshiper wishing to pray at a shrine altar has to walk through dense forest, up steep stone steps, and under many torii (wooden gateways). At the Fushimi Inari Shrine near Kyoto, for example, there are some 15,000 torii along the walkway to the altar! By the time he reaches the altar, the worshiper is steeped in the sacred atmosphere of the shrine and his soul is purified. Getting there is almost as important as the prayer itself.

In the United States, generally speaking, no matter how hard a person works, lack of results will result in a poor personal rating and lower income or status. The individual's contribution is valued only for its concrete results. Only the results count in a result-oriented society.

Bridgestone Tire Co.'s Otsubo maintains that it is process-oriented thinking that has enabled Japanese industry to attain its competitive edge in world markets and that the Kaizen concept epitomizes Japan's process-oriented thinking. Such management attitudes make a major difference in how an organization achieves change. Top management that is too process-oriented runs the risk of lacking long-term strategy, missing new ideas and innovations, instructing people ad nauseam in minute work processes, and losing sight of the forest for the trees. The result-oriented manager is more flexible in setting targets and can think in strategic terms. However, he tends to slight the mobilization and realignment of his resources for the strategy's implementation.

Otsubo suggests that the result-oriented criteria for evaluating people's performance are probably a legacy of the "mass-production society" and that the process-oriented criteria are gaining momentum in the post-industrial, high-tech, high-touch society.

The difference between process-oriented thinking and result-oriented thinking in business can perhaps best be explained with reference to Figure 1.8.

If we look at the manager's role, we find that the supportive and stimulative role is directed at the improvement of the processes, while the controlling role is directed at the outcome or the result. The Kaizen concept stresses management's supportive and stimulative role for people's *efforts* to improve the processes. On the one hand, management needs to develop process-oriented criteria. On the other hand, the control-type management looks only at the performance or the result-oriented criteria. For abbreviation, we may call the process-oriented criteria P criteria and the result-oriented criteria R criteria.

P criteria call for a longer-term outlook, since they are directed at people's efforts and often require behavioral change. On the other hand, R criteria are more direct and short term.

The difference between P criteria and R criteria may be better

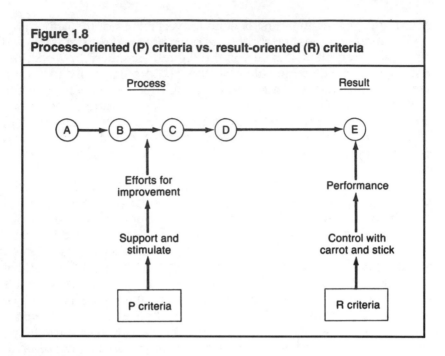

Figure 1.8
Process-oriented (P) criteria vs. result-oriented (R) criteria

Process

Result

A → B → C → D → E

Efforts for
improvement

Performance

Support and
stimulate

Control with
carrot and stick

P criteria

R criteria

understood by looking at Japanese management's approach to the activities of QC circles.

QC-circle activities are usually directed toward improvements in the workplace, yet the supporting system is crucial. It is reported that QC circles formed in the West are often short-lived. This appears to be attributable mostly to the lack of a system that addresses the real needs of the QC-circle members. If management is interested only in the results, it will be looking only at R criteria for QC-circle activities. The R criteria in this case often mean the money saved as the result of their activities. Accordingly, management's interest and support will be geared directly to the savings made by members of the QC circle.

On the other hand, if management is interested in supporting the QC circle's efforts for improvement, the first thing management has to do is to establish P criteria. What kind of P criteria are available to measure the effort made by QC-circle members?

Some obvious possibilities are the number of meetings held per month, the participation rate, the number of problems solved (note that this is not the same as the amount of money saved), and the number of reports submitted. How do QC-circle members approach their subjects? Do they take the company's current situation into consideration in selecting the subject? Do they consider such factors as safety, quality, and cost in working out the problem? Do their efforts lead to improved work standards? These are among the P criteria to be used in evaluating their efforts and commitment.

If the average QC circle meets twice a month and a particular QC circle averages three meetings a month, this indicates that the members of this group made a greater-than-average effort. The participation (attendance) rate is another measure to check the level of effort and commitment of the QC-circle leader or facilitator.

It is often easy to quantify R criteria. In fact, in most companies, management has only R criteria available, since R criteria typically relate to sales, cost, and profit figures. However, in most cases it is also possible to quantify P criteria. In the case of QC circles, for instance, Japanese management has developed elaborate measures to quantify the effort level. These and other numbers are added together and used as the basis for recognition and awards.

At one of Matsushita's plants, the waitresses in the cafeteria formed QC circles and studied the tea consumption during the lunch period. When large tea pots were placed on the tables with no restrictions on use, the waitresses noticed, tea consumption differed greatly from table to table. Therefore, they collected data on the tea-drinking behavior of employees during lunch. For one thing, they found that the same people tended to sit at the same table. After taking and analyzing data for days, they were able to establish an expected consumption level for each table. Using their findings, they started putting out different amounts of tea for each table, with the result that they were able to reduce tea-leaf consumption to half. How much were their activities worth in terms of the actual amount of money saved? Probably very little. However, they were awarded the Presidential Gold Medal for the year.

Most Japanese companies also have a suggestion system, which incorporates incentives. Whenever a suggestion yields savings, management provides rewards in proportion to the savings realized. Such rewards are paid both for suggestions made by individuals and those made by groups such as QC circles.

One of the distinctive features of Japanese management has been that it has made a conscious effort to establish a system that supports and encourages P criteria while giving full recognition to R criteria. At the workers' level, Japanese management has often established separate award systems for P criteria. While the rewards for R criteria are financial rewards directly geared to the savings or profits realized, those for P criteria are more often recognition and honor geared to the effort made.

At Toyota Motor, the most coveted QC award is the Presidential Award, which is not money but a fountain pen presented to each recipient personally by the president. Each recipient is asked to submit the name he wants engraved on the fountain pen. One person might ask for his wife's name to be printed, another his daughter's name. Bachelors sometimes ask for their girlfriends' names. And of course, many recipients ask to have their own names on their pens. The award carries prestige because top management has implemented a carefully planned program to show workers that their active participation in QC projects is important to the company's success. In addition, top executives attend these meetings, showing their active involvement and support. Such clear demonstrations of commitment go beyond the tokens of the awards to bind management and worker together in the program.

The process-oriented way of thinking bridges the gap between process and result, between ends and means, and between goals and measures, and helps people see the whole picture without bias.

Thus, both P criteria and R criteria can be and have been established at every level of management: between top management and division management, between middle managers and supervisors, and between supervisors and workers.

A manager, by definition, must take an interest in the results. However, when we observe the behavior of successful managers at a successful company, we often find that such managers are also process oriented. They ask process-oriented questions. They make decisions based on both P criteria and R criteria, although they may not always be aware of the distinction between the two sorts of criteria.

A process-oriented manager who takes a genuine concern for P criteria will be interested in:
- Discipline
- Time management
- Skill development
- Participation and involvement
- Morale
- Communication

In short, such a manager is people-oriented. Further, the manager will be interested in developing a reward system that corresponds to P criteria. If management makes positive use of the process-oriented way of thinking and further reinforces it with Kaizen strategy, it will find that the overall corporate competitiveness will be greatly improved in the long term.

REFERENCES
1. Kamban as a word simply means signboards, cards, or chits. With just-in-time production, a worker from the following process goes to collect parts from the previous process leaving a kamban signifying the delivery of a given quantity of specific parts. When all the parts have all been used, the same kamban is sent back, at which point it becomes an order for more. Because this is such an important tool for just-in-time production, kamban has become synonymous with the just-in-time production system. The just-in-time system was first employed by Toyota Motor Corp. to minimize inventory and hence cut waste. The underlying principle is that the necessary parts should be received "just in time" for the manufacturing process.

IMPROVEMENT EAST AND WEST

From *Kaizen, The Key to Japan's Competitive Success*

MASAAKI IMAI

KAIZEN VS. INNOVATION (1)

There are two contrasting approaches to progress: the gradualist approach and the great-leap-forward approach. Japanese companies generally favor the gradualist approach and Western companies the great-leap approach—an approach epitomized by the term innovation:

	KAIZEN	Innovation
Japan	Strong	Weak
West	Weak	Strong

Western management worships at the altar of innovation. This innovation is seen as major changes in the wake of technological breakthroughs, or the introduction of the latest management concepts or production techniques. Innovation is dramatic, a real attention-getter. Kaizen, on the other hand, is often undramatic and subtle, and its results are seldom immediately visible. While Kaizen is a continuous process, innovation is generally a one-shot phenomenon.

In the West, for example, a middle manager can usually obtain top management support for such projects as CAD (Computer-Aided Design), CAM (Computer-Aided Manufacture), and MRP (Materials Requirements Planning), since these are innovative projects that have a way of revolutionizing existing systems. As such, they offer ROI (Return On Investment) benefits that managers can hardly resist.

However, when a factory manager wishes, for example, to make small changes in the way his workers use the machinery, such as working out multiple job assignments or realigning production processes (both of which may require lengthy discussions with the union as well as reeducation and retraining of workers), obtaining management support can be difficult indeed.

Figure 2.1 compares the main features of Kaizen and of innovation. One of the beautiful things about Kaizen is that it does not necessarily require sophisticated techniques or state-of-the-art technology. To implement Kaizen, you need only simple, conventional techniques such as the seven tools of quality control (Pareto diagrams, cause-and-effect diagrams, histograms, control charts, scatter diagrams, graphs, and check sheets). Often, common sense is all that is needed. On the other hand, innovation usually requires highly sophisticated technology, as well as a huge investment.

Kaizen is like a hotbed that nurtures small and ongoing changes, while innovation is like magma that appears in abrupt eruptions from time to time.

One big difference between Kaizen and innovation is that while Kaizen does not necessarily call for a large investment to implement

Figure 2.1 Features of KAIZEN and innovation

	KAIZEN	Innovation
1. Effect	Long-term and long-lasting but undramatic	Short-term but dramatic
2. Pace	Small steps	Big steps
3. Timeframe	Continuous and incremental	Intermittent and non-incremental
4. Change	Gradual and constant	Abrupt and volatile
5. Involvement	Everybody	Select few "champions"
6. Approach	Collectivism, group efforts, systems approach	Rugged individualism, individual ideas and efforts
7. Mode	Maintenance and improvement	Scrap and rebuild
8. Spark	Conventional know-how and state of the art	Technological breakthroughs, new inventions, new theories
9. Practical requirements	Requires little investment but great effort to maintain it	Requires large investment but little effort to maintain it
10. Effort orientation	People	Technology
11. Evaluation criteria	Process and efforts for better results	Results for profits
12. Advantage	Works well in slow-growth economy	Better suited to fast-growth economy

it, it does call for a great deal of continuous effort and commitment. The difference between the two opposing concepts may thus be likened to that of a staircase and a slope. The innovation strategy is supposed to bring about progress in a staircase progression, as depicted in Figure 2.2. On the other hand, the Kaizen strategy brings about gradual progress. I say the innovation strategy "is supposed to" bring about progress in a staircase progression, because it usually does not. Instead of following the staircase pattern of Figure 2.2, the actual progress achieved through innovation will generally follow the pattern shown in Figure 2.3 if it lacks the Kaizen strategy to go along with it. This happens because a system, once it has been installed as a result of new innovation, is subject to steady deterioration unless continuing efforts are made first to maintain it and then to improve on it.

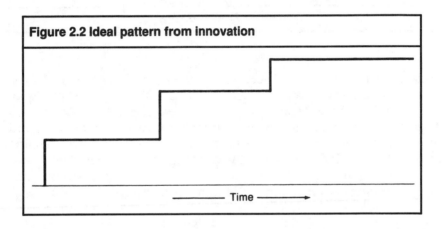

Figure 2.2 Ideal pattern from innovation

— Time ⟶

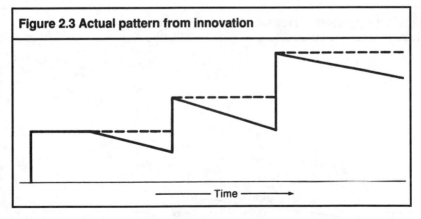

Figure 2.3 Actual pattern from innovation

— Time ⟶

In reality, there can be no such thing as a static constant. All systems are destined to deteriorate once they have been established. One of the famous Parkinson's Laws is that an organization, once it has

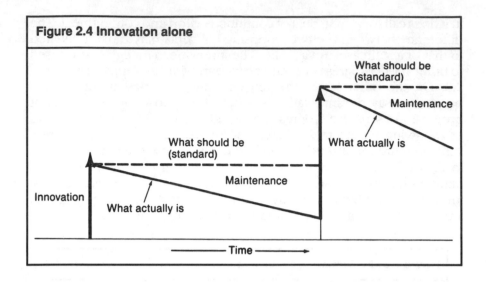

Figure 2.4 Innovation alone

built its edifice, begins its decline. In other words, there must be a continuing effort for improvement to even maintain the status quo. When such effort is lacking, decline is inevitable. (See Figure 2.4.) Therefore, even when an innovation makes a revolutionary standard of performance attainable, the new performance level will decline unless the standard is constantly challenged and upgraded. Thus, whenever an innovation is achieved, it must be followed by a series of Kaizen efforts to maintain and improve it. (See Figure 2.5.)

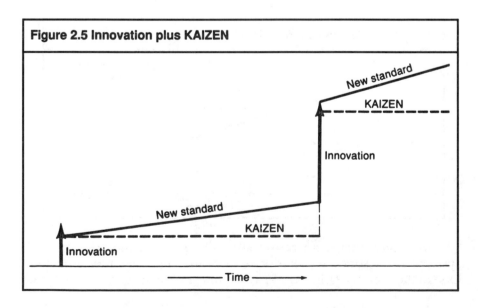

Figure 2.5 Innovation plus KAIZEN

Whereas innovation is a one-shot deal whose effects are gradually eroded by intense competition and deteriorating standards, Kaizen is an ongoing effort with cumulative effects marking a steady rise as the years go by. If standards exist only in order to maintain the status quo, they will not be challenged so long as the level of performance is acceptable. Kaizen, on the other hand, means a constant effort not only to maintain but also to upgrade standards. Kaizen strategists believe that standards are by nature tentative, akin to stepping stones, with one standard leading to another as continuing improvement efforts are made. This is the reason why QC circles no sooner solve one problem than they move on to tackle a new problem. This is also the reason why the so-called PDCA (Plan-Do-Check-Action) cycle receives so much emphasis in Japan's TQC movement.

Another feature of Kaizen is that it requires virtually everyone's personal efforts. In order for the Kaizen spirit to survive, management must make a conscious and continuous effort to support it. Such support is quite different from the fanfare recognition that management accords to people who have achieved a striking success or breakthrough. Kaizen is concerned more with the process than with the result. The strength of Japanese management lies in its successful development and implementation of a system that acknowledges the ends while emphasizing the means.

Thus Kaizen calls for a substantial management commitment of time and effort. Infusions of capital are no substitute for this investment in time and effort. Investing in Kaizen means investing in people. In short, Kaizen is people-oriented, whereas innovation is technology- and money-oriented.

Finally, the Kaizen philosophy is better suited to a slow-growth economy, while innovation is better suited to a fast-growth economy. While Kaizen advances inch-by-inch on the strength of many small efforts, innovation leaps upward in hopes of landing at a much higher plateau in spite of gravitational inertia and the weight of investment costs. In a slow-growth economy characterized by high costs of energy and materials, overcapacity, and stagnant markets, Kaizen often has a better payoff than innovation does.

As one Japanese executive recently remarked, "It is extremely difficult to increase sales by 10 percent. But it is not so difficult to cut manufacturing costs by 10 percent to even better effect."

At the beginning of this chapter, I argued that the concept of Kaizen is nonexistent or at best weak in most Western companies today. However, there was a time, not so long ago, when Western management also placed a high priority on Kaizen-like improvement-consciousness. Older executives may recall that before the phenomenal economic growth of the late 1950s and early 1960s, management attended assiduously to improving all aspects of the business, particularly the factory. In those days, every small improvement was counted and was seen as effective in terms of building success.

People who worked with small, privately owned companies may recall with a touch of nostalgia that there was a genuine concern for improvement "in the air" before the company was bought out or went public. As soon as that happened, the quarterly P/L (profit/loss) figures suddenly became the most important criterion, and management became obsessed with the bottom line, often at the expense of pressing for constant and unspectacular improvements.

For many other companies, the greatly increased market opportunities and technological innovations that appeared during the first two decades after World War II meant that developing new products based on the new technology was much more attractive or "sexier" than slow, patient efforts for improvement. In trying to catch up with the ever-increasing market demand, managers boldly introduced one innovation after another, and they were content to ignore the seemingly minor benefits of improvement.

Most Western managers who joined the ranks during or after those heady days do not have the slightest concern for improvement. Instead, they take an offensive posture, armed with professional expertise geared toward making big changes in the name of innovation, bringing about immediate gains, and winning instant recognition and promotion. Before they knew it, Western managers had lost sight of improvement and put all their eggs in the innovation basket.

Another factor that has abetted the innovation approach has been the increasing emphasis on financial controls and accounting. By now, the more sophisticated companies have succeeded in establishing elaborate accounting and reporting systems that force managers to account for every action they take and to spell out the precise payout or ROI of every managerial decision. Such a system does not lend itself to building a favorable climate for improvement.

Improvement is by definition slow, gradual, and often invisible, with effects that are felt over the long run. In my opinion, the most glaring and significant shortcoming of Western management today is the lack of improvement philosophy. There is no internal system in Western management to reward efforts for improvement; instead, everyone's job performance is reviewed strictly on the basis of results. Thus it is not uncommon for Western managers to chide people with, "I don't care what you do or how you do it. I want the results—and now!" This emphasis on results has led to the innovation-dominated approach of the West. This is not to say that Japanese management does not care about innovation. But Japanese managers have enthusiastically pursued Kaizen even when they were involved in innovation, as is evident, for example, in the case of Nissan Motor.

THE CASE OF NISSAN MOTOR

At the No. 2 Body Section at Nissan's Tochigi plant, the first welding robot was introduced around 1973. During the following decade, the section's automation rate was pushed up to 98 percent, and the robotization rate for welding work has been increased to 60 percent. During this period, the standard work time in this section was reduced by 60 percent and production efficiency improved 10 percent to 20 percent.

These improvements in productivity were the combined result of the increased automation and the various Kaizen efforts made in the workshop during that period.

According to Eiichi Yoshida, who formerly headed this section and is now deputy general manager of the plant's production control and engineering department, there have been numerous Kaizen campaigns implemented in this section.

Each year has its own campaign for improvement programs. In 1975 for instance, the campaign was named the "Seven-up Campaign," and improvements were sought in the seven areas of standard time, efficiency, costs, suggestions, quality assurance, safety, and process utilization. The campaign chosen for 1978 was the "3-K 1, 2, 3 Campaign," the 3-K standing for *kangae* (thought), *kodo* (action), and *kaizen* and the 1, 2, 3 standing for the hop-step-jump sequence of thinking, acting, and improving.

While management makes decisions involving large investment outlays such as for automation and robotics, Kaizen campaigns involve both management and workers in making small, low-cost improvements in the way work is done.

Reduction in standard time has always been a highly effective way to increase productivity. At the Tochigi plant, efforts in this area included employing the work-factor method and standardizing virtually every motion workers made in performing their tasks.

In terms of each individual's work, the smallest unit of work time considered in a Kaizen strategy is 1/100th of a minute, or 0.6 seconds. Any suggestion that saves at least 0.6 seconds—the time it takes a worker to stretch out his hand or walk half a step—is seriously considered by management.

Aside from encouraging the QC-circle activities that had been going on in the plant for some time, the section started giving awards and other recognition for workers' Kaizen efforts in such areas as safety, error reduction, and number of suggestions.

A special Kaizen sheet is made available to the worker for this purpose, and each suggestion for improvement, whether it is brought by a group (QC circle) or by an individual, is "registered" on the sheet and submitted to the section manager. Most of these suggestions are handled within the same section and by the section manager.

Yoshida says that the majority of the workers' suggestions are for changes that the workers can implement on their own. For instance, a worker may suggest that the height of his tool rack be adjusted to make it easier to use. Such a suggestion can be taken care of within the section, and in fact, the section has bought welding equipment to do just such small repair work. This section has been engaged in continuous Kaizen all the time that the production processes were being automated and robotized.

Norio Kogure, staff engineer in the section, recalls what his new boss told him when he was transferred into the section: "There will be no progress if you keep on doing the job exactly the same way for six months."

Thus the SOP in the workplace is subject to constant change and improvement. At the same time, management tells the workers that the SOP is an absolute standard to which they should strictly conform until it is improved.

Both management and workers find room for improvement every day. It typically starts with studying the way workers perform their jobs to see if the standard time can somehow be shortened by 0.6 seconds or more. Next, the search is on for a way to improve the production processes. Sometimes the subassembly work that has previously been conducted off the line can be incorporated in the line so that the few seconds required to move the subassembly to the line can be saved. Kogure says that more than 90 percent of the engineers' work in the manufacturing department is directed at some form of Kaizen.

Yoshida believes that it is the manager's job to go into the work place, to encourage the workers to generate ideas for job improvement, and to be genuinely interested in their suggestions. He also believes that these efforts at the grassroots level were behind the plant's success in halving robot breakdowns in 1980 and 1981.

KAIZEN VS. INNOVATION (2)

Figure 2.6 represents the sequence from the scientists' laboratories to the marketplace. Scientific theories and experimentation are applied as

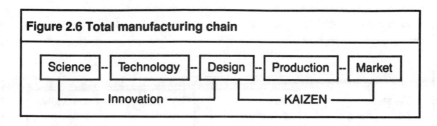

Figure 2.6 Total manufacturing chain

Science -- Technology -- Design -- Production -- Market

└── Innovation ──┘ └── KAIZEN ──┘

technology, elaborated as design, materialized in production, and finally sold on the market. The two components of improvement, innovation and Kaizen, may be applied at every stage in that chain. For instance, Kaizen has been applied to R&D activities while innovative ideas were applied to marketing to create the supermarkets and discount stores that dominated U.S. distribution in the 1950s. However, Kaizen's impact is normally more visible closer to production and market, while innovation's impact is more visible closer to science and technology. Figure 2.7 compares innovation and Kaizen in this sequence.

Looking at this list, we find that the West has been stronger on the innovation side and Japan stronger on the Kaizen side. These differences in emphasis are also reflected in the different social and cultural heritages, such as the Western educational system's stress on individual initiative and creativity as against the Japanese educational system's emphasis on harmony and collectivism.

I was recently talking with a European diplomat posted to Japan, who said that one of the most conspicuous differences between the West and Japan was that between the Western complacency and overconfidence and the Japanese feelings of anxiety and imperfection.

Figure 2.7 Another comparison of innovation and KAIZEN

Innovation	KAIZEN
Creativity	Adaptability
Individualism	Teamwork (systems approach)
Specialist-oriented	Generalist-oriented
Attention to great leaps	Attention to details
Technology-oriented	People-oriented
Information: closed, proprietary	Information: open, shared
Functional (specialist) orientation	Cross-functional orientation
Seek new technology	Build on existing technology
Line + staff	Cross-functional organization
Limited feedback	Comprehensive feedback

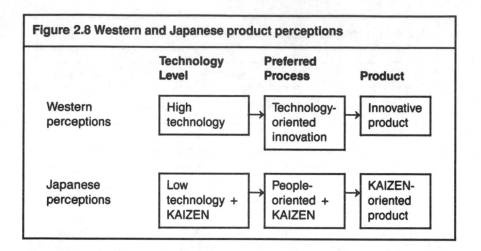

Figure 2.8 Western and Japanese product perceptions

	Technology Level	Preferred Process	Product
Western perceptions	High technology	Technology-oriented innovation	Innovative product
Japanese perceptions	Low technology + KAIZEN	People-oriented + KAIZEN	KAIZEN-oriented product

The Japanese feeling of imperfection perhaps provides the impetus for Kaizen.

In looking at the relations between Kaizen and innovation, we can draw the comparison expressed in Figure 2.8. However, as Japanese industry turns to the high-technology areas, it will lead to the situation depicted in Figure 2.9.

Once perceptions of new products have been changed this way, the Japanese competitive edge will become even greater. This change is already under way. Japanese companies have made major advances in Kaizen-related development even in the technologically most advanced areas, says Masanori Moritani, senior researcher at Nomura Research Institute.

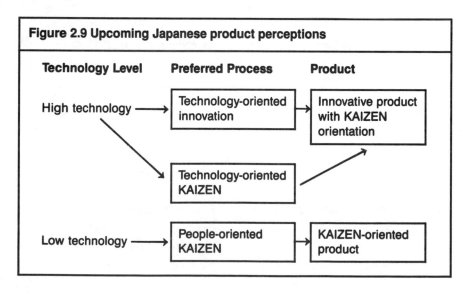

Figure 2.9 Upcoming Japanese product perceptions

Technology Level	Preferred Process	Product
High technology	Technology-oriented innovation	Innovative product with KAIZEN orientation
	Technology-oriented KAIZEN	
Low technology	People-oriented KAIZEN	KAIZEN-oriented product

Moritani points to the semiconductor laser as an example. The goal of semiconductor-laser development was to improve power levels and at the same time reduce manufacturing costs. Once this goal was achieved, it became possible to apply the semiconductor laser to mass-produced products such as compact discs and videodiscs.

At one major Japanese electronics company, the semiconductor laser developed for use in compact-disc players cost 500,000 yen in 1978. In 1980, it was down to 50,000 yen, and by the fall of 1981, it had been reduced to 10,000 yen. In 1982, when the first compact-disc players were put on the market, the semiconductor laser cost only 5,000 yen. As of 1984, it was down to the 2,000-to-3,000 yen level.

During the same period, the semiconductor laser's useful life was extended from 100 hours for some early models to more than 50,000 hours for later models. Most of these developments can be attributed to improvements in materials and production engineering, such as making thinner layers of semiconductors (which requires precision control to the less-than-one-micron level) and adopting the gaseous MOCVD (Molecular Oxidization Chemical Vapor Deposition) method. At the same time, the discs themselves were improved and pit error was reduced.

Reflecting all these efforts, compact disc players themselves underwent many changes for the better during this period. Prices also fell. In 1982, early models were priced around 168,000. In 1984, the mass-market model was selling for 49,800. During this same two-year period, the size of the player was reduced by five-sixths and the power consumption by nine-tenths. Since the basic technology for the semiconductor laser had been established by the mid-1970s, these developments represent engineering efforts in R&D, design, and production to improve on an existing technology.

Super LSI memories, fiber optics, and CCD (Charge-Coupled Devices) also represent high technology that has been successfully applied through the Kaizen approach. The main thrust of technological development today is shifting from the great-leap-forward approach to the gradual-development approach. Technological breakthroughs in the West are generally thought to take a Ph.D., but there are only three Ph.D.s on the engineering staff at one of Japan's most successfully innovative companies—Honda Motor. One is founder Soichiro Honda, whose Ph.D. is an honorary degree, and the other two are no longer active within the company. At Honda, technological improvement does not seem to require a Ph.D.

There is no doubt about the need for new technology, but it is what happens after the new technology has been developed that makes the difference. A product coming out of an emerging technology starts off very expensive and somewhat shaky in quality. Therefore, once a new technology has been identified, the effort must be increasingly directed at such areas as mass production, cost reduction, yield improvement, and quality improvement—all areas requiring doggedly tenacious efforts. Moritani says Western researchers typically show enthusiasm in tackling challenging projects and are very good at such work, but they will be at a great disadvantage in meeting the Japanese challenges in mass-produced high-technology products if they concentrate only on the great-leap-forward approach and forget everyday Kaizen.

An analysis of the semiconductor industries in Japan and the United States reveals the two countries' respective competitive advantages and illustrates the difference between Kaizen and innovation. Professor Ken'ichi Imai (no relation) and Associate Professor Akimitsu Sakuma at Hitotsubashi University have argued that:

> In greatly simplified terms, nearly all major innovations that determine the direction of future product and process development originate in U.S. firms. Japanese firms display their strength in incremental innovations in fields whose general contours have already been established.... A dominant design is an authoritative synthesis of individual innovations formerly applied separately in products. The economic value of a dominant design is its ability to impose itself as a standard in the creation of products. By virtue of standardization, economies of scale can be sought in production. This leads to a shift in the nature of competition. While initially the performance characteristics of a product are the deciding factor in competition, mass production leads to a second deciding factor: the cost of the product.
>
> Since a dominant design synthesizes past technologies, after its appearance major innovations no longer occur frequently. From then on, the center stage is occupied by incremental innovations aiming at product refinements and at improvements in the manufacturing process. The innovations conceived by Japanese firms correspond exactly to these incremental innovations. The reputation earned by Japan's l6K RAMs when they captured a large share of the American market was precisely one of high performance and low price.[1]

Paul H. Aron, vice chairman at Daiwa Securities America and professor of international business at New York University's Graduate School of Business Administration, recently said:

> Americans stress innovation and sophistication, and many companies complain that they cannot retain engineers if they

are assigned only to state-of-the-art applications. The dream of the American engineer is to establish an independent company and make an important breakthrough. After the breakthrough, the engineer expects his company to be acquired by a large conglomerate. The engineer anticipates receiving an ample financial reward and then, if he is young, to proceed to create another high technology company and repeat the process. Thus the production engineer often has less prestige, and this field does not attract "the best and the brightest" students.

The Japanese engineer largely expects to remain with the large company. Production engineers in Japanese companies often enjoy at least as much prestige as researchers.

Thus the preference for Kaizen over innovation may also be explained in terms of management's use of engineering skills, as well as the engineer's own perception of his job.

In the West, the engineer takes pride in doing his job as a theoretical exercise, and he is not necessarily concerned with maintaining rapport with the production site. On visiting an American plant recently, I was told that the machines installed there were designed by engineers at the head office who had never visited the plant. These machines often had to undergo lengthy adjustment and reworking before they were put to use.

In his book *Japanese Technology* (Tokyo, The Simul Press, 1982. Reprinted by permission.), Masanori Moritani states:

PRIORITY ON PRODUCTION
A third strength of Japanese technology is the close connection between development, design, and the production line. In Japan this is considered simple common sense, but that is not always the case in the United States and Europe.

In Japan, production runs take off with a bang, quickly reaching yearly outputs of a million units or more. American and European companies are amazed by this. Cautious in their expansion of production, often contenting themselves with simply doubling yearly output over three or four years, these companies are incredulous of the Japanese pace.

The principal element in this rapid expansion is active investment in plant and equipment, but what makes this technologically feasible is the unification of development, design, and production. In the case of home VCRs, development and design were conducted with full appreciation of the need for mass production. Easy mass production was the key design objective, and close consideration was given to parts availability, precision processing, and set assemblage....

Outstanding college-educated engineers are assigned in large numbers to the production line, and many are given an important say in business operations. Many manufacturing-industry executives are engineers by training, and a majority have had extensive first-hand experience on the shop floor. In Japanese firms, the production department has a strong voice in development and design. In addition, engineers involved in development and design always visit the production line and talk things over with their counterparts on the floor.

In Japan, even researchers are more likely to be found on the shop floor than in a research center; the majority of them are assigned to factories and operational divisions. Hitachi has about 8,000 R&D staff, but only 3,000 work at its research center. The remaining 5,000 are distributed among the various factories and operational divisions.

Nippon Electric Company (NEC) employs 5,000 technicians who are engaged either directly or indirectly in research and development. As many as 90 percent work in the factories. What this means is that the connection and understanding between development and production is very smooth indeed....

THE SHOP-FLOOR ELITE

In certain respects, French television manufacturers outshine their Japanese competitors in the development of top-of-the-line models. Soft-touch and remote control were introduced by the French well before the Japanese began using them. But while France may spend a great deal on producing splendid designs for their deluxe models, the quality of the actual product is inferior to Japanese sets. This is because French designers do not fully understand the problems encountered on the shop floor, and because the design work is not done from the perspective of the person who actually had to put the machine together. In short, there is a serious gap between development and production, a product of gaps between various strata in the company hierarchy itself....

My own career began in shipbuilding, as I worked first for Hitachi Shipbuilding & Engineering Company. Immediately after graduating from the University of Tokyo, I was assigned to the factory, where I took my place on the shop floor and, wearing a uniform like all the other employees, joined them at their work.

At the time, shipyard workers had a distinctive style of

dress; they would wrap a towel around their necks and tuck it into the front of their uniforms. In the world of shipbuilding, I suppose it was the fashion equivalent of wearing a scarf or muffler, although it also had the practical function of keeping the sweat from running down one's back and chest. No doubt these sweat-stained towels did not look like the height of fashion to outsiders, but I used to think of that dirty towel around my neck as a proud symbol of my work as an on-site technician.[2]

Thus one of the strengths of Japanese managers in designing new products is that they can assign capable engineers to both Kaizen and innovation. In general, the Japanese factory has a far higher ratio of engineers assigned to it than the American or European factory. Even so, the trend in Japan is to transfer more engineering resources to the plant to ensure even better communication with the production people.

Various practical tools, such as quality tables, have also been developed to improve cross-functional communication among customers, engineers, and production people. They have contributed greatly to creating products that meet customer requirements.

KAIZEN AND MEASUREMENT

Productivity is a measure, not a reality, says Gerald Nadler, professor and chairman of the Industrial and Systems Engineering Department, University of Southern California. And yet we have often sought the "secret" of productivity, as if the key were in defining the measures of productivity. According to Nadler, it is like finding that the room is too cold and looking at the thermometer for the reason. Adjusting the scale on the thermometer itself does not solve the problem. What counts is the effort to improve the situation, such as throwing more logs on the fire or checking the furnace—in other words, invoking the PDCA cycle. Productivity is only a description of the current state of affairs and the past efforts of people.

We might say that quality control, too, is a measure and not reality.

Quality control was started as a post-mortem inspection of defects produced in the production process. It goes without saying that no matter how hard one may work at inspecting the products, this does not necessarily lead to improvements in the product quality.

One way to improve quality is by improving the production process. Toying with the figures is not going to improve the situation. This is why quality control in Japan was started from the inspection phase, moved back to the phase of building quality in the production processes, and has finally come to mean building quality into the product at the time of its development.

If productivity and quality control are not the reality and serve only as a measure for checking the results, then what is the reality and what has to be done? The answer to this question is that the efforts put in to improve both productivity and quality are the reality. The key words are efforts and improve. This is the time to be liberated from the spell of productivity and quality control, get down to the basics, roll up our sleeves, and start working on improvement. If we define the manager's job as that of managing processes and results, then the manager should have yardsticks or measures for both of them. When Nadler said productivity is only a measure, he actually meant that productivity is a result-oriented index (R criterion). When we deal with improvement, we should be working on process-oriented indices (P criteria).

However, in most Western companies, many executives are not even aware that there are such things as process-oriented indices, because such indices have never been available in the company. The questions that the Western manager asks are always directed at the result-oriented indices, such as monthly sales, monthly expenses, number of products produced, and eventually the profits made. We only have to look at the reporting figures employed by the typical Western company, such as the cost-accounting data, to see how true this is.

When the manager is looking for a specific result, such as quarterly profits, productivity indices, or quality level, his only yardstick is to see whether the goal has been achieved or not. On the other hand, when he uses process-oriented measures to look into the efforts for improvement, his criteria will be more supportive and he may be less critical of the results, since improvement is slow and comes in small steps.

In order to be supportive, management must have rapport with the workers. However, Western management often refuses to establish such rapport. Often, the supervisors in the workplace do not know how to communicate with the workers. They are afraid to talk to them, as if they did not speak the same language (which is literally true in many countries where "guest workers" are employed).

According to Neil Rackham, president of the Huthwaite Research Group, American managers put forward their own ideas nine times for every one time they build on, improve, or support other people's ideas in meetings. The amount of supportive behavior (supportive statements) varies widely but on the average is less than half the level of supportive behavior seen in groups from Singapore, Taiwan, Hong Kong, and Japan. It is essential that Western managers develop a more supportive style in dealing with each other and with workers.

Quite recently, after a day-long discussion on the Kaizen concept, William Manly, senior vice president of the Cabot Corporation, quipped: "I thought they had two major religions in Japan: Buddhism and Shintoism. Now I find they have a third: Kaizen!" Facetious though this sounds, one should have a religious zeal in promoting the Kaizen strategy and not be concerned with the immediate payout. This is a behavioral change requiring missionary zeal, and the proof of its value is in the satisfaction it brings and in its long-term impact. Kaizen is based on a belief in people's inherent desire for quality and worth, and management has to believe that it is going to "pay" in the long run.

Such things as sharing, caring, and commitment are important in Kaizen. Just as various rituals are needed in religion, Kaizen also requires rituals, since people need ways to share their experiences, support one another, and build commitment together. This is why reporting meetings are so important for QC circles. Fortunately, one does not have to wait until the next life before seeing his reward in Kaizen, as the benefits of Kaizen may be felt within four or five years, if not immediately. The punishment for not adhering to the Kaizen creed is to be left out of the enjoyment of the progress every individual and organization must experience to survive.

Kaizen also requires a different kind of leadership, leadership based on personal experience and conviction and not necessarily on authority, rank, or age. Anybody who has gone through the experience himself can become a leader. For proof, one only has to note how enthusiastically QC circle leaders, young and old, make their presentations at meetings. This is because improvement brings many truly satisfying experiences in life: identifying problems, thinking and learning together, tackling and solving difficult tasks, and thus being elevated to new heights of achievement.

REFERENCES
1. Economic Eye, June 1983, published by Keii Koho Center. Reprinted by permission.
2. Op cit., pp. 42-43, 46-48.

II

QUALITY AND PEOPLE

THE SOFT TECHNOLOGIES OF QUALITY

What do human factors have to do with quality?
Just as much as measurement standards

C. PHILIP ALEXANDER

There is a new wind blowing through the quality profession. It is bringing some very different messages to those of us who manage and support the quality functions of our organizations. These messages tell us about quality in ways that are hard to reconcile with our traditional understanding of quality. They are messages like "quality is customer satisfaction" or even "quality is customer delight"; "quality people do quality work" and "quality is the expression of human excellence."

We have difficulty with the messages because, as one quality professional noted, "I don't know how to develop specifications from these ways of thinking about quality." It is a real dilemma because our history and technology have been built upon our ability to specify, measure, and control. As long as these specifications have been based on objectively measurable phenomena like length, weight, hardness, frequency, etc., we can set standards and develop control procedures based on these standards. Now we are confronted with a way of understanding that is expressed as customer satisfaction or even customer delight. How are we to translate this into specifications and standards?

We learn from psychologists and organization development professionals that the quality of work life is highly important in producing quality goods and delivering quality services. We believe that it takes quality people to do quality work. What is the process that generates quality of work life (QWL) and supports the development of quality people? Are the human systems in our organizations capable, as quality professionals understand the term, of providing high quality of work life? Are they under control? If not, what does it take to get them under control?

These are strange ways of thinking for quality professionals. They are beginning to take shape, however, and the outlines of a new dimension of quality are coming into view. In its broadest sense, this new dimension is couched in the subjective understanding of quality rather than the objective understanding of quality. It refers to the unfamiliar inner dimensions of quality rather than the familiar outer dimensions.[1]

It is useful to refer to this as "soft" or inner quality as compared to the "hard" or objective quality with which we are more familiar. Hence, the study of this new dimension of quality leads to "soft technologies" of quality.

THE QUALITY TRANSACTION

To better understand the soft technologies of quality, consider a concept called the quality transaction.[2] Figure 1 shows the simplest quality transaction, a supplier of goods and/or services and a customer who pays for them and provides information (feedback) to the supplier. The quality transaction provides a framework for examining the relevant quality issues from both the customer's and the supplier's standpoint. It integrates all of the usual organizational functions.

In Figure 1, the supplier creates a product or service or a combination of both, as shown in the lower box. The product and the process by which it is made are objectively measurable and are the focus for the hard technologies of quality. These include sampling plans, SPC and SQC, analysis of variance (ANOVA), design of experiments, and other techniques familiar to quality professionals. This area is also the focus for the functions of manufacturing, engineering, design, and quality as we generally think of them.

A similar but less familiar part of the quality transaction is the reciprocal flow of payment and information, the upper box in Figure 1. Payment and feedback are integral parts of the quality transaction. Reduce the flow of money from the customer to the supplier, and the quality and/or volume of the product will be reduced. Reduce the flow of information from the customer to the supplier, and the quality as perceived by the customer will decline, particularly in a competitive situation. These elements of the quality transaction are generally regarded as the domain of the accounting, marketing, and human resource functions. They are also important to the quality professional.

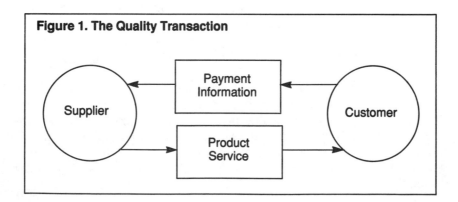

Figure 1. The Quality Transaction

The customer, on the right side of the figure, is the target of the distribution and sales functions. The supplier, on the left, is the focus of the human resources and industrial engineering functions. Using the quality transaction framework we can see how the various organizational functions have roles in the transaction.

Allowing the organizational functions to maintain a certain exclusivity (called turf) in their areas of interest ignores the interrelatedness of all of the elements of the quality transaction. Only in recent years has there been movement to integrate these functions. Quality function deployment (QFD) is an excellent example in which the design, manufacturing, and quality functions are integrated with the customer. Similarly, quality of work life programs integrate the functions of human resources, industrial engineering, and manufacturing on the supplier's side.

THINKING OBJECTIVELY

Now consider the quality transaction on the basis of an objective vs. a subjective perspective. For those who are comfortable with left brain/right brain terminology, those terms can also be used to make the comparison.

Objectively, or from the linear, rational left brain perspective, the elements of concern are only those that can be described and measured objectively. The main focus is on the box in the lower center—the product and the production process by which it is made. Services are generally described in terms of associated products or objectively measurable parameters, such as time. The roles of the customer and supplier are limited to their objective, rational, left brain behavior.

From this perspective the customer makes rational choices based on objective information about the product or service in much the same way a computer would. Such things as defects and frequency of repair records will be compared with costs and expected product life. Purchasing decisions on competitive products will then be made accordingly by the rational customer. These concerns add the area of reliability to the quality professional's portfolio and expand the definition of quality to include "fitness for use."

Similarly, from the objective or left brain perspective, the supplier is an extension of the production process. The supplier collects information on the product and process, makes rational decisions based on comparison with specifications or objectives, and controls the process to maximize quality and productivity. The supplier also calculates cost-benefit ratios for alternative employment opportunities, thereby creating a need for wage, salary, and benefit administrators, labor relations professionals, safety engineers, and others in the human resources field. Also, physical constraints require that the production and other equipment be tailored to match the requirements of the individual supplier to maximize quality and productivity. This becomes the domain of the industrial or human factors engineer.

If this were a full representation of the situation, appropriate software could be written for the supplier and customer and the whole thing could be let go at that. Obviously it is not, even though scientific management tends to work from this perspective. Let's now examine the quality transaction from a subjective or right brain perspective.

THINKING SUBJECTIVELY

From this perspective the quality transaction takes on a very different look. The transaction is now better understood in terms of a relationship. What is important now are the values, beliefs, and emotions of the supplier and customer. The product becomes the tangible expression of the supplier's values, commitments, and creative abilities. Service becomes the intangible expression. Similarly, the returning payment and information are expressions of gratitude by the customer. The physical elements in the transaction are important mainly as perceptions affected by the values, beliefs, and emotions of the customer and supplier, who share a unique relationship. These elements are now simply means of enhancing this relationship.

From this perspective, quality looks more like trust in the sense of mutual positive regard. It is not enough that the product meets specifications and is fit for use. It must also enhance the customer's feelings of well-being in light of his or her own particular values, beliefs, emotions, and perceptions. This is called customer satisfaction and even customer delight.

Similarly, the supplier also perceives the return of payment and information and integrates it with his or her perception of the working environment, difficulty of the work, feeling of accomplishment, relationship with associates, and other subjective factors. The result is the supplier's perceived quality of work life. It could just as easily be called supplier satisfaction, but the quality of work life label is generally applied to this area. Customer satisfaction and quality of work life, then, become the main areas of focus for the soft technologies of quality. It is important to remember, however, that these are perceptions and not objective measurements. I will discuss this point later.

It is worth noting that even the hard technologies of quality take on a different perception when viewed subjectively. They are no longer techniques to be used to improve process capability or product quality. From this perspective they become potential means for enhancing the supplier's creative abilities and feelings of competence and self-worth. Thus these techniques can contribute to the supplier's quality of work life, but only when they mesh with his or her values, beliefs, and perceptions.

Summarizing this exploration of the quality transaction, the hard technologies of quality focus on products, production processes, objectively measurable phenomena, and the rational, left brain aspects of customer and supplier. The soft technologies of quality focus on the inner, subjective perceptions of customer and supplier that cannot be objectively measured in the usual sense. The quality transaction takes on the character of a relationship in which quality itself takes on the nature of trust. Quality products and services become the tangible and intangible expressions of human excellence.

These two complementary perspectives are quite different from each other. Quality professionals must understand and be able to use both.

PRACTICAL APPLICATIONS

Having reviewed the general framework for the soft technologies of quality, what do they look like in practice? The information in Figure 2 covers the major elements of the soft quality technologies and their related applications.

This list is meant to convey the general nature of the area and show the more important and better-known programs, activities, and techniques. Many of these are well known to professionals in the fields of psychology, organizational development, human resources, marketing, and sales. Quality professionals must be familiar with these areas to meet their responsibilities in improving product and service quality. Managers must also understand them to support the work of quality professionals in their firms.

MISAPPLICATION OF HARD QUALITY TECHNOLOGY

In examining the soft technologies of quality, it is useful to look at some of the ways that the hard technologies have been misapplied. Probably the most important is in the area of measurement. The hard technologies are based on objective measurements, so it seems reasonable to attempt to make similar measurements in the subjective area and use these as a basis for statistical techniques and other methods. Unfortunately, in the subjective arena, each person's perceptions and internal values are the criteria. They are typically not laid out in neat, logical relationships subject to simple measurement. These values are interrelated in dynamic and ever-changing ways.

For example, imagine what would happen if all of the standard 12-inch rulers in the desk drawers of your company were replaced by the "psychological yardsticks" of their owners. First, we would notice that the actual lengths of these scales varied over a wide range. Some would be several times longer than the others. Then we would notice that the 12 units would not be uniformly distributed along the scale. On some they would be bunched up at the high end, on others at the low end. On some they would be bunched up at both ends, and on others in

---

Figure 2.
The soft technologies of quality and related applications

1. Measurement and Information Gathering Techniques
a. Quantitative
   • Customer satisfaction surveys and quantitative market research techniques
   • QWL, employee, and organizational surveys
b. Qualitative
   • Customer panels, interviews, and focus groups
   • Employee interviews, "sound off" groups, and suggestion programs

2. Improvement Programs
a. Team or group involvement—quality circles, employee involvement (EI) teams, corrective action teams, self-managing work groups, socio-technical systems (STS), participative management, and consensus decision making
b. Individual involvement—management by wandering around (MBWA), performance management, career management, and suggestion programs
c. Rewards and incentives—gainsharing programs, individual and group bonus and incentive programs
d. Recognition and communication—recognition banquets and occasions, employee and customer-of-the-month awards, circle of excellence awards, newsletters, appreciation letters, sharing rallies

3. Education and Training
a. Measurement of training quality and effectiveness
b. Inclusion of the soft technologies of quality in undergraduate- and graduate-level curricula in both technology and business

4. Standards and Certification
a. Standards—development and inclusion of soft technologies and human system aspects into quality standards
b. Certification
   • Development of the appropriate body of knowledge for the soft technologies of quality
   • Upgrade quality professional certification examination questions for inclusion of soft technologies
   • Develop certification for quality circle and EI team facilitators
c. Human factors—determine objective and subjective aspects of person/machine interface on quality
d. Leadership and management—improve management understanding of both hard and soft technologies of quality

the middle. And finally, if this were not complex enough, all of the scales would stretch and bend like rubber, some very easily and others with difficulty. It would help to keep this in mind if you're trying to design a simple 10-point scale to measure customer satisfaction or quality of work life.

Not only does measurement itself illustrate a fundamental difference between the hard and soft technologies, but the use of measurements is also different. The primary use of measurements in the hard technologies is to control and reduce variability in products and processes. Accuracy of measurement and the use of proper statistical procedures are essential.

In the soft technologies, the main objectives are to improve customer satisfaction and quality of work life. Actually, these two objectives have much in common. Within the organization, everyone is both customer and supplier. Each person is a supplier to someone else, and is also someone else's customer. Thus, improving the internal quality of the person accomplishes both objectives.

However, in improving the internal quality of the person, we are not trying to reduce variability. We want to increase the capabilities of each person to express his or her unique set of values, purposes, intents, and creativity within the organizational context. When seen in this light, we are actually trying to increase variability in the human system.

The difficulty occurs when we mistakenly try to equate the human system or organization with the production process. People are not machines or parts. While this certainly seems self-evident, there are many cases in which people are treated like machines.

Consider the simple act of taking a measurement. Most production processes are highly automated with an assortment of measuring devices that continually measure and, through manual or automatic controls, adjust the variables influencing the process, thereby reducing variability in the output. These measuring devices are routinely calibrated to ensure a high degree of accuracy.

It seems reasonable to think of the human system as a production process. In so doing we can measure the critical variables like pay, benefits, working conditions, etc., and use this information to reduce variability and improve human performance. However, the simple act of measurement in the human system introduces a significant variable. It changes expectations, and expectations make a considerable difference to most people.

Consider this illustration. In the late 1960s and early '70s, a major refinery took a series of surveys to measure the quality of work life. Survey questionnaires were administered to the entire work force of several thousand employees and managers. The first two surveys were taken about a year apart and showed almost no statistically significant differences. The third survey, taken three years later, showed appreciable deterioration in the results.

This was a considerable surprise to the management. From their perspective there had been little or no change in the overall operations or the business climate during the entire period. To validate the findings of the third survey, a series of interviews was undertaken. The results were best explained by one refinery worker's comment: "We told them twice (the first two surveys) what the problems were and management didn't do a thing about them."

Products and processes can be measured as often as one likes and the results will only show normal operational or measurement variation. With people this is not the case. Machines and products do not care what is done with the measured information. People do. This is not to say that surveys cannot be used. Rather, in the soft technologies, it cannot be assumed that the familiar understandings of the hard technologies will apply.

Another common misapplication of hard quality technology is in trying to apply common statistical procedures to human system processes. All of us are familiar with the bell-shaped curve of standard distribution. We know what percentage of the area under the curve is within plus or minus one sigma unit, or plus or minus two or three sigma units.

This information is very useful. But we forget that an essential feature of the standard curve is that it is based on measurements generated by a random process. People functioning in organizations are motivated. Hence, the measured results of their activities can rarely meet the test of random generation. Therefore, one would not expect to find a distribution pattern resembling the standard curve when examining a large number of performance measures, for example, unless these were machine paced.

Unfortunately, many firms assume that performance variations must have some relationship resembling the standard curve and force fit them on this basis to classify them for merit pay increases. Quite apart from variability in individual performance created by management or the system, and the problems of measuring performance subjectively, we simply cannot assume that performance is based on random behavior. Therefore, all we can say about it is that it will probably vary. The pattern of variation is unknown and can change based on motivation, experience, skill, and ability.

Problems arising from trying to measure subjective things like QWL and customer satisfaction, and from misapplying statistical concepts based on random processes to motivate human behavior, are the kinds of problems that an understanding of the soft technologies of quality will reduce or eliminate.

NEW PERSPECTIVE ON HARD QUALITY TECHNOLOGY

In the soft technologies, the familiar hard quality technologies and statistical procedures take on a different meaning. They are not applied to the human system as they are in the production process or in determining product quality. They are now thought of as new tools and techniques that will enhance the inner quality of some (but probably not all) individuals. They will enable people to better express their values, purposes, and beliefs in creative ways through the production of goods and services. In the hard technologies we focus on the product or process. In the soft technologies we focus on the person.

Consider this example. The person chosen as facilitator for a quality circle program in a manufacturing plant had considerable production experience but none in quality or statistical processes. As part of his training he received training in SPC/SQC and "discovered" variability. It was a real revelation to him. He was excited by the opportunity this new knowledge gave him to improve plant operations through the use of control charts and other statistical techniques. And, more important from his perspective, to share this new and exciting discovery with others in the organization through the quality circle program.

With knowledge gained from the soft technology, he did not immediately set up training programs for all of the employees. Rather, he told them about the quality circle program, what was in it for them, and asked them if they would like to volunteer. Those that did were taught the statistical processes and learned to use them for solving problems that they selected in their work area. After they became familiar with the statistical processes, they were introduced into the production operations. However, the quality circles still discussed the production applications in their circle meetings.

This facilitator was using soft quality technology to implement hard quality technology. The statistical processes are the same in both cases. However, in the hard technology, the statistical processes are mainly a means for improving the production process. In the soft technology, these processes are mainly a means for improving the employees' internal quality and productive capabilities. In both cases an improved product results, but the difference is the focus.

These ideas might sound strange to managers and quality professionals in the United States, but the basic philosophy has been well developed and integrated into companywide quality control (CWQC) as practiced in Japan. The late Kaoru Ishikawa made these observations about the practice of CWQC in 1985:

> CWQC requires a move from top-down management to a management philosophy of respect for humanity....Top-

down management must play an active leadership role even though the company's philosophy promotes respect for humanity, volunteerism, creativity, and ideas in a bottom-up manner...

A QC education should seek to give workers the satisfaction of achieving their goals and doing their jobs well, the happiness of cooperating with others and being recognized by others, and the joy of personal growth.

The real growth, in my opinion, is human happiness through CWQC.[3]

In the United States we have a high regard for the quality of Japanese products, but we do not yet understand that the quality of Japanese products is an outcome of a CWQC system in which the real aim is human happiness—the satisfaction of achievement, the good feelings of cooperation, the pride of being recognized, and the joy of personal growth. These are clearly the dimensions of inner quality and the cornerstones of the soft technologies.

Ishikawa's soft words are backed up with hard yen. A typical world-class Japanese manufacturing company is investing 4% of total plant capital investment costs in selecting and training employees for a new operation in the United States. This is equivalent to 18% of their first year's gross payroll. This is an awesome measure of commitment to people, but this is the kind of commitment it will take from firms that want to compete in world-class markets.

THE NEW QUALITY PARADIGM

This has been a very broad overview of the soft quality technologies and their applications. Perhaps by the turn of the century the soft technologies of quality will be as routine and as well understood by quality professionals as sampling plans and control charts. By the year 2000 we might have technical, undergraduate-, and graduate-level programs that cover both the hard and soft quality technologies. We might also have certification for facilitators in quality circles, employee involvement, and related programs. We might have quality system standards that encompass the human system. And we might even have ways of thinking about quality in the human system that are as yet entirely unknown. It is a new and exciting arena for the quality professional.

Let me conclude by sharing a vision of the future for the quality profession. It enhances the existing hard technologies of quality by placing them on a foundation comprised of the inner or soft dimensions of quality and the needs and priorities of the person in the human system. I believe it is a vision worthy of our profession.

In the new quality paradigm, we will shift our focus from seeing quality as something "out there" to understanding it as something "in here." Quality will begin not as conformance to specifications, fitness for use, or even customer satisfaction. Quality will begin internally as a vision, as an awareness of a creative impulse to express values and ideals. It will begin as the shaping and expression of our dreams. Quality will become the manifestation of human intellect and ability in its myriad forms. And we will know the quality product or service for what it truly is—the visible and tangible expression of human excellence.

REFERENCES

1. C. Philip Alexander, "Quality's Third Dimension," *Quality Progress,* July 1988.

2. C. Philip Alexander, "Reconceptualizing Quality," *Quality Progress,* October 1987.

3. Kaoru Ishikawa, "How to Apply Companywide Quality Control in Foreign Countries," *Quality Progress,* September 1989.

ORGANIZATION-WIDE QUALITY PROGRAMS

How to avoid common pitfalls and create competitive advantage

ROLAND A. DUMAS, PH.D.

How to Bake a Cake

After several years of investigating organization-wide quality programs, I and some of my colleagues facetiously use an unusual analogy. If a company were to bake a cake in the same way that it introduces a quality system, the recipe would read like this:

> Find an expert and ask what ingredient is key to a good cake. Get that ingredient and bake it. Throw it out. Find another expert and ask what ingredient he believes is most critical. Get that ingredient and bake it. Throw out the mess. Repeat. Repeat.

Managers would process a series of perfectly good ingredients in a "logical" manner, and serially discard them, occasionally polluting the tools and the environment. It almost sounds like a bad ethnic joke: "How does a corporation bake a cake? One ingredient at a time and then it reorganizes."

This "serial cake baking" method parallels what we see happening in the typical company-wide program where a company adopts the program of a "guru," including the bias toward a single tool. When the program does not achieve the desired outcome, it is replaced by another guru, and so forth. In the end, there is a lot of experience, a lot of expenditure, and a fair amount of frustration at the total cost and the elusiveness of total quality.

The Investigation

During the past several years, I and my colleagues have investigated company quality systems. The formal studies were conducted while I was employed by Zenger-Miller, Inc., a training company. In that process, we have learned a lot about how organizations evolve quality awareness, and how they almost predictably take a series of easy tactical solutions, before facing up to the reality of the culture change inherent in quality improvement. During this period, we collected information from a variety of sources. This reflects information from more than 1000 organizations. It covers all industries and regions, including service companies. We gathered this information from interviews with people at various job levels (from executives to front-line employees) and from surveys that covered practices, expenditures, and experiences in wider numbers of companies.

We have, out of necessity, become students of the major quality disciplines in order to understand the points of view of the quality "teachers", as well as to be able to track the outcomes of the instruction and programs. In a sense, we have taken on the role of "disciple" of several gurus, and become conversant in the rationale and philosophy of each, as well as familiar with the "techniques" that each has to offer.

Drawing from this enormous quantity of information, we often find that the most valuable information is gained from people working in organizations that have quality programs, but who are not the primary directors of those programs. Confidential interviews, sometimes off-site, have provided invaluable information about quality programs that was not available from program "owners," top level managers, and people who have political interests in the programs. It is often the case that the perceived and promoted results of a quality program are not representative of what one finds by digging into the real experience of people working in the system.

What We Found: The Serial Cake Baking Recipe
Historically, a typical organization goes through a series of efforts that are correct, but which frequently betray poor assumptions or poor integration with other efforts. The typical company first understands that there is a quality problem based on complaints or a competitive comparison of quality.

Executives interpret the problem as a worker motivation problem. That is, they see it as a poor work ethic, a union issue, lack of attention, or other interpretation that infers attentional or motivational shortcomings of front-line employees.

The organization then progresses through a series of programs based on the assumption that it is the fault of one group or another that quality is not competitive. The series often includes several, if not all, of this list:
- Employee motivation programs
- Employee skill programs (quality circles, SPC, sales training etc.)
- Employee incentive programs (financial, awards)
- Work teams and autonomous teams
- Robotics and automation to replace labor
- MRPII, cost of quality, information integration systems
- Just in time, supplier management systems

In many cases, an organization works right through this list in serial fashion. Previous programs are either discontinued, or given little attention after the initial thrust.

As we observed the efforts in these series, the thinking of many executives became obvious (and is corroborated in interviews). Despite public statements to the contrary, their behavior indicates that they believe that the solution to quality problems is to change some group of people. Initially, it is the workers: motivate them, train them, reward them, clump them, and then, in frustration, replace them with machines. Next under scrutiny are supervisors and middle managers.

The second wave involves tightening management controls and pushing the problem upstream to suppliers. In many cases, companies have spun off operations that had intractable quality problems, and then held them accountable to higher quality standards.

There is nothing wrong with any one of these methods (in fact, total quality companies may be doing all of them). They are, however, often done in a fragmented fashion without commitment or integration, and are frequently done for the wrong reasons. Rather than being parts of a larger effort to adopt a new philosophy, they appear to be part of a witch hunt in which upper management is determined to fix or eliminate the offending party.

Whether this is the intention or not (we have no way of knowing), the target populations tend to resist rather than welcome the improvements. Manufacturing managers obey the letter of the law in installing SQC systems, but don't use them in making decisions, preventing breakdowns, or scheduling maintenance. They are simply recorded and stored, or replaced with traditional inspection methods. Passive acceptance, pocket vetoes, and other resistance methods are not uncommon.

Quality professionals find themselves outrageously frustrated when they attempt to install quality improvement and cost saving-systems, only to find their customers unexcited or passively resistant. The issue is not resistance to quality, but often to the implied inference that they are the cause of the problem and have been singled out as the party in need of repair. The quality professional often finds himself or herself able to install new testing machines, but not change minds of production management or financial controllers.

While this is a "typical" learning effort, the real situation is not quite so bleak. As companies travel through whatever serial cake baking recipe they may have, they aren't just trying and discarding fads. Through the process of elimination, the problem eventually comes home as a leadership issue. *That systems need to be integrated and led evolves as the long-term learning.*

Tracking Expenditures: Pareto on His Head
Validating this conclusion was a study that tracked the kinds of outside training and development expenditures that were made in total quality

efforts compared to the problems that typical companies experience. We found that about 80 percent of outside expenditures went for technical training and installing new systems, such as cost of quality. Less than 20 percent was related to management leadership and involvement in the programs.

When respondents were asked where the major problems were, the ratio reversed. Eighty percent of the problems were associated with management leadership, support and involvement, and 20 percent related to technical skills. In other words, the Pareto principle was stood on its head: 80 percent of the effort was going to fix 20 percent of the problem.

The real issues that quality implementors reported in our investigation was that management bought "systems" to "install" in the organization, but did not really understand the underlying philosophy, much less support the quality programs that they had initiated. The most frequent experience was that the top levels of the company delegated responsibilities too quickly and continued to demand actions that were not compatible with the new quality standards. It is this contradictory example that undermines others' willingness to make change.

In interviews with senior management, they showed belief that they had bought technical and management systems that would be strategic additions or changes to their businesses. They are generally not aware that most total quality systems require a change in their attitude and behavior as a critical element of success.

Implementation and Instructional Methods

Most total quality programs are brought in from outside companies or are adapted from proprietary packaged programs that are in widespread use. The most widely used or imitated packages are associated with well known quality gurus, each with a different emphasis and a system of seminars, training sessions, and techniques. One may stress SQC, another quality functional deployment, and a third cost of quality.

While we developed clear preferences for the sense and utility of some programs over others, we found some common gaps in these programs. The gaps seemed to emanate from the experience of the initial developers of the programs. These fell into two groups: management-originated programs and engineering-originated programs.

The management-originated programs suffered from excessive awareness-building and expectation-raising without adequate skill-building or support. There were lots of events, meetings, affirmations, and rules and bureaucracies, but little connection to daily life on the job and few of the underlying skills so an employee could follow the rules.

The engineering-oriented programs had technical methods and skills that were up to the job, but were not able to capture the attention of nontechnical employees, including managers. The common logical methods that technical professionals are used to and prefer tend to be deadly for everyone else in the world.

Both types of effort suffer from problems of instructional methodology, and consequently don't get their messages across effectively.

The larger problem that plagues most total quality efforts is the absence of a realistic implementation program. Some packaged systems come with numerically listed "steps." The inference is that if all of the steps are accomplished, then quality will be improved. These generate a false sense of accomplishment, as organizations race to get to the bottom of the list as quickly as possible. Each step is taken as more of a procedure or an event to be staged.

Most of these programs want for a method of assuring that systems, culture, skills, and other important variables are deployed sensibly and effectively. The process is a genuinely profound organizational change, not a corporate chain letter. It needs thoughtful, competent leadership and planning, complete with a voice strong enough to call senior managers to task for their own behavior.

Role of Quality and Training Professionals

We found it curious that the major gaps in most programs, integration of awareness with technology, training methods, and implementation skills, call for a significant role for two types of people: Human resource professionals, and quality professionals. Organizational development and training skills are the hallmark of a competent human resource professional. The ability to identify the technical system and technical skills required for a given job are second nature to quality engineers.

When we looked at the leadership of most total quality programs, we found an ironic evolutionary process. The origins of the typical program are found in executive initiative—the purchase of a packaged program or the declaration that there would be a given emphasis. The early stages of organization-wide efforts often exclude both human resource and quality professionals.

These individuals typically are brought in to administer the program after key decisions are made, including the outside expertise that forms the frame of the program. They generally have little opportunity to make their respective contributions until it is "rework" time.

Service Quality Parallels

In a separate investigation, we studied organization-wide service quality programs, principally in the financial, retail, and health care industries. We found that organizations with no hard product have problems determining the quality of their products, as some aren't consumed until a distant future date (insurance), and others are consumed at the time of transaction with no objective trace of the relative quality level (a retail transaction).

Increasingly, service sector companies and white collar areas of manufacturing companies are under pressure to demonstrate quality gains just as are the production areas. Under the banner of "white collar productivity," many organizations are expressing frustration over the inability to achieve either quality improvement or efficiency derived from investments in automated administrative systems.

The efforts that we saw in the service quality investigation were amazingly similar to what we saw when we looked at the course of quality programs. The first efforts were largely targeted at motivating front-line employees. They were trained subsequently to initiate customer contacts and cross sell "products." With variable results, later efforts increasingly recognize the role of systems, management, and leadership in the effort. Organizations are realizing that you cannot expect higher quality service from the front-line employees when the internal service quality is substandard.

Second generation service quality programs bear little resemblance to old-style customer service training. No longer are they focused on the front line employee exclusively, and less and less are they focused on smiling and selling, but on discovering and meeting customers' real needs.

OBSERVATIONS AND RECOMMENDATIONS

Some issues are common enough that we can confidently make some general recommendations in the area of developing and implementing an organization-wide quality effort. These points are by no means substitutes for guidelines that Deming, Juran, or other experts offer.

Rather, they are empirically derived recommendations that may reinforce or supplement the company-wide guidelines. They are the points that, though they may be stated in formal programs, often aren't understood by many companies:

1. *Quality is a Management Leadership Issue.* How management thinks, behaves and structures systems is the pivotal issue.

2. *Take care of the basics.* Introducing new systems and technologies when people don't have the fundamental skills to work in the new systems is a prescription for disaster.

3. *Implement systems and technical change WITH social change.* People are more receptive to new ways of management and working together when the systems are changing. Implementing social and technical change is synergistic.

4. *Focus on some basic concepts.* The definition of quality should

relate easily to everyone's job. It should be simple and practical.

5. *Join the post-charismatic generation.* Don't abrogate responsibility to make decisions to famous experts. None of them has a complete answer, and they all have something worthwhile to say. Learn from them all, and then become your own guide.

6. *Broaden scope.* We all can learn from organizations in a wide variety of industries, even those which are not doing as well as you believe you are. Broaden the scope of your effort to include quality of management decisions, the sales process, hiring and promotion, training, and every aspect of the business. They all influence customer satisfaction.

7. *Concentrate on a value-driven approach.* Above all, quality is an ethic, a value more important than financial return. When held as a higher standard, then there is more buy-in from employees, and the actual financial return will reflect the higher customer satisfaction and market acceptance than a cost reduction approach.

TRENDS AND PREDICTIONS

In conducting the investigation on quality, we noted some general trends that transcend individual company programs. Obviously, there is a greater awareness of the issue today than a decade ago, and greater specific skill in more people.

What may not be obvious is that *the definition of quality is evolving* in a predictable fashion, and that is being driven by the marketplace.

We often hear that consumers are continually pressing for higher levels of quality. Our interpretation of the history of quality suggests that the marketplace not only demands increasing quality to stay competitive, but that the very definition of quality is evolving also. That is, there is within each market, a periodic upheaval in which a more powerful definition of quality turns the market upside down. Those who were formerly quality leaders find themselves "trumped" by new players.

We see this progression as a hierarchy. A definition of quality represents both the objectives and the upper limits of achievement. For instance, the lowest level of quality definition is that quality is synonymous with more features.

This standard of definition was common in the 1950's and 1960's in the automobile industry, and may characterize the financial services industry today. With this kind of definition, better quality is achieved by adding more features to a base product or by differentiating products on the basis of feature elements. When all competitors accept this definition, then it is easy to pick out the higher quality producers.

This definition fails, however, when customers become aware that extra features are superfluous if the base product is unreliable. This

```
┌─────────────────────────────────────────────────────────┐
│  Quality Definitions: A Hierarchy                         │
│                                                           │
│                                  4. It Develops           │
│                                                           │
│                       3. It Satisfies                     │
│                                                           │
│              2. It Works                                  │
│                                                           │
│     1. Extra Features                                     │
│                                                           │
└─────────────────────────────────────────────────────────┘
```

realization is often precipitated by a new market entry that offers products or services that are simple and that work. The definition of "it works" trumps the definition of "extra features."

This is what happened when Volkswagen thumbed its nose at Detroit and sold a basic product that had none of the features which characterized the old quality standard. It simply changed the definition. There are lots of ways of expressing "it works," such as "meets customer specifications," and "right the first time."

Just as "it works" trumps "extras," "satisfaction" trumps "it works." When quality definitions express the responsibility to satisfy customers or satisfy customer expectations, they go beyond meeting the articulated needs (fitness for sale) to the customers' real needs (fitness for use). Juran's definition, "Quality is fitness for use" or 3M's "Quality is meeting customer expectations 100 percent of the time" are good examples of this level of awareness and competitiveness. They compel a different set of measures, ones that focus on customers' experiences rather than producers' "self serving" (as put by 3M) standards.

Organizations that actually respond to such definitions find themselves with distinctive competitive advantages over those who meet specifications or requirements. After all, there are products that meet requirements that turn out to be non-functional or even dangerous in the long run. Consumers don't always know what they need at the time of purchase, but have a right to expect that the producer does and will take responsibility to provide for fitness for use.

However, the progression of quality demands, awareness, and definition should not be expected to stay still. If we extrapolate from what we are currently seeing to project future trends, there is another level of quality that should appear as a trump card to the "satisfaction" level.

This is that products and services develop customers. That is, they make customers better consumers by educating them and exposing them to greater value from the products and services. This would not just be product use training as is currently generally offered, but service that appreciably enhances the value of the product to the customer.

There are examples of this level of quality already in practice, although it is far from widespread. 3M's overhead projectors, for example, when sold to corporate customers, come with training on the conduct of better business meetings. Not just the use of the projector, but better management. Their correct assumption is that better quality meetings will create more received value from their products. This comes from the awareness that they are not selling a bag of features, nor just properly working features that meet the expectations of projected images. They are providing better business decisions.

In our investigation, we see that different industries are at different stages in the definition of quality. Within industries, there is competition within a definition and competitive advantage when one competitor elevates the operating definition of quality to the next level.

Organization-wide quality programs are also helped or hampered by their operating definitions of quality. When the practiced and promoted definition of quality is on a lower level, it puts a ceiling on the awareness of members of that environment and represents an upper limit to the achievements that can be expected. When the definition as practiced and promoted is at the high end of the spectrum, it makes possible greater levels of improvement.

We believe that there is also a strong motivating effect on employees when the definition of quality takes on the tones of consumer rights that the higher levels have. It makes one's responsibility clearer, and related to higher social morals.

SUMMARY

This on-going exploration into organization-wide quality programs is not characterized by comparisons of technical sophistication of systems but, rather, the effectiveness of programs as wholes. In this investigation, we found some patterns that typify an average company's involvement in total quality, complete with frequently occurring false steps.

If there are general learnings, beyond the points described above, they are that the understood, promoted, and practiced definition of quality is critically important. It is probably worthy of special attention in the formative stages of a program, including industry comparisons.

This definition, along with the observation that management leadership practices and management systems have avoided key elements in many efforts leads us to strongly suggest: *No organization-wide system should be adopted until management understands its role in leading by example and creating a quality ethic that is supported by management systems and daily behavior.* Multi-step programs should not be initiated until the environmental conditions created by management are addressed.

JOIN FORCES FOR TOTAL QUALITY CONTROL

Or: Take a trainer to lunch

ROLAND A. DUMAS, PH.D.

We are, without a doubt, undergoing a quality revolution in America. Companies are searching for the latest quality technologies to incorporate into everything from manufacturing to government services.

In interviews with professional quality engineers and managers, however, we have developed a sense that many identify closely with the mythological figure, Sisyphus. Sisyphus was condemned to push a heavy stone up a long hill, only to have it roll down again in a never-ending cycle.

In the same way, quality professionals often report extreme frustration over setting up easy-to-use and sophisticated QC systems, only to find them disabled, overridden, or "buried" by their internal customers. Their customers are managers who are up to their eyes in quality problems, yet are unable to see the significance of the potential impact of a total quality system.

Many managers and executives see quality systems as "techniques" to be incorporated into their traditional portfolio of management tools. Quality professionals see the systems as not so much "tools," but rather as an essential viewpoint in the development of competitive businesses.

The Impact of Individuals

When we looked into these situations, we found cases like this one:

> Tony Montegue, 27, is a quiet, bespectacled production worker in a new plant of an established midwestern manufacturing company. Its high-tech look and participative management make this factory different from anything Tony or his friends have known before. They're all survivors of a turbulent economy in America's rust belt. Dubbed "associates" rather than workers (or, as many deprecatingly refer to themselves in older companies, "slugs"), the company is betting its future on high tech run by highly involved employees.
>
> A key feature of the company's success formula is a Total

Quality Management system. The "cost of quality" is tracked in every department, and analyzed scrupulously to find ways to get higher quality at lower cost. At the same time, a statistical process control system tracks hundreds of variables, including white collar and management systems. When the statistics indicate that something might be out of adjustment, someone is expected to hit the panic button, regardless of what might be the cause or who might be responsible for the problem.

The systems are in place, reports are issued regularly and accurately and reviewed, with frequent and intense trouble-shooting meetings with managers and production workers. Still, beneath the surface, there is skepticism about the company's ability to actually live up to the super-efficient and high quality goals it has set for itself. Not that people don't want it to happen or don't personally believe in it; it's just that the day-to-day experience of employees and managers doesn't measure up to the public image or to the formal plans.

In Tony's situation, it comes down to a decision of whether or not to hit the button. "The Button" (oftentimes a figurative button) is accessible to every employee and, when hit, stops production in that immediate area and signals adjacent work teams to whirl into impromptu trouble-shooting activities. They are under the gun to find the cause of the problem and cure it so that the delicate scheduling of the whole plant doesn't get tangled up. Everyone knows that when the button is hit, it's the result of a statistical calculation about the machines' tendency to start going out of whack. Still, the button-pusher, while doing a great service to quality and the official plan, is no folk hero.

As Tony describes it, "When you hit the button, fifty pairs of eyes are suddenly on you. You've jeopardized single-handedly the productivity of the next team down the line, and blown the whistle on either the team upstream or the maintenance group, not to mention the managers. Just-in-time starts to look like 'Not-quite-in-time.' It's bad news, no matter how you cut it."

There is a tendency to "shoot the messenger," no matter how right the message. It's worse than the older plant where another department (Quality Control) would give a formal report criticizing your quality. Now, the 'enemy' isn't from another department, but is a member of your own team.

Tony's predicament is the conflict between following the company's very clear high-tech quality objectives, and its almost ideological promotion of team work and "fellowship" as the means to attain those objectives. Mutual congratulations for all achievements, and a positive attitude about the company are as standard an apparel as the white jumpsuits worn by associates and their managers in the plants. This attitude is seen as being an essential component of the total quality program.

Montegue notes, however, that "good fellowship" sometimes gets in the way of pushing the button. There are lots of ways of avoiding pushing the button, including feigning overwork, "losing" a sample of data, or even falsifying the data. This pushes the problem downstream, and saves a worker from taking a bit of risky initiative.

Tony Montegue is a composite character, created during a study of company-wide quality systems. Many manufacturing employees and managers feel they know him personally. The more experience companies have had with implementing quality programs, the more real Tony is.

Troubles aren't encountered only at the worker level. Just as likely, managers are simply reluctant to give up old ways of doing things, and are apprehensive about solving problems "before they occur" (as they understand the purpose of SPC). They conceptually buy off on installing sophisticated QC methods, but they balk at the idea of fixing things that are not, to them, currently broken.

When companies have installed quality systems, sometimes very sophisticated ones, personal issues have ever greater influence on the effect of technological solutions. In many ways, Tony Montegue represents an all too common experience with well planned quality systems. They universally rely on employee and management skills that are not part of the official quality system; they rely on initiative, and the day-to-day skills to make the initiative understandable and effective.

The Investigation

Since 1982, I have conducted research for Zenger-Miller, a developer of training programs. In the very pragmatic sense, Zenger-Miller seeks to provide the right training programs to meet the needs of companies taking on major quality improvement efforts. It has been clear for some years that quality will be the greatest competitive force in the marketplace, and also the greatest force in changing the skills required to work in competitive companies. If a training company is to be competitive in the future, it will have to provide organizations with training to develop these new skills.

Throughout this period, we have followed the introduction of everything from quality circles to just-in-time and autonomous work groups, as well as the typical behavioral responses to managers and workers to new technologies. This investigation has included personal interviews, surveys, analyses of quality audits, and analyses of the various new systems. We looked for what worked, what didn't, what new skills were needed, and what old behaviors needed to be replaced.

Technologies Versus Human Skills

Our findings have, to some extent, been counterintuitive. In this technological revolution, one would expect that the greatest need would be bringing people up to speed on new methods, such as SQC, and installing new systems, such as MRP II or a cost-of-quality system. In fact, this is the *priority*. Most companies are using some form of work teams or employee action teams, along with SQC, CIM, or just-in-time. These activities, along with cost-of-quality measurements, are where effort and attention are being devoted.

The experience of those involved in these efforts, however, suggests that new technologies and new systems are the relatively easy part. It's getting people to them that ends up being the problem. In the area of critical needs, the list contains no technical or systems issues, but exclusively behavioral and management practice issues. Leading the list of obstacles to total quality control are:

1. TURNING LIP SERVICE INTO ACTUAL MANAGEMENT COMMITMENT

Support, even to the point of spending large sums of money, does not have the persuasive punch of setting a personal example. When management agendas and behaviors remain essentially unchanged, all the training and systems installation will have little effect.

As one front line worker put it, "They can spend millions on the outside consultant, spend years in meetings and presentations, and rent the biggest band in the biggest tent for ZD day. But I watch what they do." Employees have long ago broken the code on management messages. They listen to the words, attend training, and read the posters. They actually change how they do things when they see managers and executives toeing the corporate line, and discontinuing practices that counteract or contradict the new message.

2. STICKING TO THE PROGRAM

Companies see programs come and go, and quickly get jaded about the latest trend. With the attitude of "this too shall pass", they wait for the changes to blow over. So even when managers do the right thing, they must unwaveringly continue to do it for a protracted period before they will earn the trust of the rank and file.

Those chartered with delivering either the technology or the participation in quality programs have major problems making managers understand that this is not something that they should "give a try." Doing it has no meaning until employees are persuaded that managers won't desert the cause under pressure or that the managers themselves won't be hung out to dry.

3. MANAGEMENT PRACTICES THAT SUPPORT THE TECHNOLOGIES AND SYSTEMS

When we look at every major system, including SPC, cost of quality, just-in-time, Juran's methods, Taguchi's methods, quality circles, and several others, there is a basic evolution: The systems have their origins in a specific technology or collection of tools. Each toolbox is extremely powerful. When users of the various tool boxes try to make these skills normative in an organization, they encounter cultural opposition that pure logic cannot overcome.

The gurus then formulate "general" cases of their methods, describing the actions or conditions that must be present in an organization if it is to derive benefit from the tool boxes. So, you get Deming's 14 points, Juran's 10, Crosby's 14, and so on. They are the environmental preconditions to the successful use of quality technologies and systems.

Most organizations, however, assume that they are taking care of basic management practices, and that the only thing they have to do is take on the new systems and methods. This is not the case. It is the observation of most implementors of quality systems that too much effort has been made for rapid technical improvement without the necessary groundwork. Deming's seventh point, "Institute modern methods of supervision," is a good example of the absolute necessity to clean up management methods before installing quality systems. If the management methods contradict quality principles, the life expectancy for a quality system will be short.

Practice Tends to be a Reversal of the Pareto Principle

When you look at where the real needs are in new quality systems, the irony emerges: The problems with high-technology systems are found in low-technology areas—human behavior. The focus and effort of most companies is, as stated above, on new technical methods, while the greatest need remains in the management practice area. Expenditures follow this pattern where five dollars are spent on technical and systems training for every dollar spent on management practices training.

This is a reversal of the Pareto Principle, with the least resource going to the most critical issue. This is not to argue that organizations do not need a fast and massive infusion of quality methods, but that there needs to be a balance and a planned synergy between new technical systems and the social environments in which they function.

The Higher the Tech, the Higher the People Emphasis

What our investigation uncovers is an irony of epic proportions. Corporate executives are investing heavily in high tech solutions to marketplace, economic, and social problems. Replacing workers with machines, in the view of many, is the solution to productivity, quality, and flexibility problems. In reality, however, as you install new systems, you are captive to the skills and expectations of the people remaining in the systems. As you actually reduce the absolute number of employees, you are increasingly dependent on their skills, awareness, and knowledge, not to mention the trust of those remaining.

Needless to say, trust is not engendered when a new system is introduced, complete with training, while management openly discusses reductions in force and salary roll backs for workers while appropriating new benefits, bonuses, and precious metal parachutes for themselves.

THE MISSING ELEMENTS

Instructional Methods

In addition to the needs identified by implementors of quality systems, we also found that the method of introducing new techniques often has gaps. Most programs are developed either by engineers or by line managers, rather than by professional educators. We learn a rather straightforward way of teaching in engineering schools (yes, I attended one of them): Derive and prove a new approach, spin off corollaries, turn them into applications, construct algorithms, and turn those into programmed learning. Simple, straightforward, and logical. The first thing one learns when teaching outside of engineering schools is that the straightforward method of introducing new skills and new methods typically is the hardest way to get a point across. There are situational, personal, and value connections that should be made so that people are willing to learn the new methods. As one person put it, the methods may be as easily learned as balancing a checkbook, and as hard as balancing a checkbook when you don't understand what money is. Teaching adults—as smart as they may be—new behaviors is different from teaching students or introducing a new engineering method.

Also, there are instructional methods based on advanced learning theory that have a significantly better track record than the straight didactic method. Although derived from university research, the methods typically have not been used in university level education and training. Applied cognitive social learning, known as behavior modeling, focuses on replacing "natural" behaviors with "appropriate" responses to situations. That is in distinction to teaching skills to students who have no pre-existing behaviors, skills, or expectations.

Implementation Programs

To be fully integrated into the way a company operates, a company-wide quality system must be generally accepted as a worthy replacement for the existing, comfortable, and well-known way of doing business. Something that starts as a simple "Get those people up to speed on SQC" has widespread ramifications in terms of who does what first, how decisions will be made differently, and a host of other issues.

There is an unstated question asked by every affected employee, "What does this mean for ME?" As people look for answers and attempt to create sense and stability of the new system, there is organizational upheaval. There is also a strong tendency to draw back toward the comfortable ways things were before the change.

Any quality program, no matter how straightforward or limited in scope, is an organizational change. It needs the thoughtful, experienced and structured guidance of leadership familiar with the processes of organizational change.

In the grand schemes of quality gurus, there is a sense of this change in their "general" cases. But none deal explicitly with management of organizational change. Most tell you what must be done; none tell you how.

THE ROLE OF HUMAN RESOURCE DEVELOPMENT

We have outlined three critical functions that are typically missing in company-wide quality efforts: 1. Management and interpersonal skills that parallel the rapid increase in technical change. 2. Instructional and developmental methods that employ current technologies for training and changing adult behavior. 3. Implementation strategies that take into consideration the complexity of introducing new systems into the organization.

When one looks at the list of critical needs of quality programs, and at the missing elements in the delivery of training on new quality systems, there is an uncanny overlap with the strengths of most human resources departments. It is also typical that the human resources function plays a very minor supporting role in large quality programs, and is generally not involved in sorting out issues, planning, and making the up-front decisions about what must happen, when, and with whom.

Perhaps there is a residual sense that HR is the just the old-fashioned personnel function, largely focused on maintaining records and delivering basic training to employees. This is regrettable, as many quality programs would greatly benefit from the partnership with organizational development and training functions. In many ways, human resources professionals are trying to grow out of an outdated image, just as quality control professionals must deal with old images of inspectors.

Regardless of why we found HR typically underinvolved, this is a situation that, if rectified, could dramatically accelerate acceptance and implementation of advanced quality systems. There are a number of companies that have incorporated training and organizational development resources into the planning and execution of quality systems. The early results indicate major cost savings in training and use of outside packaged services, increased acceptance of change, and successful anticipation of common pitfalls, such as those listed in this article.

Tektronix, of Beaverton, Oregon, has experienced much of the turmoil of the electronics industry in the last few years. Faced with a need to continue developing new products and control costs in a soft market, a variety of changes and systems have been introduced. Decision-making has been decentralized, the number of layers of management dramatically reduced, and decision-making driven down as far as possible.

To make the employee side of new quality systems effective, the fundamental unit, the work team, is empowered to make a lot of key decisions, including hiring into the team. To prepare employees to not only accept, but excel, in the new structure, they are likely to receive training in Zenger-Miller's *Working* course in working with team members, "internal customers," working smarter, and other communications skills. Harve Ballard, materials manager for the Laboratory Instruments Division says, "The importance of good communication skills increase as you move away from a procedural structure, where every job and responsibility is clearly defined. Before, you knew where your responsibility began and ended. But in moving to the team concept, a lot can fall through the cracks."

Ballard says that managers must learn new skills and demonstrate new levels of leadership, leading by example rather than by dictate in order to make new systems work. "You can't force improvement and innovation, you must create the environment and lead by example. The leader's job is to kick the barriers out of the way, giving employees a chance to fail, even." For this reason, systems and technological change are implemented in conjunction with management and employee training.

Allentown, Pennsylvania-based Air Products and Chemicals is emphasizing company-wide quality as a key element in its plan to remain competitive in a very tumultuous industry. Each division is given a good deal of autonomy in selecting the method and plan by which quality improvement will occur. All, according to Al Greene, Corporate Director for Quality Systems, are committed to addressing management and employee skills and behaviors as pivotal areas where quality will be strengthened.

In the Chemicals Group, the second largest group of Air Products, Vice President Frank Ryan selected a manager from the corporate HR department (albeit with a strong quality background) to design and implement that division's total quality plan. Jim Ranieri, Manager of Integrity Systems, as it is called, outlined some of the key elements of an integrated program.

Beginning with a pre-existing vendor-supplied cost-of-quality management program, and widespread SQC training, those with titles of facilitator, coordinator, or internal consultant will be rigorously trained in methods of adult learning, group leadership and facilitation, and the basics of organizational dynamics. Managers, from first-line supervisors to senior managers will receive a basic curriculum of "foundation" skills, drawn largely from Zenger-Miller curricula. The performance appraisal system will be integrated with the quality system. Managers will be appraised on their performance in supporting quality practices, group problem-solving, innovation and teamwork. Says Ranieri, "If you don't link the performance appraisal system with the strategic objectives, then you may find yourself rewarding outmoded behavior while encouraging new approaches."

Air Products is also developing a "soft side" quality audit, to complement the manufacturing audit that exists. The soft side audit addresses the application of quality methods to white collar areas. The title of "integrity systems" is, for Air Products, a symbol of a commitment to create consistency and synergy among the various management systems.

St. Paul, Minnesota-based 3M has become one of the few American examples of high quality standards and market niche domination with a quality strategy. 3M has become, in a sense, a "living laboratory" of quality methods. They have experimented with many methods developed in the U.S. and abroad, adapted them to 3M's culture, and integrated them into a total quality management process.

The overall process differs from the guru-authored systems in that it is clearly driven by personal and cultural values rather than by the need to apply a particular quality technology. Jim Thompson, Manager of Quality Management Services, and co-developer of 3M's process, acknowledges the critical need to use SPC, JIT, and other methods. However, he feels they must follow a carefully planned course of organizational change.

3M's blend of value-driven messages, organizational change models, and specific technologies has paid off. The combination of heightened awareness and diligence has helped many internal divisions dramatically reduce quality problems and successfully implement the introduction of JIT, continuous flow manufacturing, and other major advances. More importantly, this process has integrated staff support groups into the quality process to provide better internal customer service.

In the five years I tracked the needs of companies engaging in quality improvement efforts for Zenger-Miller, we saw a wide variety of approaches, and a wide range of success. The common denominator among the more successful efforts is that they consider technical and human systems to be inextricably linked, and that a true partnership between quality and human resource professionals is one of the best ways to model this belief.

We have repeatedly found that there are foundation skills, general leadership and interpersonal management skills, that consistently make or break a quality effort. Without these skills in place, the role of quality management will likely include rolling stones back up Sisyphus' hill.

III

IDEAS AND ISSUES

ROBUST QUALITY

Design products not to fail in the field; you
simultaneously reduce defectives in the factory

GENICHI TAGUCHI AND DON CLAUSING

When a product fails, you must replace it or fix it. In either case, you must track it, transport it, and apologize for it. Losses will be much greater than the costs of manufacture, and none of this expense will necessarily recoup the loss to your reputation. Taiichi Ohno, the renowned former executive vice president of Toyota Motor Corporation, put it this way: Whatever an executive thinks the losses of poor quality are, they are actually six times greater. How can manufacturing companies minimize them? If U.S. managers learn only one new principle from the collection now known as Taguchi Methods, let it be this: Quality is a virtue of design. The "robustness" of products is more a function of good design than of on-line control, however stringent, of manufacturing processes. Indeed—though not nearly so obvious—an inherent lack of robustness in product design is the primary driver of superfluous manufacturing expenses. But managers will have to learn more than one principle to understand why.

ZERO DEFECTS, IMPERFECT PRODUCTS

For a generation, U.S. managers and engineers have reckoned quality losses as equivalent to the costs absorbed by the factory when it builds defective products—the squandered value of products that cannot be shipped, the added costs of rework, and so on. Most managers think losses are low when the factory ships pretty much what it builds; such is the message of statistical quality control and other traditional quality control programs that we'll subsume under the seductive term "Zero Defects."

Of course, customers do not give a hang about a factory's record of staying "in spec" or minimizing scrap. For customers, the proof of a product's quality is in its performance when rapped, overloaded, dropped, and splashed. Then, too many products display temperamental behavior and annoying or even dangerous performance degradations. We all prefer copiers whose copies are clear under low power; we all prefer cars designed to steer safely and predictably even on roads that are wet or bumpy, in crosswinds, or with tires that are slightly under or overinflated. We say these products are robust. They gain steadfast customer loyalty.

Design engineers take for granted environmental forces degrading performance (rain, low voltage, and the like). They try to counter these effects in product design—insulating wires, adjusting tire treads, sealing joints. But some performance degradations come from the interaction of parts themselves, not from anything external happening to them. In an ideal product—in an ideal anything—parts work in perfect harmony. Most real products, unfortunately contain perturbations of one kind or another, usually the result of a faulty meshing of one component with corresponding components. A drive shaft vibrates and wears out a universal joint prematurely; a fan's motor generates too much heat for a sensitive microprocessor.

Such performance degradations may result either from something going wrong in the factory or from an inherent failure in the design. A drive shaft may vibrate too much because of a misaligned lathe or a misconceived shape; a motor may prove too hot because it was put together improperly or yanked into the design impetuously. Another way of saying this is that work-in-progress may be subjected to wide variations in factory process and ambience, and products may be subjected to wide variations in the conditions of customer use.

Why do we insist that most degradations result from the latter kind of failure, design failures, and not from variations in the factory? Because the ambient or process variations that work-in-process may be subjected to in the factory are not nearly as dramatic as the variations that products are subjected to in a customer's hands—obvious when you think about it, but how many exponents of Zero Defects do? Zero Defects says, The effort to reduce process failure in the factory will simultaneously reduce instances of product failure in the field. We say the effort to reduce product failure in the field will simultaneously reduce the number of defectives in the factory.

Still, we can learn something interesting about the roots of robustness and the failures of traditional quality control by confronting Zero Defects on its own ground. It is in opposition to Zero Defects that Tiguchi Methods emerged.

ROBUSTNESS AS CONSISTENCY

According to Zero Defects, designs are essentially fixed before the quality program makes itself felt; serious performance degradations result from the failure of parts to mate and interface just so. When manufacturing processes are out of control, that is, when there are serious variations in the manufacture of parts, products cannot be expected to perform well in the field. Faulty parts make faulty connections. A whole product is the sum of its connections.

Of course, no two drive shafts can be made *perfectly* alike. Engineers working within the logic of Zero Defects presuppose a certain amount of variance in the production of any part. They specify a target for a part's size and dimension, then tolerances that they presume will allow for trivial deviations from this target. What's wrong with a drive shaft that should be 10 centimeters in diameter actually coming in at 9.998?

Nothing. The problem—and it is widespread—comes when managers of Zero Defects programs make a virtue of this necessity. They grow accustomed to thinking about product quality in terms of acceptable deviation from targets—instead of the consistent effort to hit them. Worse, managers may specify tolerances that are much too wide because they assume it would cost too much for the factory to narrow them.

Consider the case of Ford vs. Mazda (then known as Toyo Koygo), which unfolded just a few years ago. Ford owns about 25% of Mazda and asked the Japanese company to build transmissions for a car it was selling in the United States. Both Ford and Mazda were supposed to build to identical specifications; Ford adopted Zero Defects as its standard. Yet after the cars had been on the road for a while, it became clear that Ford's transmissions were generating far higher warranty costs and many more customer complaints about noise.

To its credit, Ford disassembled and carefully measured samples of transmissions made by both companies. At first, Ford engineers thought their gauges were malfunctioning. Ford parts were all in-spec, but Mazda gearboxes betrayed no variability at all from targets. Could *that* be why Mazda incurred lower production, scrap, rework, and warranty costs?[1]

That was precisely the reason. Imagine that in some Ford transmissions, many components near the *outer limits* of specified tolerances—that is, fine by the definitions of Zero Defects—were randomly assembled together. Then, many trivial deviations from the target tended to "stack up." An otherwise trivial variation in one part exacerbated a variation in another. Because of deviations, parts interacted with greater friction than they could withstand individually or with greater vibration than customers were prepared to endure.

Mazda managers worked consistently to bring parts in on target. Intuitively, they took a much more imaginative approach to on-line quality control than Ford managers did; they certainly grasped factory conformance in a way that superseded the pass/fail, in-spec/out-of-spec style of thinking associated with Zero Defects. Mazda managers worked on the assumption that robustness begins from meeting exact targets *consistently*—not from always staying within tolerances. They may not have realized this at the time, but they would have been even better off missing the target with perfect consistency than hitting it haphazardly—a point that is illuminated by this simple analogy:

Sam and John are at the range for target practice. After firing ten shots, they examine their targets. Sam has ten shots in a tight cluster just outside the bull's-eye circle. John, on the other hand, has five shots in the circle, but they are scattered all over it—as many near the perimeter as near dead center—and the rest of his shots are similarly dispersed around it (see the "Who's the Better Shot?" diagram).

Zero Defects theorists would say that John is the superior shooter because his performance betrays no failures. But who would you really rather hire on as a bodyguard?

Sam's shooting is consistent and virtually predictable. He probably knows why he missed the circle completely. An adjustment to his sights will give many perfect bull's-eyes during the next round. John has a much more difficult problem. To reduce the dispersion of his shots, he must expose virtually all the factors under his control and find a way to change them in some felicitous combination. He may decide to change the position of his arms, the tightness of his sling, or the sequence of his firing: breathe, aim, slack, and squeeze. He will have little confidence that he will get all his shots in the bull's-eye circle next time around.

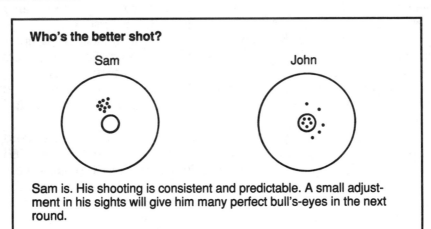

Who's the better shot?

Sam   John

Sam is. His shooting is consistent and predictable. A small adjustment in his sights will give him many perfect bull's-eyes in the next round.

When extrapolated to the factory, a Sam-like performance promises greater product robustness. Once consistency is established—no mean feat, the product of relentless attention to the details of design and process both—adjusting performance to target is a simple matter: stack-up can be entirely obviated. If every drive shaft is .005 centimeters out, operators can adjust the position of the cutting tool. In the absence of consistent performance, getting more nearly on target can be terribly time-consuming.

But there is another side to this. There is a much higher probability of catastrophic stack-up from random deviations than from deviations that show consistency. Assuming that no part is grossly defective, a product made from parts that are all off target in exactly the same way is more likely to be robust than a product made from parts whose deviations are in spec but unpredictable. We have statistical proofs of this, but a moment's reflection should be enough. If all parts are made consistently, the product will perform in a uniform way for customers and will be more easily perfected in the next version. If all parts are made erratically, some products will be perfect, and some will fall apart.

So the case against Zero Defects begins with this: Robustness derives from consistency. Where deviation is consistent, adjustment to the target is possible; catastrophic stack-up is more likely from scattered deviation within specifications than from consistent deviation outside. This regard for consistency for being on target, has a fascinating and practical application.

THE QUALITY LOSS FUNCTION

Analysis of Ford's *overall* losses as compared with Mazda's suggests that when companies deviate from targets, they run an increasingly costly risk of loss.

Overall loss is quality loss plus factory loss. The more a manufacturer deviates from targets, the greater its losses.

From our experience, quality loss—the loss that comes after products are shipped—increases at a geometric rate. It can be roughly quantified as the Quality Loss Function (QLF), based on a simple quadratic formula. Loss increases by the square of deviation from the target value, L=D2C, where the constant is determined by the cost of the countermeasure that the factory might use to get on target. If you know what to do to get on target, then you know what this action costs per unit. If you balk at spending the money then with every standard deviation from the target, you risk spending more and more. The greater the deviation from targets, the greater the compounded costs.

Let's say a car manufacturer chooses not to spend, say $20 per transmission to get a gear exactly on target. QLF suggests that the manufacturer would wind up spending (when customers got mad) $80 for two standard deviations from the target ($20 multiplied by the square of two), $180 for three, $320 for four and so forth.

This is a simple approximation, to be sure, not a law of nature. Actual field data cannot be expected to vindicate QLF precisely, and if your corporation has a more exacting way of tracking the costs of product failure, use it. But the tremendous value of QLF, apart from its bow to common sense, is that it translates the engineer's notion of deviation from targets into a simple cost estimate managers can use.

QLF is especially helpful in the important early stages of new product development, when tolerances are set and quality targets are established.

SONY TELEVISIONS: TOKYO VS. SAN DIEGO

The compelling logic of QLF is best illustrated by the performance of Sony televisions in the late 1970s. The case demonstrates how engineering data and economic data can (and should) be seen in tandem. Sony product engineers had ascertained that customers preferred pictures with a particular color density, let's call it a nominal density of 10. As color density deviated from 10, viewers became increasingly dissatisfied, so Sony set specification limits at no less than 7 and no more than 13.

Sony manufactured TV sets in two cities, San Diego and Tokyo. Sets shipped from San Diego were uniformly distributed within specs, which meant that a customer was as likely to buy a set with a color density of 12.6 as one with a density of 9.2. At the same time, a San Diego set was as likely to be near the corporate specification limits of 13 or 7 as near the customer satisfaction target of 10. Meanwhile, shipments from Tokyo tended to cluster near the customer satisfaction target of 10, though at that time, about 3 out of every 1,000 sets actually fell outside of corporate standards.

Akio Morita, the chairman of Sony reflected on the discrepancy this way: "When we tell one of our Japanese employees that the measurement of a certain part must be within a tolerance of plus or minus five, for example, he will automatically strive to get that part as close to zero tolerance as possible. When we started our plant in the United States, we found that the workers would follow instructions perfectly. But when we said make it between plus or minus five, they would get it somewhere near plus or minus five all right, but rarely as close to zero as the Japanese workers did."

If Morita were to assign grades to the two factories' performances, he might say that Tokyo had many more A's than San Diego, even if it did get a D now and then; 68% of Tokyo's production was in the A range, 28% in the B range, 4% in the C range, and 0.3% in the D range. Of course, San Diego made some out-of-spec sets; but it didn't ship its F's. Tokyo shipped everything it built without bothering to check them. Should Morita have preferred Tokyo to San Diego?

The answer, remember, must be boiled down to dollars and cents, which is why the conventions of Zero Defects are of no use here. Suppose you bought a TV with a color density of 12.9, while your neighbor bought one with a density of 13.1. If you watch a program on his set, will you be able to detect any color difference between yours and his? Of course not. The color quality does not present a striking problem at the specification limit of 13. Things do not suddenly get more expensive for the San Diego plant if a set goes out at 13.1.

The losses start mounting when customers see sets at the target value of 10. Then, anything much away from 10 will seem unsatisfactory, and customers will demand visits from repairpeople or will demand replacement sets. Instead of spending a few dollars per set to adjust them close to targets, Sony would have to spend much more to make good on the sets—about two-thirds of the San Diego sets—that were actually displeasing customers. (Dissatisfaction certainly increases more between 11.5 and 13 than between 10 and 11.5.)

What Sony discovered is that you gain virtually nothing in shipping a product that just barely satisfies the corporate standard over a product that just fails. San Diego shipped marginal sets "without defects," but their marginal quality proved costly.

Using QLF Sony might have come up with even more striking figures. Say the company estimated that the cost of the countermeasure required to put every set right—an assembly line countermeasure that puts every set at a virtual 10—was $9. But for every San Diego set with a color density of 13 (three standard deviations from the target), Sony spent not $9 but $81. Total quality loss at San Diego should have been expected to be *three times* the total quality loss at the Tokyo factory.

DEVIATION: SIGNAL TO NOISE

If Zero Defects doesn't work, what does? We have said that quality is mainly designed in, not controlled from without. In development work, engineers must discipline their decisions at virtually every step by comparing expected quality loss with known manufacturing cost. On the other hand, the reliability of QLF calculations is pretty obviously restricted by the accuracy of more preliminary measures. It is impossible to discern any loss function properly without first setting targets properly.

How *should* design engineers and manufacturing managers set targets? Let us proceed slowly, reconsidering what engineers do when they test components and subassemblies and how they establish what no particular part "wants to be" in the context of things that get in its way.

When Sony engineers designed their televisions, they assumed that discriminating customers would like a design that retained a good picture or "signal" far from the station, in a lightning storm, when the food processor was in use, and even when the power company was providing low voltage. Customers would be dismayed if the picture degraded every time they turned up the volume. They would reject a TV that developed snow and other annoying "noises" when afflicted by nasty operating conditions, which are themselves considered noises.

In our view, this metaphorical language—signal as compared with noise—can be used to speak of all products, not just televisions. The signal is what the product (or component or subassembly) is trying to deliver. Noises are the interferences that degrade signal, some of them coming from outside, some from complementary systems within the product. They are very much like the factors we spoke of as accounting for variations in product performance—environmental disturbances as well as disturbances engendered by the parts themselves.

And so it seems reasonable to define robustness as the virtue of a product with a high signal-to-noise ratio. Customers resent being told, "You were not expected to use our product in high humidity or in below-freezing temperatures." They want good performance under actual operating conditions—which are often less than perfect. We all assume that a product that performs better under adverse conditions will be that much more durable under normal conditions.

Signal-to-noise ratios are designed into products before the factory ramps up. The strength of a product's signal—hence, its robustness—is primarily the responsibility of the product designers. Good factories are faithful to the intention of the design. But mediocre designs will always result in mediocre products.

CHOOSING TARGETS: ORTHOGONAL ARRAYS

How, then, do product designers maximize signal-to-noise ratios? World-class companies use a three-step decision-making process:

1. They define the specific objective, selecting or developing the most appropriate signal and estimating the concomitant noise.

2. They define feasible options for the critical design values, such as dimensions and electrical characteristics.

3. They select the option that provides the greatest robustness or the greatest signal-to-noise ratio.

This is easier said than done, of course, which is why so many companies in Japan, and now in the United States, have moved to some form of simultaneous engineering. To define and select the correct signals and targets is no mean feat and requires the expertise of all product specialists. Product design, manufacturing, field support, and marketing—all of these should be worked out concurrently by an interfunctional team.

Product designers who have developed a "feel" for the engineering of particular products should take the lead in such teams. They can get away with only a few, limited experiments, where new people would have to perform many more. Progressive companies make an effort to keep their product specialists working on new versions rather than bump them up to management positions. Their compensation schemes reward people for doing what they do best.

But the virtues of teamwork beg the larger question of how to develop an efficient experimental strategy that won't drain corporate resources as you work to bring prototypes up to customer satisfaction. Intuition is not really an answer. Neither is interfunctionality or a theory of organization. Product designers need a scientific way to get at robustness. They have depended too long on art.

The most practical way to go about setting signal-to-noise ratios builds on the work of Sir Ronald Fisher, a British statistician whose brilliant contributions to agriculture are not much studied today. Most important is his strategy for systematic experimentation, including the astonishingly sensible plan known as the "orthogonal array."

Consider the complexity of improving a car's steering. Customers want it to respond consistently. Most engineers know that steering responsiveness depends on many critical design parameters—spring stiffness, shock absorber stiffness, dimensions of the steering and suspension mechanisms, and so on—all of which might be optimized to achieve the greatest possible signal-to-noise ratio.

It makes sense, moreover, to compare the initial design value to both a larger and a smaller value. If spring stiffness currently has a nominal value of 7, engineers may want to try the steering at 9 and at 5. One car engineer we've worked with established that there are actually 13 design variables for steering. If engineers were to compare standard, low, and high values for each critical variable, they would have 1,594,323 design options.

Proceed with intuition? Over a million possible permutations highlight the challenge—that of a blind search for a needle in a haystack—and steering is only one subsystem of the car. In Japan, managers say that managers "like to fish with one rod"; engineers are optimistic that "the next cast will bring in the big fish"—one more experiment and they'll hit the ideal design. Naturally, repeated failure leads to more casts. The new product, still not robust to customers' conditions, is eventually forced into the marketplace by the pressures of time, money and diminishing market share.

To complete the optimization of robustness most quickly, the search strategy must derive the maximum amount of information from a few trials. We won't go through the algebra here, but the key is to develop a system of trials that allows product engineers to analyze the *average* effect of change in factor levels under different sets of experimental conditions.

And this is precisely the virtue of the orthogonal array (see the insert, "Orthogonal Arrays: Setting the Right Targets for Design"). It balances the levels of performance demanded by customers against the many variables—or noises—affecting performance. An orthogonal array for 3 steering performance levels—low, medium, and high—can reduce the experimental possibilities to 27. Engineers might subject each of the 27 steering designs to some combination of noises, such as high/low tire pressure, rough/smooth road, high/low temperature. After all of the trials are completed, signal-to-noise values may be used to select the best levels for each design variable.

If, for example, the average value for the first nine trials on spring stiffness is 32.4, then that could characterize level one of spring stiffness. If the average value for the second group of trials is 26.7, and the average for the third group 28.9, then we would select level one as the best value for spring stiffness. This averaging process is repeated to find the best level for each of the 13 design variables.

The orthogonal array is actually a sophisticated "switching system" into which many different design variables and levels of change can be plugged. This system was conceived to let the relatively inexperienced designer extract the *average* effect of each factor on the experimental results, so he or she can reach reliable conclusions despite the large number of changing variables.

Of course, once a product's characteristics are established so that a designer can say with certainty that design values—that is, optimized signal-to-noise ratios—do not interact at all, then orthogonal arrays are superfluous. The designer can instead proceed to test each design variable more or less independently without concern for creating noise in other parts or subassemblies.

SYSTEM VERIFICATION TEST: THE MOMENT OF TRUTH

After they've maximized signal-to-noise ratios and optimized design values, engineers build prototypes. The robustness of the complete product is now verified in the System Verification Test (SVT)—perhaps the most critical event during product development.

In the SVT, the first prototypes are compared with the current benchmark product. Engineers subject both the prototype and the benchmark to the same extreme conditions they may encounter in actual use. Engineers also measure the same critical signal-to-noise ratios for all contenders. It is very important for the new product to surpass the robustness of the benchmark product. If the ideal nominal voltage is 115 volts, we want televisions that will have a signal of 10 even when voltage slips to a noisy 100 or surges to an equally noisy 130. Any deviations from the perfect signal must be considered in terms of QLF that is, as a serious financial risk.

The robust product, therefore, is the one that minimizes the average of the square of the deviation from the target—averaged over the different customer-use conditions. Suppose you wish to buy a power supply and learn that you can buy one with a standard deviation of one volt. Should you take it? If the mean value of output voltage is 1,000 volts, most people would think that, on average, an error of only one volt is very good. However, if the average output were 24 volts, then a standard deviation of one seems very large. We must always consider the ratio of the mean value divided by the standard deviation.

The SVT gives a very strong indication, long before production begins, of whether customers will perceive the new product as having world-class quality and performance. After the new design is verified to have superior robustness, engineers may proceed to solve routine problems, fully confident that the product will steadily increase customer loyalty.

BACK TO THE FACTORY

The relationship of field to factory proves to be a subtle one—the converse of what one might expect. We know that if you control for variance in the factory, you reduce failure in the field. But as we said at the outset, a concerted effort to reduce product failure in the field will simultaneously reduce the number of defectives in the factory.

Strive to reduce variances in the components of the product and you will reduce variances in the production system as a whole. Any strengthening of a design—that is, any marked increase of a product's signal-to-noise ratio—will simultaneously reduce a factory's quality losses.

Why should this be so? For many reasons, most importantly the symmetries between design for robustness and design for manufacture. Think of how much more robust products have become since the introduction of molded plastics and solid-state circuitry. Instead of serving up many interconnected wires and tubes and switches—any one of which can fail—engineers can now imprint a million transistors on a virtually indestructible chip. Instead of joining many components together with screws and fasteners, we can now consolidate parts into subassemblies and mount them on molded frames that snap together.

All of these improvements greatly reduce opportunities for noise interfering with signal; they were developed to make products robust. Yet they also have made products infinitely more manufacturable. The principles of designing for robustness are often indistinguishable from the principles of designing for manufacture—reduce the number of parts, consolidate subsystems, integrate the electronics.

A robust product can tolerate greater variations in the production system. Please the customer and you will please the manufacturing manager. Prepare for variances in the field and you will pave the way for reducing variations on the shop floor. None of this means the manufacturing manager should stop trying to reduce process variations or to achieve the same variations with faster, cheaper processes.

And there are obvious exceptions proving the rule—chip production, for example, where factory controls are ever more stringent—though it is hard to think of exceptions in products such as cars and consumer electronics.

The factory is a place where workers must try to meet, not deviate from, the nominal targets set for products. It is time to think of the factory as a product with targets of its own. Like a product, the factory may be said to give off an implicit signal—the consistent production of robust products—and to be subject to the disruptions of noise— variable temperatures, degraded machines, dust, and so forth. Using QLF, choices in the factory like choices for the product, can be reduced to the cost of deviation from targets.

Consider, for instance, that a cylindrical grinder creates a cylindrical shape more consistently than a lathe. Product designers have argued for such dedicated machines; they want the greatest possible precision. Manufacturing engineers have traditionally favored the less precise lathe because it is more flexible and it reduces production cost. Should management favor the more precise cylindrical grinder? How do you compare each group's choice with respect to quality loss?

In the absence of QLF's calculation, the most common method for establishing manufacturing tolerances is to have a concurrence meeting. Design engineers sit on one side of the conference room, manufacturing engineers on the opposite side. The product design engineers start chanting "Tighter Tolerance, Tighter Tolerance, Tighter Tolerance," and the manufacturing engineers respond with "Looser Tolerance, Looser Tolerance, Looser Tolerance." Presumably the factory would opt for a lathe if manufacturing chanted louder and longer. But why follow such an irrational process when product design people and manufacturing people *can* put a dollar value on quality precision?

Management should choose the precision level that minimizes the total cost, production cost plus quality loss—the basics of QLF. Managers can compare the costs of competing factory processes by adding the manufacturing cost and the average quality loss (from expected deviations) of each process. They gain economical precision by evaluating feasible alternative production processes, such as the lathe and cylindrical grinder. What would be the quality loss if the factory used the lathe? Are the savings worth the future losses?

Similar principles may be applied to larger systems. In what may be called "process parameter design," manufacturers can optimize production parameters—spindle speed, depth of cut, feed rate, pressure, temperature—according to an orthogonal array, much like the spring stiffness in a steering mechanism. Each row of the orthogonal array may define a different production trial. In each trial, engineers produce and measure several parts and then use the data to calculate the signal-to-noise ratio for that trial. In a final step, they establish the best value for each production parameter.

The result? A robust process—one that produces improved uniformity of parts and often enables managers to simultaneously speed up production and reduce cycle time.

HOW MUCH INTERVENTION?

Finally there is the question of how much to intervene *during* production.

Take the most common kind of intervention, on-line checking and adjusting of machinery and process. In the absence of any operator monitoring, parts tend to deviate progressively from the target. Without guidance, different operators have widely varying notions of (1) how often they should check their machines and (2) how big the discrepancy must be before they adjust the process to bring the part value back near the target.

By applying QLF, you can standardize intervention. The cost of checking and adjusting has always been easy to determine; you simply have to figure the cost of downtime. With QLF, managers can also figure the cost of *not* intervening, that is, the dollar value to the company of reduced parts variation.

Let's go back to drive shafts. The checking interval is three, and the best adjustment target is 1/1,000th of an inch. If the measured discrepancy from the target is less than 1/1,000th of an inch, production continues. If the measured discrepancy exceeds this, the process is adjusted back to the target. Does this really enable operators to keep the products near the target in a way that minimizes total cost?

It might be argued that measuring every third shaft is too expensive. Why not every tenth? There is a way to figure this out. Say the cost of intervention is 30 cents, and shafts almost certainly deviate from the target value every fifth or sixth operation. Then, out of every ten produced, at least four bad shafts will go out, and quality losses will mount. If the seventh shaft comes out at two standard deviations, the cost will be $1.20; if the tenth comes out at three standard deviations, the cost will be $2.70; and so on. Perhaps the best interval to check is every fourth shaft or every fifth, not every third. If the fourth shaft is only one standard deviation from the target value, intervention is probably not worth the cost.

The point, again, is that these things can and should be calculated. There isn't any reason to be fanatical about quality if you *cannot* justify your fanaticism by QLF. Near the target, production should continue without adjustment; the quality loss is small. Outside the limit, the process should be adjusted before production continues.

This basic approach to intervention can also be applied to

preventive maintenance. Excessive preventive maintenance costs too much. Inadequate preventive maintenance will increase quality loss excessively. Optimized preventive maintenance will minimize total cost.

In Japan, it is said that a manager who trades away quality to save a little manufacturing expense is "worse than a thief"—a little harsh, perhaps, but plausible. When a thief steals $200 from your company there is no net loss in wealth between the two of you, just an exchange of assets. Decisions that create huge quality losses throw away social productivity, the wealth of society.

QLF's disciplined, quantitative approach to quality builds on and enhances employee involvement activities to improve quality and productivity. Certainly, factory-focused improvement activities do not by and large increase the robustness of a product. They can help realize it, however, by reducing the noise generated by the complex interaction of shop-floor quality factors—operators, operating methods, equipment, and material.

Employees committed to hitting the bull's-eye consistently cast a sharper eye on every feature of the factory environment. When their ingenuity and cost-consciousness are engaged, conditions change dramatically, teams prosper, and valuable data proliferate to support better product and process design. An early, companywide emphasis on robust product design can even reduce development time and smooth the transition to full-scale production.

Too often managers think that quality is the responsibility of only a few quality control people off in a factory corner. It should be evident by now that quality is for everyone, most of all the business's strategists. It is only through the efforts of every employee, from the CEO on down, that quality will become second nature. The most elusive edge in the new global competition is the galvanizing pride of excellence.

REFERNCES
1. See Lance A. Ealey's admirable account of this case in *Quality by Design: Taguchi Methods and U.S. Industry* (Dearborn, Mich.: ASI Press, 1985), pp. 61-62.

10 REASONS WHY TOTAL QUALITY IS LESS THAN TOTAL

The road to total quality is paved with good intentions — and littered with potholes. Here are some detours for skirting them

LAWRENCE HOLPP

As greater numbers of American managers place their oil-resistant, steel-toed size 12s over the line separating lip service from total quality improvement, they often step in things that give them cause to regret the move.

Their misgivings result in part from a backlash against the quick-fix, management-fad mentality so maligned in business books for years—the kind of thinking that leads us to see all problems as nails ready to be pounded by the latest technological hammer.

But it's not just a fad backlash that produces those misgivings about total quality improvement (TQI). Equally fundamental problems arise from the fact that TQI requires massive change in an organization. TQI means that quality becomes everyone's responsibility. Traditionally, most quality efforts have been attempts to "control" it, "assure" it, "inspect" it or "guarantee" it. These approaches were designed to make sure that product defects were caught before they left the plant, warranteed after they left, or recalled if they threatened life or liability.

Quality nowadays means making sure that customers' needs are identified early in the process of designing and producing a product or service. Total quality means redesigning the organization itself to keep it responsive to those needs as the product goes from one department to another—from marketing or research-and-development (R&D), to design, to engineering and manufacturing, to sales and to service.

There are no shortcuts around the long-term commitment needed to drive a TQI effort. But there are some common snags that seem to thwart many good intentions. Knowing the danger areas is half the battle. Once they have been identified, careful, systematic efforts at managing them will avoid the skepticism and lack of trust that otherwise can undermine even the best quality-improvement solutions.

Here are 10 saboteurs that can waylay TQI. Alone they are irritants. In concert they're deadly.

1. Uncorrected Vision

Most companies that launch TQI efforts develop a vision statement. Good idea. But too many wind up with a statement that reads like a textbook—pages of copy, punctuated with bylaws and conditional clauses, that give off the musty smell of a policy manual. This is not a vision. Vision statements that are disconnected from values and behaviors are more akin to hallucinations.

To empower people at all levels of the organization, visions must be short, to the point and possess a strong emotional component everyone can support. More important, they must be linked to visible *actions* obvious to everyone.

At Miami-based Florida Power and Light, for example, the vision is short and sweet: becoming the "...best-managed utility and recognized as such." But it drives a sustained effort at communicating the quality improvement program to other companies. This process has influenced many manufacturing organizations to get involved in TQI. After all, if a Florida utility can do it, why not a Pennsylvania steelmaker?

Douglas Aircraft has taken a different tack. The company asks all employees on a new project to sign a "commitment statement," which links the overall vision ("quality is the supreme value") to specific behaviors such as "cooperating with all my teammates in this new way of working together to build airplanes."

Vision statements must be closely coupled with behaviors that can be picked out, reinforced and practiced by employees. In this way, a vision becomes a realistic goal toward which everyone can work.

2. Poor Objectives

For some time now, management by objectives (MBO) has suffered bad press because it has been misused by people who take performance objectives and turn them into short-term, limited, quantifiable goals. This has the effect of encouraging functional groups within the organization to battle one another for resources and recognition, rather than working in concert for the long-term benefit of the customer or the organization.

Policy deployment (or quality function deployment) is a specific management method that can help link customer needs to daily activities within even the most layered organizations. This system breaks customer requirements into clearly defined projects, creates a trail of responsibility throughout the organization, and sets goals for everyone based on their ability to meet customers' needs.

Quality function deployment looks a lot like MBO, but the main point of it is to make sure everyone's objectives harmonize. Communication and involvement must run throughout the organization. A successful system meets these criteria:

• Projects are visible and well-represented. Everyone knows what other teams and departments are doing that may affect them. Management shows progress on projects by posting updates in common areas where teams meet.

• Management is involved. Rather than delegating projects as though they were goals for particular subordinates to meet, managers participate in the problem-solving process. They attend meetings in order to know what's going on. Managers representing different functions must also meet to keep each other informed about the progress of projects.

• The policy deployment process uses targets and indicators that are easily interpreted. If not, communication among departments and levels will become a Tower of Babel. It helps to use a standard format. Some companies are using a "storyboard" format borrowed from Walt Disney. It uses graphs, pictures and common symbols to show the status of various projects.

• Those responsible for projects see them as important daily activities, not as extra work. Everyone must understand that quality-improvement projects *are* their jobs, not an overlay. The only way to accomplish this is by example: The leaders in the organization must care enough to reinforce quality-related activities.

3. Loose Cannons

Two kinds of loose cannons are likely to clatter across the decks during a total quality campaign. The first are people who use quality as an excuse to establish fiefdoms. The second are people who remain in powerful positions but don't get with the program. Both types are dangerous—empire builders to the positive thrust of TQI, foot-draggers to the morale of their people.

Because it commands resources, TQI has political allure. Departments and staff in key areas grow, budgets increase, senior management spends time on quality-related activities, and opportunities for recognition and rewards abound. TQI can be fertile ground indeed for political manipulators.

This is not necessarily bad. You do need champions, and calculated self-interest may motivate them to step forward. But to control potential empire builders, make sure that the guidelines for judging the success of TQI are measurable and team-focused. Asking ambitious managers some of these questions should help channel their energies into positive directions:

• What data do you have to support your results?

• How many of your projects are cross-functional, involving and benefiting other departments?

• To what extent have you used successful ideas from other areas?

• What do your customers say about your improvement efforts?

• How committed are employees at the team level? What data do you have to prove it?

These questions assess how well managers are working with people inside and outside their departments. Even the most politically ambitious managers can contribute to TQI if they are able to work as team players.

The other loose cannons, managers who have found subtle anchors to drag, are in some ways even more dangerous. These types stifle their employees' efforts. (Meanwhile, their people can see that others around them are making the transition to a different kind of organization with the support and encouragement of their managers.) Often these resisters have a long history with the company and have seen other big-deal programs come and go. Their best instincts tell them to wait and see before plunging in.

They can't be blamed for that. Nevertheless, the only thing that will motivate them—besides seeing that this latest parade is not going to pass on by—is a kick in the pants. They need to see their bosses getting with the program in word and deed. They need to have their job duties translated into quality-improvement terms so that the only way to fulfill them is to learn to develop and track quality indicators and use problem-solving processes.

Over time, many resisters will come around. Those who don't will have to be replaced. Some may retire. Others will have to transfer to assignments where they can't do the TQI effort any harm.

4. Wandering Teams and Lost Supervisors

To some cross-functional teams that have no clear charter, TQI must seem like a bizarre management dream. "Generate workable ideas for improving quality" sounded like a neat goal when the team formed, but that was then—this is now. Wandering about many a company, these demoralized teams have spawned a host of problems. For instance:

• What to do about low team productivity after the "cherry-picking" ideas that lie on the surface have been harvested.

• What to do about "team burnout," which often occurs about two years into a program.

• How to judge team suggestions that require complex statistical measurements when few in the organization have any real familiarity with data analysis.

• How to address raised expectations on the part of employees for additional involvement and training.

Along with wandering teams, many supervisors and middle managers get lost in the shuffle. The momentum of quality improvement has swept by them. Their subordinates are working on foreign-sounding problems with tools and techniques that remain mysterious. Their traditional roles of authority have declined as functional groups approach greater levels of autonomy. They have been disenfranchised.

Yet, as with all changes, opportunities arise. Organizations are beginning to recognize that they face two distinct choices: Either they must develop a new role for supervisors and team leaders in managing the quality-improvement activities of various groups of people, or they must abandon the traditional role of supervisor entirely and move toward semiautonomous teams.

At Ibis, a producer of industrial enzymes in Kingstrcc, SC, teams have become largely autonomous. Former supervisors are now called "technical resources." They are expected to serve as trainers, researchers, facilitators and coaches to the teams they once managed. Likewise, in the massive new C-17 aircraft project that will employ nearly 10,000 people at Douglas Aircraft in Long Beach, CA, traditional supervisors will now act as brokers between assemblers, and technical and administrative support groups. Other organizations, such as Best Food Co.'s Skippy peanut butter plant in Little Rock, AR, have eliminated the supervisory role entirely and farmed out its duties to team members.

Another solution retains the traditional supervisor title, but expands the role. Enhancing the role of supervisors usually means training them in the skills and abilities they need to serve as coaches in developing their teams and leading the problem-solving process.

One of the reasons "quality circles" have gotten a bad name is that they create parallel structures that encourage both employees and management to see TQI as something disconnected from the *real* work. Quality meetings can turn into coffee klatches or gripe sessions. Making supervisors and managers responsible for maintaining and building their teams gives them a stake in the success of the process as well as a clearly defined role to play every day: coach and facilitator.

5. Nonstatistical Thinking

Since few senior managers have any training in statistics, they cannot be expected to look at the world in terms of data rather than gut feeling. Only extensive training can change this view.

Unfortunately, technicians who conduct training in statistics often don't realize how difficult it is to teach managers new tricks. Lectures are rarely enough. To learn to use statistics comfortably, participants need practice with realistic situations.

Statistical thinking is more than numbers. It is a way of looking at the world, of managing people and of deducing the root causes of problems. This orientation is required of both managers and employees in investigating problems. And it runs counter to many popular knuckles-and-know-how notions of leadership that focus on willpower, vision and charisma. In an essay for *The Wall Street Journal,* "Leadership...More Doing Than Dash," management theorist Peter Drucker lambasted the idea that showmanship is the key trait of the effective modern leader, while plain, solid competence is gray and unfashionable.

Statistical thinking can appear dull and actuarial to managers who want to get to the heart of problems, solve them and move on to the next. Yet their role is not to play statistician; achieving *real* statistical fluency is like mastering a second language. Instead, their job is to act as coach, getting players to think problems through.

One way to do that involves mastering the art of asking questions, or the "Five Whys," as they are sometimes called. Asking why over and over again gets to the root cause of problems, and determining root causes is the ultimate purpose of statistical analysis. By asking why again and again, a manager can get an employee to think deductively.

Here is an illustration of how the five whys work, from *Kaizen* by Masaaki Imai.

Question 1: *Why did the machine stop?*
Answer: Because the fuse blew due to an overload.
Question 2: *Why was there an overload?*
Answer: Because the bearing lubrication was inadequate.
Question 3: *Why was the bearing lubrication inadequate?*
Answer: Because the lubrication pump wasn't functioning right.
Question 4: *Why wasn't the pump working right?*
Answer: Because the pump axle was worn out.
Question 5: *Why was it worn out?*
Answer: Because sludge got in it.

While sludge might not be the final explanation for problems affecting the machine shop's productivity, it is certainly a more useful explanation than a blown fuse. The "Five Whys" should not be used as a cross-examination method, but they should push both managers and subordinates to delve for causes beyond the obvious. Used as part of a coaching process, this sort of questioning helps drive a data-oriented culture, which provides fertile ground for TQI.

6. New-Program Syndrome

In these turbulent times, management has often fallen victim to a host of scams—or well-intentioned but useless techniques—designed to motivate workers. Each one promises to fire up the employees and change their attitudes toward quality, costs, productivity, service, safety or communication. Workers, in turn, have been subjected to successive new programs launched with posters, banners, free lunches and pins. Today, workers and managers alike eye any ambitious new initiative with suspicion. Employees sneer at the word "program." Middle managers and supervisors cringe when executives retreat to a conference center with some productivity guru.

Florida Power and Light decided to tackle the new-program syndrome head-on. The total-quality process at the Miami-based utility began as the Quality Improvement Program (QIP). Predictably, QIP suffered the scorn heaped upon all such monikers. But management has begun reinforcing a transformation that makes quality improvement part of the job. The goal now is to quit calling it a program and instill quality thinking, techniques, vocabulary and systems into everybody's day-to-day work.

This means departments do regular status reports in the quality-improvement format; individual performance objectives are written in terms of targets, limits and customer requirements; staff meetings and QIP meetings are held simultaneously, not separately as had been the case. Most important, perhaps, the old quality-circle technique of having staff facilitators lead teams has begun to change. Managers and supervisors are taking on the role of facilitator and directly leading their own teams. Thus, the work of quality is becoming more closely integrated into the daily work of each unit.

7. What, More Training?

Unquestionably, training is the glue that binds TQI efforts. Unfortunately, past practices of ignoring performance objectives when designing courses have not helped training departments attain the prestige they must have to drive TQI.

Success in a TQI environment demands very special skills. Traditional competencies—organizing, delegating, controlling—are still important, but employees must learn to operate in a vastly more complicated workplace. They must face such issues as managing values (ethics), quality, customer orientation, vision and alignment, influence, heterogeneous work groups, cultural differences in overseas markets, unfamiliar and shifting organizational structures, shrinking staffs, robotics and artificial intelligence in the office environment.

Add to this the alphabet soup of advanced manufacturing technologies—TQI, JIT, SPC, CAD-CAM—and you have a formula for total confusion. Kaoru Ishikawa, the father of TQI, once said that total-quality control begins with education and ends with education. The only way out of the woods is through training.

Many organizations concerned with TQI are making a startling commitment to training:

• At NUMMI, the Toyota-General Motors joint venture in Fremont, CA, every employee receives 48 hours of training in four areas: problem solving, *kaizen*, quality and safety. Much of the curriculum is developed and taught by hourly team members.

• At McDonnell Douglas' massive start-up in Columbus, OH, all 15,000 new employees will attend a three-week assimilation program.

• Japanese-American start-ups routinely send hundreds of their production workers to Japan to improve both technical and interpersonal skills.

- To emphasize its commitment to quality improvement, Florida Power and Light has sent nearly 400 managers and specialists through a three-week statistics course.

Why are companies making this kind of investment in training? There are a variety of reasons. The skills and knowledge needed in TQI companies are not readily available in the work force. Top-level employees must be supported in their own efforts toward constant improvement. And the fact is, according to a study done for the Department of Labor, the dollars invested in training yield a faster and bigger payback than most investments, including new capital equipment.

The content and focus of training is going to be as diverse as the needs it addresses. But increasingly, training must be:

- Delivered on the job, with lots of application time and real-world relevance.
- Delivered "just in time," coordinated with the needs of teams that are developing greater autonomy.
- Conducted by line people—team members, leaders, supervisors, managers and executives.
- Provided to employees at all levels simultaneously so that clear messages are reinforced all at once.
- Skill-based, with measurable, observable and attainable outcomes. Theory is fine, but it must be conveyed in an application-oriented fashion.
- Reinforced by performance measures that make the training stick and seem important. Don't train supervisors to coach, for instance, and then fail to appraise their coaching performance.

Training is becoming too important a commodity to be left solely in the hands of training departments or external consultants. Though both can be helpful, *management* must take an active role in diagnosing training needs, overseeing program development and delivering the training. In a TQI organization, employee development cannot be delegated.

8. Double-Crossed Functional Management

When does cross-functional management become double-crossed management? When some failure of support, training, clear goals or individual performance measures drives people apart.

Cooperative, cross-functional management and teams are critical to any organization. They are especially vital for success in a TQI company because policy deployment projects will nearly always require several departments to work together. Clearly, cross-functional management strikes at the heart of traditional organizations. It is the essence of Point 9 in quality expert W. Edwards Deming's "14 Points": Break down barriers between departments.

In order to combat the natural tribal inclinations of functional units, management must play sink or swim with them. This means throwing cross-functional problems at teams staffed by some of the top people from several departments—even though their initial reaction may be panic, followed by inaction. To motivate these teams, management can provide training that:

• Teaches people how to communicate in a group. Team members must learn how to influence one another—and how to influence other groups over which they have no control.

• Teaches team leaders to run effective meetings that adhere to systematic agendas. Leaders must learn to handle team dynamics to increase involvement, develop individuals, focus on results and encourage problem solving.

• Enhances team members' ability to analyze problems, evaluate alternative actions, plan and implement solutions, and use data in all phases of their investigation.

Finally, training and organizational changes must be reinforced through the performance-management process. The real problem hindering cross-functional management is not the ability or willingness of team members to cooperate. It is the long history of not being rewarded for cooperation, or being punished for sharing information or involving others.

Management must reinforce the idea that it's OK to work with other units both formally and informally. Team play should be considered a performance dimension, and individuals selected for important cross-functional projects should be recruited not only for their competence but also for their ability to work with others. Being assigned to a project team should become a mark of special regard, and a route to promotions and other rewards.

9. Electronic Management

Too often senior executives appear only on television screens in cafeterias or in front of large audiences at big corporate meetings. In the former, they cannot be heard over the clink of forks; in the latter, they act as a powerful sleeping pill. In either case, employees realize that if the message were really important, senior management would be there to reinforce it in the flesh.

While it is difficult to imagine CEOs and other corporate officers kicking off every training program, orientation seminar or team meeting, senior managers must play a more active role than reading carefully scripted speeches into television cameras. Like everyone else in a TQI organization, they must put quality into every aspect of their jobs.

For many senior managers this means:

• Asking their lower-level managers for quality-related data as the top priority—ahead of cost, sales or inventory-activity information. This will drive the demand for quality data down into the organization as subordinates at all levels scramble to prepare their bosses to meet with *their* bosses.

- Using quality techniques such as storyboarding, brainstorming, sampling or other methods in meetings with shareholders and customers.

- Making "executive visits" like senior managers do at Florida Power and Light. In these visits, officers, including the president, actually coach department "lead teams" in the details of the problem-solving process, and give them resources, feedback and encouragement.

- Involving suppliers in the TQI process. Many companies are narrowing their cadre of suppliers to those vendors who adhere to strict quality standards.

- Aggressively seeking out and recognizing employees who achieve high quality in their work. Don't limit this activity to paternalistic gestures directed at line employees. Reward managers and executives who take leadership roles in TQI as well.

TQI is not something for caretaker managers. It is a full-time job and, for many, becomes a personal crusade. To get the message out and to make converts, senior managers must take an active role in selling TQI throughout the organization. In short, they must both talk and walk TQI.

10. 1, 2, 3...Change
TQI and dramatic change go hand-in-hand. It is naive to expect employees to abandon long-held values and behaviors in favor of new ones simply because we want them to. It's a little like introducing the metric system on...oh, say, Thursday. Change is a gradual process that must be managed with compassion, understanding and a full range of options for the resisters and real losers. As with a society, one measure of an organization's compassion is how it treats those who get lost in the shuffle of change.

We don't resist (for long) changes that benefit us. We only resist those that threaten us. Encourage people to see the benefits of the change to come, help them identify the WIIFM (what's in it for me) of the change. You will discover that change that's anticipated and managed is not change...it's innovation.

A SHORT HISTORY OF CONSTANT IMPROVEMENT
Managers are all clamoring for constant improvement. "We read that book," they say. "You know, the one that talks about *kaizen*. We want some of that."

The "that" they refer to is the process of self-critique and work-skills improvement that Masaaki Imai describes in his book *Kaizen*. Managers who embrace the new religion want their teams to exercise more initiative, to figure out how to improve all sorts of processes, and then go ahead and improve them. In short, they want employees to act empowered.

But the idea of constant improvement is not new. We used to call it "work ethic," "spirit of innovation" or "achievement motivation." We do not need to import lots of rigorous work rules and time and motion improvements from Japan in order to make better mousetraps. We're quite capable of doing it on our own.

If you doubt that, review the development of a quintessentially American innovation: the Big Squeeze. You may know the Big Squeeze by some other name—the 32-ounce Giant Mug, the Non-Drip Sippy Liter, the Big Shot or some name as yet unknown to me—but you probably know what I mean. For those who don't, go down to your local Rax or Atlantic station or some fast-food place and look at the soft-drink promotions. Many will be advertising a 32-ounce plastic container that features a screw-on lid with a hole just large enough for a thick straw to poke through tightly.

The Big Squeeze first appeared on the scene about two years ago. When I spotted one for the first time, I felt with heart-stopping certainty that here was a true breakthrough. It is an innovation that has solved many nagging problems for serious soda drinkers. It holds a lot of liquid. It doesn't wear out. It can be used to hold various drinks. It can even be frozen and thawed.

The straw is great. It's big. It never bends or crimps. It comes with a little cap to prevent spills. All this and it's healthy, too. An acquaintance of mine says she likes to chew on the straws all day instead of smoking cigarettes.

Now, if one were guided by the notion that quality is customer satisfaction, one would, as the sayings go, leave well enough alone, don't mess with success, and don't fix what ain't broke, insofar as the Big Squeeze is concerned.

Nevertheless, some genius decided to tinker with the process. The first innovation I discovered was at Rax, the fast-food place. One day I discovered that the end cap for the straw was now attached by a little plastic cap holder. No longer would I be plagued with the problem of what to do with it.

But that was only the beginning. Another Edison was hard at work.

Last week I visited my local Atlantic convenience store/gas station and saw a whole new species of Big Squeeze. This one had a dazzling array of innovations. The straw was sealed through the lid to eliminate leaks. It had a little landing pad for the straw cap on the top of the lid where you could place it neatly while drinking. But the greatest improvement of all was a small breather valve on the lid. By closing the valve, you can seal off the contents of the container so that it absolutely, positively won't leak. In addition, the container, which is opaque, has a transparent strip running its length that allows you to see the level of liquid left in the cup.

Having gleefully purchased this new "Big Shot" for 99 cents (with a fill-up of soda included), I sat transfixed as I experimented with all its wonderful features. Here was the epitome of customer satisfaction: Not only were my valid requirements met, my wildest expectations were exceeded.

I realized right then that the power of constant improvement is not just its ability to transform products, but to transform people. I was transformed. This Big Shot stirred in me a primeval longing for still more improvements. I even began to think of some myself. Suppose they came up with a new kind of squeeze cup that held hot liquids with a special wide straw for soup? Or how about a cup that was insulated and wouldn't sweat? Ideas came to me in a flash. I could see some quality team in Indiana or Ohio, where the cups are made, brainstorming new ideas. "What else can we do with this gizmo?" someone asks. "Well, suppose we... ."

That's what constant improvement is all about. In dreams begin reality.—**Lawrence Holpp**

QUALITY GURUS: THE MEN AND THEIR MESSAGE

Deming, Juran and Crosby differ in their approaches to quality improvement. But their similarities may be more important

JOSEPH OBERLE

"Improve quality [and] you automatically improve productivity. You capture the market with lower price and better quality. You stay in business and you provide jobs. It's so simple."—W. Edwards Deming

When Deming talks about the success that results from quality improvement, it sounds as simple as falling off a log. All you need to do is define quality for your organization, train your employees accordingly and voila! Your organization is quality-conscious, productive and competitive.

In concept, of course, Deming is right. So are Joseph M. Juran and Philip B. Crosby. They are, of course, the Big Three in quality consulting, the best-known names in the business. Each has spent a good portion of his life telling companies that quality improvement is simple—and critical for survival in the global marketplace. All three insist that quality improvement is a never-ending process. Their philosophies have been dissected and examined in a legion of business magazines and books, yet the concepts are articulated in such straightforward language that they are understandable to everyone from line operator to CEO.

But when their ideas are coupled with the various techniques they provide and then customized to suit particular organizations, the results are myriad applications that can appear like a quality quagmire. When you learn, for instance, that Company A has adopted a "modified Crosby approach" to quality improvement while Company B is going with "basically straight Juran," what have you learned?

A LITTLE HISTORY

After 10 years of quality improvement efforts in some U.S. organizations and almost four decades of quality as a virtual lifestyle in Japan, the quality movement has grown enormously. The word "quality" is touted by innumerable vendors of products and services, some of whom actually deliver the thing itself. Organizations that were once students of quality—such as General Motors, Florida Power and Light,

Corning Inc. and many others—have now become teachers, providing programs, models and techniques to other organizations.

Indeed, the list of those who qualify as "quality experts" has expanded to include names such as Dorian Shainin, William Conway, Armand Feigenbaum and Kaoru Ishikawa. Yet the trio of Deming, Juran and Crosby are the real leaders—the big three who have achieved guru status and made QC (quality control), TQI (total quality improvement), COQ (cost of quality) and SPC (statistical process control) familiar workplace acronyms. Most other quality improvement programs are generally considered derivatives or combinations of these gentlemen's ideas and owe a great deal of their success to them.

Deming was the pioneer, the ground breaker, the American who took his message to Japan in 1950 and was instrumental in turning Japanese industry into an economic world power that still has many U.S. organizations reeling. The Japanese heeded Deming's advice about SPC, a statistical method for examining work processes. They also embraced his 14-point program for managing productivity and quality—which gave them about a 30-year head start on the United States.

Perhaps because he was ignored in his own country for so long—or maybe due to years of dealing with cocksure managers losing buoyancy in a pool of their own ignorance—Deming has acquired a reputation for delivering his message with venom. Although he has mellowed as he nears the end of his ninth decade, he has been known to walk into a gathering of CEOs anxiously awaiting his message and ask them sarcastically if they need him to run their businesses for them. Deming's style is confrontative, and he tends to lose patience with those who resist the learning. At the same time, his approach is philosophically humanistic; it treats workers as humans rather than as cogs in a machine. Nothing draws Deming's scorn faster than an allegation that lazy or incompetent workers are responsible for quality problems. His message to top managers: If your company makes lousy products, it's your fault, nobody else's.

Juran pulled ashore in Japan a few short years after Deming and built an equally formidable reputation in quality improvement, albeit with a less vitriolic style. Juran defines quality as "fitness to use," which stresses the reliability of a product or service for its users. He espouses the Juran Trilogy—quality planning, quality contol and quality improvement. He advocates an accounting system that measures the costs of waste and defective products, calling these the costs of poor quality—an idea designed to appeal to upper management. In 1979 he established the Juran Institute in Wilton, CT, to deliver his programs and develop and distribute his quality materials.

The year 1979 was important for Crosby as well. After beginning his career in industry as an inspector and then working up to vice president of quality at ITT, he left the company in '79 to form Philip Crosby Associates Inc. and the Crosby Quality College in Winter Park, FL. Crosby's methods are marked by popular slogans such as "zero defects," "conformance to requirements" and "quality is free"—the last of which is the title of his first and most popular book.

Crosby, like Deming, has a 14-point program for quality management. To this he adds four "quality absolutes": a definition of quality, a prevention (rather than appraisal) system of quality, a performance standard (zero defects) and the measurement of quality (the cost of nonconformance). Unlike Deming and Juran, Crosby is a formidable motivational speaker, known for whipping his audience into an emotional frenzy that leaves them waving his quality banner in evangelical fervor.

THE MESSAGE IS COMMITMENT

The fundamental message of all three gurus is basically the same: Commit to quality improvement throughout your entire organization. Attack the system rather than the employee. Strip down the work process—whether it be the manufacturing of a product or customer service—to find and eliminate problems that prevent quality. Identify your customer, internal or external, and satisfy that customer's requirements in the work process or the finished product. Eliminate waste, instill pride and teamwork, and create an atmosphere of innovation for continued and permanent quality improvement.

This process, they say, will naturally lead to increased competitiveness and profit.

Quality improvement really does sound simple; it has been called by some "a blinding flash of the obvious." Even applying these concepts is simple, as we will see. But simple does not mean easy. None of these experts offers a quick fix to heal years of mismanagement. Their programs require continuous commitment rather than a "program-of-the-day" outlook. Crosby, Deming and Juran provide assistance in developing that attitude; they just go about it in slightly different ways.

Some of the differences are clear. For example, the means by which an organization is introduced to the respective programs vary. You can send your top managers to Crosby's college, order Juran's videotapes and materials from his institute, or join a waiting list to pay for Deming to tell you, in person, what a fool you've been (at 89, he still lectures).

According to Bill Cronk, quality improvement coodinator of Caterpillar Tractor Co. in Peoria, IL, that distinction was important to his organization. When Caterpillar sought a quality improvement program in 1982, it chose Juran because it could purchase books, videotapes and materials right off the shelf. Juran "talks our language," says Cronk, so Caterpillar established a quality institute to educate its worldwide network of employees, suppliers and dealers.

The gurus also differ in concept. One of Crosby's slogans calls for zero defects in a product, while Deming's 10th point is to "eliminate slogans, exhortations and targets for the work force asking for zero defects and new levels of productivity." Deming's fourth point warns managers to "drive out fear" so that everyone can do their jobs, while Juran says, "Fear can bring out the best in people." The second point of Juran's "breakthrough sequence" calls for problem analysis to "distinguish the vital few projects from the trivial many and set priorities based on problem frequency." This differs from Crosby's 11th point on error-cause removal, which encourages employees "to inform management of any problems that prevent them from performing error-free work," implying that no problem is too small.

Other differences are not so clear cut. All three experts call for the use of statistical tools in process measurement, but Deming and Juran place more emphasis on them than Crosby. They all stress total company commitment, but Deming starts at the top and works down, while Juran says the process can begin with middle management and work up and down the ranks; Crosby, focusing on conformance to requirements and product defects, appears to put more responsibility on operators. These variances are often a matter of degree and to many observers are minor or trivial at best.

"Much is made of the differences among these three gurus, but the similarities are much more important in my view." says Dr. Don Berwick, vice president of care measurement at Harvard Community Health Plan. "People should look for the similarities, for the things they hear from all the gurus, because there is a certain core set of concepts that make up an irreducible set. If you're not following [those concepts], then you're not doing quality improvement."

Each of the consultants preach quality improvement in terms that encompass a broad spectrum of industries and types of organizations. Choosing among the three depends on the needs of a particular organization and how it prefers to adapt a quality philosophy to fit those needs.

CROSBY

In 1979 Tennant Co. of Minneapolis went shopping for a quality improvement program. According to John Davis, director of manufacturing engineering and product conformance, Tennant wanted a program that could be adopted throughout the corporation. Crosby's nontechnical approach looked as if it would be workable in both field and administrative operations. Although the company has just a couple of full-time trainers on staff, today it has 60 people capable of delivering training on 80 different topics. It also has a great reputation for quality. But the approach is no longer strictly Crosby style.

"Crosby's 14-step approach is still the foundation for our efforts," Davis says, "but if you walked into our company today, you'd see a lot of small-group involvement, which is something that Juran advocates. You'd see a lot of applications where we're using statistical process control, which is something that Deming advocates. You'd see a real mix."

Crosby provides an excellent structure to get an organization started in quality improvement, says Davis, while tools and techniques from the other gurus offer more nuts-and-bolts help. More than one organization has approached quality improvement by starting with an awareness campaign and then jumping into specific techniques.

Armstrong World Industries of Lancaster, PA, for example, sent 500 upper-level managers through Crosby's introductory program at Winter Park, and hand-picked 50 employees for two weeks of training to prepare them for their roles as quality instructors. William B. McBee, the director of quality at Armstrong, claims the initial training from Crosby gave his far-flung organization a common language and mission concerning quality, and laid the groundwork for specific improvements.

"Crosby really works on the mind and focuses on behavior among people [within the organization and among] organizations," says McBee. "He's excellent at helping to adjust your attitude toward quality. He's not as strong on specific tools [that will get the job] done. But we knew that going in. You create an attitude of change and that creates the need for tools. If you apply the tools to an organization that doesn't have a strong [perceived] need for them, you're fighting an uphill battle. You've got to prime the pump and gain the commitment of your key people. Then you can overlay the tools to keep it flowing."

According to McBee, training is a good way to gain that commitment; according to the gurus, training is essential. The eighth point in Crosby's program requires all levels of management to be trained early in the process in order to fill their roles in the quality improvement effort. Whether that role is as a trainer, an exemplar of quality commitment or a demonstrator of quality-management principles, Crosby sees the training of managers as vital. Mike Morris, director of quality improvement at Perdue Farms in Salisbury, MD, calls the Crosby program "a good tool for teaching managers how to manage."

DEMING

The gospel according to Deming is taught by Deming alone; he has neither an institute nor partners—just a secretary who has worked for him for more than 35 years. Reportedly, he is less motivated by remuneration for his work than by the desire to get his message to as many people and organizations as possible.

His sixth point calls for training on the job, and his methods tend to demand it. Deming advocates SPC, the use of complex statistical charts to plot variations from the ideal in a production process and to determine the right course to correct those variations. This concentration on statistical charting is where intensive training comes in.

At Aristech, a petrochemical and plastics manufacturer based in Pittsburgh, all 2,000 employees are trained in basic SPC. According to corporate manager of quality and productivity George Hanington, a select few are also trained in experimental design, an advanced mathematical tool that improves on the old engineering approach of examining one variable in a process at a time. In making some plastics, Aristech's process includes 50 to 100 variables, and experimental design enables the company to measure all of them simultaneously. It streamlines the process, and saves time and money.

The rigor of Deming's approach is one of its strengths, says Marian Steeples, director of quality at U.S. West Inc. She cites his insistence on constancy of purpose and continuous improvement (point 5: "Improve constantly and forever the system of production and service."). Deming also contends that quality and productivity can change the shape and scope of an organization, which creates the need for constant training and retraining (point 13: "Institute a vigorous program of education and self-improvement."). While lasting quality improvement is also preached by Crosby and Juran, Deming stresses that continuous innovation is the only way to keep customers coming back.

Ford Motor Co. has employed Deming's philosophies since 1981, and has been lauded for the improved quality of its automobiles. But Ford is not finished, says Ed Baker, director of quality planning and statistical methods. "We never reach a point where we've done everything we can because the customer is always expecting a lot more, so we have to continually improve what we're doing," he explains. "Whether it be our design, the way the car functions, the features of the car or some qualitative characteristics in terms of the interior, you can't stop. Otherwise you're going to lose the game."

Quality improvement that requires continuous training is equally at home in service industries. For example, training plays a key role in ground operations at Federal Express, says Linda Griffin, senior quality administrator. The rules and procedures necessary to meet customer needs are constantly changing, she says, which means continuous training in new billing procedures, new customer service requirements or whatever. Couriers, managers and other local station employees are trained to analyze procedures when recurring customer problems are found. Customer-contact employees also get six weeks of training in how to handle irate callers. All of these programs are focused on providing quality customer service.

U.S. West's Steeples serves as an examiner for the Malcolm Baldridge Quality Award, this country's equivalent of Japan's Deming Prize for total quality management. She says the service industry needs new ideas for quality improvement. She believes that manufacturers have made great strides in quality, but that service organizations aren't moving along fast enough. Despite some notable accomplishments in the service sector—Florida Power and Light recently won the Deming Prize for quality and was the first non-Japanese corporation to do so—she says the industry needs to cultivate more new leaders with ideas for applying the quality principles, and to do it soon.

JURAN

In the language of quality, the term *customer* can mean more than just the consumer of a product or service. On a production line, it can be the next person down the line. That's where Juran comes in.

Juran looks at quality improvement in a project-by-project, step-by-step manner. Every step in a process affects the next step in that process and so on. When work is passed on from one employee to the next, the recipient of that work is the customer, or client, in that work relationship—and the process becomes one of meeting the needs of that customer. Deming calls it "breaking down the barriers between departments." Juran calls it "identifying your customer."

At Moore Business Forms of Chicago, director of quality Sandy Park calls it "listening to our people." Quality improvement in the 107-year-old company has meant that managers and line employees attend the same training sessions. Lines of communication have opened up, and management is hearing what the employees need to operate the business. Managers and supervisors are learning to manage in a more participative environment, and employees are learning group dynamic skills to help them run meetings.

Juran's quality philosophy urges managers to examine the entire production process for problems—from material supplier to end user—and then train employees to do the same. In many organizations, that calls for breaking up into small groups, quality teams or quality circles (depending on whose terminology is being used). Juran advocates training for these groups in problem solving, brainstorming, group dynamics and teamwork. A major thrust of Juran's principles is to teach employees to work in groups to determine cause-and-effect relationships in workplace problems.

In some companies, quality training focuses on teaching employees how to examine the ways in which they perform their jobs. Howard Green, a training administrator for Southern California Edison in Rosemead, CA, employed Juran for that purpose. His department formed quality groups that were trained in statistical analysis and in ways to examine their work processes. Once the groups uncovered problems in the processes, they sorted them by the Juran method of the "vital few vs. the trivial many," according to potential cost savings. For example, the groups determined that the utility company could save substantial labor costs if it used precast trenches for electrical substations instead of digging them. As a result, instead of 16-man crews building the trenches in stages for 16 days, crews of three now work for three days to complete the task.

Southern California Edison also trains employees to negotiate with suppliers and follows up on that training by asking trainees to actually purchase labor for curb-and-gutter construction, for instance. Green reports that this method allows the company to measure the training in actual dollars, rather than merely reading the usual "smile sheet" evaluations at the end of a session. The result is a cost-effective approach to training that adheres to Juran's concept of focusing on the process.

Controlling costs to impress upper management is high on Juran's list of quality improvement techniques. Both he and Crosby address the cost of quality, and concentrate on preventing waste and defective products. Whether the defects occur because of shipping, production or poor materials, waste and defects must be eliminated—and that no longer means being tossed out by an inspector at the end of a line.

Tom Gillem is director of quality education and communication at Hospital Corporation of America, which owns 80 hospitals nationwide. He's part of a quality resource group his company formed to search for ways to translate the tools and techniques of quality improvement into the language of health care. As a result of quality training introduced by the resource group, one hospital reduced the amount of wasted intravenous antibiotics by 50 percent. Gillem says it can be reduced even further.

SAME DRAGON

All three quality champions aim at getting management's attention. Whether they advocate waving a quality flag, demonstrating cost savings or grabbing managers by the lapels, their intentions are similar.

In Deming's view, the system—not the worker—is to blame for an organization's quality problems, and management is responsible for that system. He contends that management is responsible for 85 percent of all quality problems; Juran puts the figure at 80 percent. At the same time, Juran advocates collecting data that demonstrate the extent of a problem to convince top management to improve quality. Crosby says that management must convince the entire organization of *its* commitment to quality with a written policy, films, books and posters. In other words, whatever tack they take, all mandate managerial commitment.

If they're all trying to slay the same dragon, why split hairs over their differences? Perhaps the most sensible approach is to select recommendations from each, depending on the needs of your organization. As Harvard Community Health Plan's Berwick says, "It's a rich field, and like any rich field, you can learn a lot from [all] the players."

In the end, your choice of gurus may not be crucial at all. June Barhet, district manager of quality and data management for AT&T Operator Services, likens it to picking a religion: "Does it matter what church you go to as long as you do the right thing? If you lock in with Crosby and go with Crosby's techniques, you'll get improvement. If you go with Juran, you'll get improvement. If you go with Deming, you'll get improvement. Which one is better than the other? I don't know. I don't think it makes much difference as long as you're using something."

IV

SELECTED SYSTEMS

SUPPLIER QUALITY AUDITS

Audit builds stronger business relationships between user and source

CHARLES E. BOBBITT, JR.

In today's business world, quality is beginning to be the number one objective of every company. If nothing else, "quality" is at least a buzzword. For those companies that are providing financial and people resources to achieve the best available quality materials, implementation of internal quality programs is extending to suppliers. To assist in the supplier quality implementation process, audits are developed to help the company quantify all its suppliers.

There are two main types of supplier quality audits: supplier quality rating audit (SQRA) and supplier quality improvement audit (SQIA). Similarities exist between the two audit types. For example, both contain categories that look at the supplier's quality system, and category scoring in both is similar.

Once the supplier audit has been performed, the score and other measurement criteria are used by the purchasing department to determine the best supplier to use for specific materials. These measurements are the basis for supplier selection and use.

SQRA AND SQIA CATEGORIES

Eight categories are used in the two audit schemes:

• *Quality systems management* evaluates the commitment to quality by a supplier's management. Here, the supplier's management is queried on its internal and external quality policies, principles and procedures.

• *Design information* deals with the supplier's specification and document control system. Design and process documentation, customer specifications and document change control systems are evaluated in this category.

• In *procurement,* the supplier's procured material specifications, receiving inspection facilities and procedures, and his supplier requirements are reviewed.

• *Material control* addresses the supplier's handling of incoming and in-process materials, in-process control system and the facility's appearance.

• For *final acceptance,* the supplier's handling, storage, inspection, shipping and control principles and procedures of finished materials are analyzed.

• *Calibration* procedures, facilities and standards are also evaluated with emphasis placed on measurement instrument repeatability and reproducibility and the system of instrument recall.

• *Quality information and statistical process control* (SPC) evaluate the supplier's manufacturing equipment, statistical method of process control, machine and process capability, technical support and manufacturing technology.

Table 1. Weighted quality system categories	
Category	**Weight**
Quality systems management	0.2
Design information	0.1
Procurement	0.1
Material control	0.1
Final acceptance	0.1
Calibration	0.1
Quality information	0.1
Statistical process control	0.2

The categories may or may not be weighted in scoring. By using a weighting system, SQRA and SQIA are scored according to areas considered to be more significant, as in Table 1. The system rating for the SQRA and SQIA is broken down into five classifications and ratings. Typically, suppliers scoring 70 percent and above, plus other criteria, qualify for certification wherever such programs exist. (Certification is not included in this feature; it requires separate attention.)

SQRA, SQIA DIFFERENCES

As already noted, SQRA and SQIA have similarities between them. They use similar questions, categories, classifications and ratings. There is one very significant difference between them, however. SQRA ends up being just that—a rating of the supplier's quality system. But SQIA enables the company and its suppliers to work together on continually improving the supplier's quality system.

With SQRA, a checklist of various items is generally used to judge the supplier being audited. Once the audit has been completed and a rating number established, communications between the company and its supplier stop. The company doing the audit uses the rating to determine which supplier it will conduct business with. The supplier with the highest rating then gets most of the business from the auditing company. (So that the auditing company does not encounter material shortages, two or more other suppliers are retained for a small percentage of the business.)

On the other hand, SQIA is used as a rating tool for helping the auditing company decide which company to do business with. It also allows the auditing company to work with major suppliers in making quality improvements within their operations. This type of audit contains general questions that require a written response on all categories critiqued.

Once this type of audit is completed, areas of concern are mutually addressed. To resolve these areas, a constant communications link is formed between the supplier and the auditing company. If the supplier needs help, either financial or people, then the auditing company— providing it is serious about quality improvement—must provide that help.

SQIA is the initial phase of building a working relationship with the supplier. First, it opens the door to candid discussions concerning the supplier's business operation. Suppliers who learn to understand the objective of SQIA consider the audit the first step to achieving the best quality products available. Some suppliers realize that this type of audit is actually providing a free service. Normally, they would pay consultants thousands of dollars for this service.

Next, identified problem areas give the supplier the opportunity to fix things that normally would not get fixed. By having a customer-performed audit, the supplier is given the clout to focus the necessary resources to get problems resolved.

Lastly, all of the supplier's customers will benefit from the improved quality attained through the SQIA. Even though this seems to be a deterrent to the auditing company, it must realize that it can still maintain the competitive edge by continually improving supplier programs and relationships.

As with SQRA, SQIA allows the company to determine the best supplier of a given material and rate all suppliers accordingly. The supplier with the highest rating is given the majority of the business. Again, so that the company does not run into shortages, two or more suppliers are retained.

A company's purchasing department generally establishes supplier classifications; see Table 2. Suppliers are given a rating based on specific criteria. As with all purchasing departments, material cost is very important in choosing a supplier. This cost must be kept at a minimum so that the finished product cost remains low. In some cases, however, paying a higher price for a material may prove to be more beneficial to the user company. The high-priced material must demonstrate some type of cost savings within the user's operation to

Table 2. SQRA and SQIA classifications and ratings	
Classification	**Rating (%)**
Outstanding	86-100
Satisfactory	70-85
Improvement needed	41-69
Significant deficiency	21-40
No system	0-20

offset a lower-priced, lower-quality material.

The supplier classification criteria in Table 3 show that this purchasing department is using quality as the prime indicator for choosing suppliers; 65 percent of the total calculation is devoted to quality. The supplier's parts per million (ppm) defective and lot accept rate, determined by the using company's incoming quality department, are the measurable items defining quality costs. The supplier quality audit score accounts for its percent of the total calculation.

Table 3. Supplier classification example		
Classification	**Weight (%)**	**Measurement criteria**
Quality rating	50	Defective level (ppm) and lot accept rate
On-time delivery	35	Material delivery time to point of use
Quality audit	15	Supplier audit score

The remaining 35 percent of the calculation is based on on-time delivery. On-time delivery is measured by the supplier's performance to customer-supplied shipping schedules. Once an order is shipped from the supplier's location until the time it is received by the using organization, and how this time compares with the shipping schedule is the criterion for on-time delivery.

In this example, the quality rating is weighted at 50 percent. Without the continual improvement obtained with SQIA, a supplier may never know what areas require improvement or how to make them. The feedback obtained with SQIA allows the supplier to work on these areas and obtain assistance from his customer when needed.

With SQIA, the supplier base in time will be cut to only one supplier of a specific material. The one quality supplier who has earned this status and the auditing company will have established a relationship of trust and knowledge about one another that will allow for a one-supplier base and a business future for each other.

When comparing SQRA against SQIA, with the improvement audit, an auditing company and its supplier will both benefit in the long run by working toward continuous quality improvement. To become part of this quality process, companies must realize the benefits of SQIA and take steps toward achieving the best quality products available.

BUILD A BETTER SUPPLIER-CUSTOMER RELATIONSHIP

Some simple checklists can help organize cooperative quality improvement efforts

EDWARD J. BROEKER

A better customer-supplier relationship offers a powerful opportunity to improve quality and reduce costs. Quality can be managed only when customers and suppliers are partners. The improvement process is established primarily by the customer and must be based on mutual respect, trust, and benefit.

The problem is that customers commonly have treated their suppliers as adversaries. The customer supplied the specifications, schedules, and payment while the supplier found a way to meet the customer's demands. Bids for materials too often were solicited on a continuous or semicontinuous basis; contracts were awarded on the basis of price and schedule, with some consideration, perhaps, for quality. With this scenario, there was no real need for a customer to interact with a supplier because the supplier might change the next time bids were solicited. Each party would press short-term advantages. The failings of that approach are that it fosters mutual suspicions and precludes mutual assistance, joint planning, and other forms of close collaboration.

Six steps forward

1. Build a trusting relationship.

2. Establish clearly understood requirements.

3. Select suppliers capable of conformance.

4. Be serious about conformance.

5. Develop a system of measurement.

6. Make sure each nonconformance is corrected.

BUILD A TRUSTING RELATIONSHIP

The complexity of today's business climate requires cooperation between customers and suppliers. This has to be a planned, continuing relationship based on mutual respect. Mutual respect comes from mutual understanding.

The supplier should be regarded as an extension of the customer's process. Suppliers will do their share in quality improvement when they realize that their customers take requirements seriously, and reject nonconforming products.

Many supplier-customer relationships have not developed because of a lack of trust. Some suppliers consider their processes to be proprietary and see no need to involve their customers. Customers, likewise, have seen no need to explain to suppliers how their materials are used in the customer process. Often suppliers are not trusted out of fear that they might pass on proprietary information to competitors.

No company can operate effectively, however, without an exchange of ideas. Sharing information on processes often is necessary if suppliers are to provide nonconformance-fee materials. Likewise, a customer will not be able to understand a supplier's problem without some knowledge of the supplier's processes and procedures. Trust must be the basis for exchange. As each conforms to mutually-agreed-on requirements and learns to do it right the first time, they will eliminate the cost of having to do something again. Quality improvement, will result in cost reduction.

ESTABLISH CLEARLY UNDERSTOOD REQUIREMENTS

One of the first things a customer must do before selecting a supplier is to establish clear, precise requirements for the product or service to be provided. These requirements create a basis for evaluating suppliers. Requirements are established by answering questions. In the case of supplier selection, these questions might include:

- What is required?
- What is the anticipated schedule that must be supported?
- What experience should the supplier have in producing the product?
- To what extent will the supplier participate in developing the end product?
- How many sources will the product require?
- How will conformance to requirements be measured?
- What corrective action system is required?
- What geographic location is necessary for the supplier?
- The answers to these questions will help a customer evaluate which supplier can best meet its needs.

SELECT SUPPLIERS CAPABLE OF CONFORMANCE

Other information can come from a review of past performance, tests of incoming materials, and on-site evaluation. The on-site evaluation will provide the opportunity to assess the supplier's internal quality control procedures and manufacturing control systems. Such evaluations should emphasize determining the capabilities of the process, the adequacy of the process controls, and the training and qualifications of the work force.

The evaluation also can help improve communications between the customer and supplier, and even within the supplier's organization. Such surveys frequently stimulate action by the supplier's top management on matters that the supplier's own employees have been unable to communicate.

BE SERIOUS ABOUT CONFORMANCE

For customers to adopt and realize a specific quality performance, their suppliers must do likewise. The suppliers must be told immediately that quality is non-negotiable.

Customers and suppliers must agree completely on quality performance standards. Concurrence requires the following steps:

• Make certain the supplier understands every detail involved in delivery of the product. This includes specifications, technical data, delivery, and billing procedures.

• Establish two-way communications. The customer must be ready and willing to explain the reason for requirements. Suppliers should be willing to explain their processes.

• Establish precise methods for accepting materials. The supplier's and customer's test equipment must correlate.

DEVELOP A SYSTEM OF MEASUREMENT

One of the most important steps in the supplier quality management cycle is measurement and feedback. Supplier measurement should contain all critical variables such as quality, delivery, and price. Any price measurement should include the cost of nonconformance traceable to the product.

The cost of an item should reflect the initial purchase price plus the added costs resulting from items such as scrap, rework, delays, field failures, and poor supplier quality. These costs might greatly exceed the savings achieved by buying from the lowest bidder.

Measurements provide evaluation of suppliers and customers in addition to other valuable information.

Purchasing managers generally agree that buying decisions should be based on all costs, not only the purchase price. Many times, however, they lack information on the added quality-related costs. It is highly effective to develop customer measurements along with supplier measurements for major material purchases. The pulse of both measures is to gain information. Such information is intended to work both ways: While the customer is sending the supplier this information, the supplier should provide the customer with information on how conformance will be attained.

MAKE SURE EACH NONCONFORMANCE IS CORRECTED

With each nonconformance, suppliers should be asked about the corrective action they will take. They should be able to provide answers to these questions:

- What caused the nonconformance?
- What changes in the process need to be made to achieve correction?
- When will these changes be implemented?
- How will these changes be made foolproof?
- How will the customer know the changes have been made?

It is the customer's responsibility to ensure that the supplier works to find the root cause of each nonconformance and takes the necessary action to permanently eliminate the cause. The role of the supplier in quality improvement is critical. For the supplier to achieve improvement, the customer must demand it.

MANAGING QUALITY IN STAFF AREAS—PART 2

Staff support areas like accounting and marketing must become just as competitive as manufacturing

BARBARA J. YOUNG

Members and managers of staff areas are finding their jobs and departments changing drastically. These departments are being challenged to contribute to the bottom line. Entrepreneurial groups in many areas of service are knocking on corporation doors and offering competitive services at reduced costs. In short, staff support areas are having to run leaner, become competitive, and justify the quality vs. cost of their services—and in some extreme cases, their existence.

As managers assess the situation for their groups, they are finding themselves on roads previously untraveled. What can they do? What should they do? The following ideas, which managers of staff areas can use to manage the needed changes, build upon the basics presented in Part I of this article, which appeared in the October 1989 issue. These ideas have been piloted successfully in some areas.

The major theme is to view your area as a small business. What is a business? You say you are not a profit-making enterprise. Realize, however, that you do have a budget. You are expected to break even. Therefore, you do have a small business similar to a non-profit organization. Your group must provide some value-added service—or there will be no customers for your "products"—in the long term. (Customer refers to the person or persons purchasing your group's products and services. For staff groups, these customers are mainly other internal departments.)

BACKGROUND DEVELOPMENT

As with any other small business, the following functions are embedded in your organization, whether or not you have thought of it this way:

- *Manufacturing.* This is the process in your business by which you "produce products" for your customers to purchase so they can satisfy some particular need.
- *Research and development.* This is the process in your business by which you prepare for the future and determine what tools, techniques, or "products" you will sell to meet your customers' future

142

and changing needs.

- *Marketing.* This is the process in your business by which you identify your customer base and determine your customers' needs, price and distribution requirements, etc. This also involves the element of "sales" and the process by which you let the customer know of the user benefits of your "products."

- *Market intelligence.* This is the process in your business by which you identify the current and potential share of your market and also current and potential competitors that could erode your market share.

Each of these processes must be understood and operate effectively for your area to achieve positive business results. Your reaction to this might be, "I don't have time to address all this. I have jobs to get done today." That's what the manufacturing area was saying five years ago. The internal turmoil that corporations are facing today, with ever-increasing competition, is well documented.

Or your general reaction might be, "I don't have the training for all this." If "all this" is approached at a simplistic level first, as will be demonstrated here, it becomes simpler to ease into the approach. But, undeniably, these are the skills that managers of staff support areas must develop for the future.

How might a manager ease into looking at the area more as a competitive business? Following are some simple, relatively quick

---

Worksheet 1

	Key Functions	5-Year Goals	1-Year Goals
	Manufacturing/Service 1. Products (value added) 2. Delivery		
	Marketing 1. Sales 2. Advertising/education		
Mission • What • To whom • Why	**R&D** 1. Technologies		
	Market Intelligence 1. Customer 2. Competitor 3. General trends		
	STAFFING/TRAINING FINANCIAL PERFORMANCE		

approaches for managers to try and some of the resulting benefits. Consider them as ideas and further apply your creativity in thinking of their use in your environment.

BASIC BUSINESS QUESTIONS NEEDING ANSWERS

1. *What is Your Business?*

Many staff groups find it hard to succinctly describe their value-added products and services. One useful technique to do this is for the group to put itself in the following situation.

Suppose that you are an outside contract group—that is, you do not have the luxury of being an actual part of the corporation you now

Worksheet 2

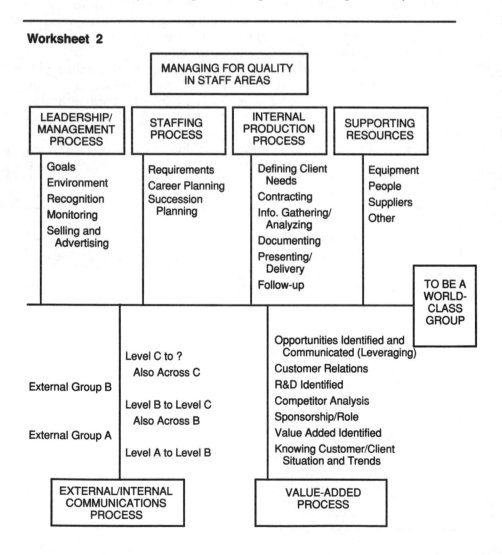

144

serve. Your group wants to renew its annual contract with the larger corporation. Unfortunately, the group cannot give a verbal presentation—it can only leave a marketing brochure with the contact person. How would you describe the group, its products, its method of service, its value to the corporation, and its competitive leverage in a convincing manner? Mock up that marketing brochure.

This exercise takes about one to four hours to do. It has proven to be a very useful exercise. It condenses the group's offerings into a short format. It forces the group into taking the customer's viewpoint of what value added means. It highlights what the group does not know about itself or about its ability to describe its offerings in simple language that can be understood by a customer. Many groups have ended up redesigning the brochure into a truly acceptable format for internal corporate marketing, and in some appropriate cases, for

---

Worksheet 3a

Client Quality Assessment Questionnaire

Client: **Date of Service:**
Project Title: **Project Number:**

Please comment candidly, pro and con, relative to the areas mentioned below. Do not be limited to the space provided—use the back of the sheet if necessary. Your time and assessment are appreciated.

Defining the need: Do you believe your objectives and constraints were understood relative to resolving your issue? Were alternative approaches provided to meet those needs? Was planning done in a timely, effective, and professional manner? Was anything missing? What could have been done differently?

Providing service: Was the service provided in an efficient and effective manner? Were the personnel flexible and effective? Do you believe total assistance was rendered to meet your needs and objectives? What else could have been done to improve the service?

Service wrap-up: Was the documentation complete and timely? What else could have been done?

Value added: What was the value added to your situation through this service? Could it have been greater? If so, how? Where else might you obtain these services? Why did you choose this group?

Other comments:

marketing its services externally.

2. *Where Are You Taking Your Business?*
If you are truly running a business, you should have some vision of where it is going—a business plan. Worksheet 1 shows an approach to this. The flow of information moves left to right and back again. As one moves to the next column to the right, the question "How will we do this?" is answered. As one moves to the preceding column, the question "Why are we doing this?" is answered.

Worksheet 3b

Client Assessment of Finance and Administration

Your help is requested to assess the performance of the finance and administration group serving your organization. This information will be used to target any services needing improvement.

Seven key activities have been defined as being performed by finance and administration:

1) Counseling—Provide appropriate insight relative to business/financial implications of particular business decisions as requested or unsolicited.
2) Special request analysis—Manage special projects involving financial analysis and business implications (i.e., new product introductions, marketing promotions, acquisitions, strategy assessment, etc.).
3) Financial performance monitoring—Provide information to monitor the financial performance of your organization. This includes scheduled reports as well as additional requested reporting.
4) Pricing—Provide information on financial and business implications of various pricing options as well as control mechanisms.
5) Billing systems—Provide and manage an appropriate billing system to meet your organization's requirements.
6) Asset reporting—Provide and manage an appropriate asset reporting system to meet your organization's requirements (i.e., inventories, receivables, and capital/fixed assets).
7) Credit service—Manage accounts receivable, which includes bookkeeping, collection, bad debt charge-offs, and credit administration (including credit worthiness). Provide information regarding terms of sale and their influence on days sales outstanding.

On the following pages, you are requested to:
  • indicate how important each of these activities is to you.
  • assess how well these activities have been performed during the last 12 months.

If you have not used a particular activity in the past 12 months, or are not aware of the activity being performed by the finance and administration group, *so indicate and skip to the next page.*

An additional sheet at the end of the questionnaire is included for any other information on activities that are performed for your unit, or that you feel should be performed but currently are not.

---

1) Counseling-Providing appropriate insight relative to business/financial implications of particular business decisions as requested or unsolicited.

(Please circle appropriate number.)

A) How important is the counseling activity to your area of responsibility within the organization?

Not important   1   2   3   4   5   Very important

B) Have you utilized this activity in the past 12 months?

Yes, have utilized.. 1
No, have not utilized, but am aware of it................................2
Am not aware of this activity.. 3

(If you circled 2 or 3 in question B, please skip to next page.)

The following questions relate to your level of satisfaction with various dimensions of this counseling activity.

(Please circle the appropriate number:
1 = very dissatisfied and 5 = very satisfied.)

Interpersonal Aspects:	Very Dissatisfied			Very Satisfied	
Responsiveness	1	2	3	4	5
Proactiveness	1	2	3	4	5
Attitude	1	2	3	4	5
Sensitive data treated confidentially	1	2	3	4	5

Technical Aspects:					
Provides objective/ independent assessment	1	2	3	4	5
Appropriateness of work (e.g., prioritizing, level of detail, etc.)	1	2	3	4	5
Problem definition-perspective and insight	1	2	3	4	5
Timeliness	1	2	3	4	5
Communications effectiveness (presentations and reports)	1	2	3	4	5
Completeness	1	2	3	4	5
Consistency of information	1	2	3	4	5
Generates an appropriate understanding of the use of financial information	1	2	3	4	5
Understands the business of your organization	1	2	3	4	5

Are there any quality attributes of services that have not been rated that should be?

_____   _____

_____   _____

The leftmost item is the group's mission. Some insight into this should have come out of the marketing brochure exercise. It is a single statement that indicates what, in general, the group does as a business, and for whom, and what value is added.

Next, the major business functions (manufacturing, marketing, R&D, and market intelligence) combine to accomplish that mission. The plans you outline for these functions will combine to make the strategy.

Moving right, the group identifies the vision five years out for each of these functions. This prepares the group to look far enough into the future to identify changing customer requirements, changing technology, and corporation trends. The group must determine how these changes will affect its business and how it should respond to them.

The last column contains the one-year goals. These goals should be developed on the premise that, if the group is to achieve the five-year goal, they must accomplish this much in the first year to remain competitive.

Operationally then, as indicated below the line on the diagram, you will have to develop staff and monitor financial performance to achieve the strategy just developed. Staff and financial performance will also have five-year and one-year goals.

The result of this form is that the various parts of the business are integrated into a long-term vision. Suddenly, the group is in control of the business; it is not just running to catch up. The strategy is all laid out on one page for visibility and reference.

Worksheet 4					
Competitors	C = Current P = Possible	Their service leverage against us	Their cost of service	Our service leverage against them	Our cost of service
1.					
2.					
3.					
4.					
5.					

This technique takes four to eight hours to draft. It helps the group understand the environment in which it operates and the forces acting upon it—both positive and negative. It is a useful communication tool for other levels within the division or the corporation because it explains what the group's plans are and why.

Another useful technique at this point is for the group to identify its critical success factors (Worksheet 2). This is a cause-and-effect diagram, showing some of the processes required for a world-class staff group. The group can look at this to point out those areas that need improving and to check that these areas are represented in the one-year and five-year goals on Worksheet 1. The information gained from the customer and employee questioning sessions, recommended in Part I of this article, could also be reviewed and built in at this time.

3. What Do Customers Think About the Products of Your Business?

The business must continually monitor the quality and value-added aspects of its products as viewed by the customer. Two popular methods are to send customers a questionnaire after every job, or at planned intervals, asking them about the quality of service.

As mentioned—in Part I, the questions should be in the areas of:

Worksheet 5

Products/Services	Percent of time	Costs				Volume of service	Cost per unit	30% Profit	Benchmarking to external providers
		adm. chgs.	salary & benefits	R&D, mtkg. intel., etc.	total				
1)		x	x	o	x	x	x	x	x
2)		x	x	o	x	x	x	x	x
3)		x	x	o	x	x	x	x	x
etc.									
R&D		o	o						
advertising/ marketing		o	o						
market intelligence		o	o						
	100%			$ x total group budget					

149

• the quality of design of the staff group's products and services. This includes effectiveness of contracting, or setting the specifications, and the appropriateness of the developed product or service.

• the quality of delivery of the staff group's products and services. This includes availability, responsiveness, timeliness, completeness, professional rapport, and packaging of the product.

An easy-to-fill-out form should be developed to send to customers (Worksheet 3a-b). Quantitative scales of zero to l0 can be used. The group can then summarize and monitor these ratings.

4. How Do You Stack Up Against the Competition?

With the entrepreneurial environment that exists, it is interesting to observe the creative services that are being developed. Your particular staff area might not have any direct competitor right now, but that does not preclude the possibility of one being developed in a garage or home office right now. There is also the chance of duplication of efforts in large organizations, which, when noted, will most likely be eliminated. Knowing your competitors, both internal and external, allows you to determine your competitive advantage and leverage. This helps you fine-tune the quality and cost of services offered and identify shortcomings within your area. Worksheet 4 is an example of a format with which comparative information can be noted and continually updated.

Another way to get information about competition is to ask the customers. In the quality survey, customers can be asked which alternative sources of service they considered, the relative advantages and disadvantages of those sources, and why your particular group was chosen to do the work.

As shown in Worksheet 4, the cost of services must be addressed. Cost does not necessarily mean quality, but it cannot be denied that internal customers will consider it when services are being contracted. Worksheet 5 shows one way you can benchmark your services. A by-product of the marketing brochure is that the products and services offered are defined. These products and services are listed in the first column of Worksheet 5.

The worksheet then asks you to distribute your group's time across these products. In addition, you must allocate "costs" for R&D, market intelligence, and marketing efforts within your area. These costs must be reallocated across the charge of your products, as shown, to recover these costs and break even. An estimate of volume is then made. Dividing dollars by volume provides an estimate of your charge-out rate, priced so that you will break even. This can be benchmarked against competitors' rates. From this you can determine whether you are competitive in cost or not, or whether you should be the brokering service to obtain the desired quality services, but for the reduced price offered externally.

When comparing yours to outside prices, consider the fact that external competitors are profit businesses. If your rates are similar to theirs, you obviously have some room for improvement in your internal costs—and these should be isolated as to their source. It is enlightening to determine the overhead costs within a large corporation and their contribution to the cost of your services.

This process should take four to eight hours, depending on the availability of budget information and the complexity of your product and service offerings.

5. What Have You Done to Include Your Employees in the Business?

Involving staff employees, at all levels, in these processes can increase productivity. Enthusiasm will grow as the group works through the processes—they feel part of the business. They understand better the business of which they are a part and can give ideas on improvements. Also, the employees better understand the need for quality from a customer's perspective as they see that their salaries are paid by the customer's repeat requests for service.

START NOW

Given the changing corporate environment, the quality, cost, and value added of staff products will be looked at with ever-increasing care. It behooves managers, therefore, to look at their areas of responsibility as non-profit businesses. These quick-and-easy techniques for a group to use to better understand itself as a competitive business can result in:

- a basic marketing brochure.
- a basic business plan.
- prioritized concerns to address needed improvements.
- initial monitoring of the customer's reaction to the staff group's products and services.
- initial monitoring of competitive position.
- benchmarking of cost of service.
- increased productivity.

A challenge remains. Currently, staff areas spend a lot of time firefighting—a sign of problems further up in the process of events. The competitive environment facing staff groups might not be great enough yet for them to want to envision and acquire skills to run a competitive business. However, if lessons can be learned from corporations and the challenges they have had to face, staff support managers might want to start early and avoid the high-pressure crunch that happens when market share suddenly erodes.

V

CASE STUDIES

CRAZY ABOUT QUALITY

CEO Marshall McDonald made excellence a passion at Florida Power. His successor, John Hudiburg, is making it a religion

GARY JACOBSON AND JOHN HILLKIRK

Marshall McDonald was always the quirky idea man when he was CEO of Florida Power & Light Company. But around 1980, when he suddenly developed an interest in quality—no, make that a passion for quality—his managers' eyebrows went up. And when he prodded his company to take its first steps toward a program, skepticism spread rapidly through the ranks.

Management, as a rule, can be reluctant to change, and Florida Power's top executives were no exception. C.O. Woody, the executive vice president who heads the company's nuclear division, for example, remained an unbeliever until fall of 1984. Then a team from the St. Lucie 2 nuclear plant cut its refueling shutdown time to half the usual 75 days, saving the company $28 million, and Woody decided to find out how the team pulled it off. "I needed to talk to the workers without the plant managers around to get the real story on how this process was working," he says. One day he followed the workers into the "hot" locker room—where they change into their anti-contamination clothing—and got his answer. The method they used had grown out of their quality-management teamwork, they told him, and they had never worked so hard or enjoyed themselves more.

These days Woody and most of the 15,000 executives and employees of Florida Power & Light, the fourth-largest and fastest-growing utility in the country, have abandoned their doubts and embraced quality efforts with a quasi-religious zeal. Not that the early doubts about McDonald's plans were entirely unwarranted. What the now-retired executive and his successor, John J. Hudiburg, set about doing was nothing less than to bring to a service company the exacting standards that had been used almost exclusively by manufacturing companies. Management wasn't even sure it could be done. A manufacturer has a real product whose quality can be standardized by measuring and testing. But how does one "quantify" the quality of a service?

Grappling with these and a host of other questions set McDonald and Hudiburg on a journey that has brought them to the forefront of the quality movement in this country. McDonald, 71, a Wharton School MBA with a weakness for new management schemes, practiced law and served as a top executive at several major oil companies—

including Sinclair and Union—before taking the top post at Florida Power in 1971. He retired last year but remains chairman of FPL Group, the holding company for Florida Power, which accounts for $4.6 billion of the group's $5.8 billion in annual revenues. Hudiburg, 61, joined Florida Power in 1951 as an engineer straight out of the Georgia Institute of Technology and has worked there since. He became CEO in 1983.

Under the leadership of McDonald and Hudiburg, Florida Power, a monopoly utility whose profit margin is set by the Florida Public Service Commission, has become what is widely regarded as the very model of a modern quality-conscious company. In the past few years, more than 400 companies and municipal governments—and even the Internal Revenue Service—have sent representatives to Florida to see what can be accomplished when quality becomes more than just the latest management fad.

Florida Power considers its transformation anything but a fad. In fact, management now believes it has mastered the form sufficiently to compete for Japan's most coveted quality award, the Deming Prize. The award is named after W. Edwards Deming, the American management expert who helped turn Japan Inc. into a world power. No company outside Japan has won the prize.

McDonald first seized on the notion that a commitment to quality could transform a company about 10 years ago. At the time, leading lights in the field were drawing large crowds to symposiums, where they instructed managers on the wonders that could be achieved by applying quality-management techniques to manufacturing. It was at such a symposium in Chicago that McDonald heard the news.

Unlike the traditional product-oriented bias in manufacturing—make it, inspect it, ship it—"total quality," as it is sometimes called, grew out of the work of Deming and J.M. Juran, both renowned management gurus who spent years in Japan preaching their gospel to eager listeners, and Philip B. Crosby, author of the best-seller *Quality Is Free.*

In their pursuit of high manufacturing standards, Deming and Juran advocated an array of statistical methods and measuring techniques to ensure uniform standards of quality; Crosby pushed zero defects. The Japanese went a step farther and encouraged workers to form small groups—quality teams—that would employ a step-by-step process to identify a manufacturing problem, analyze the cause and develop a permanent solution. The solution should always lead to improved quality.

But just what is the measure of quality? Simple: It's making products that meet customers' expectations. If a customer wants a Chevrolet, don't give him a Cadillac—or a Yugo. The operative word here is "customer." Customers aren't just the people who buy a company's products. They are the people on both sides of a transaction—inside or outside the company. At Florida Power, for example, cable pullers are the customers of linemen. The linemen at one service center laid plastic pipes into which cable pullers had to insert electrical wiring. The cable pullers often found that the pipes had slipped out of position when they were ready to perform their task, resulting in costly delays. In quality-speak, the customer's expectations weren't being met. So the linemen designed and constructed a template that held as many as 10 pipes firmly in place and saved the cable pullers the trouble of having to redo their work. The result was an estimated saving of more than $5,000 a year in labor costs.

When McDonald first brought these ideas back from Chicago, the response was less than enthusiastic. He pressed copies of Crosby's book, which was intended for manufacturers, on his top executives, hoping its lessons could somehow be adapted to a service company. They balked. "The initial reaction from the vast majority of people at the company was 'Here's another wild hare of Marshall's,'" says McDonald. "And it's true, I've had my share." Hudiburg doesn't disagree. "Down through the years we've tried them all," he says, ticking off some of McDonald's past enthusiasms: education and training, high-powered consultants, short courses on management at Harvard, management-by-objectives. Most didn't work—and those that did had limited impact. This time McDonald was determined to see the changes through.

Florida Power already had a rudimentary quality system in its nuclear division. After the Three Mile Island disaster in 1979, utilities around the country found themselves battered by long construction and licensing delays. To avoid similar problems, the utility, which at the time was constructing the St. Lucie 2 plant, set up special groups of workers that were essentially quality teams. Their job was to anticipate the critical periods during construction, solve problems that loomed ahead and maintain contact with the Nuclear Regulatory Commission. The strategy worked. By 1981 the project was winding down well ahead of the industry's average schedule. McDonald encouraged the St. Lucie team leaders to help set up similar groups at the utility's fossil-fuel plants. In a real sense, they would also advance his crusade to bring a quality program to Florida Power & Light.

Under McDonald's constant proselytizing, quality teams began to appear here and there. By 1981, they had formed not only at fossil-fuel plants but also at service centers and among distribution engineers, who work on transmission lines. The following year, meter readers in the Melbourne, Florida, area took up the new approach. By the end of 1982, 160 teams were scattered around the company. But just what were they accomplishing? The answer was by no means clear—especially with a minimum of specialized training, varying degrees of commitment and continuing uncertainty about the ways to measure quality in a service company.

Still, McDonald kept pushing. Deming was invited to speak to Florida Power's senior management. So were Juran and Crosby. But there still wasn't a workable formula for applying their methods, says Kent Sterett, who had helped lead the quality teams at St. Lucie and had taken charge of the budding program. "We decided that a blend or hybrid was the best approach for us," says Sterett, who began devising his own training material for the teams. Juran's concept of continuous improvement, for instance, was better suited to a service company than was Crosby's notion of zero defects. In fact, as Florida Power's program took shape, the idea of continuous improvement became its centerpiece. Given enough time and effort, a manufacturer might be able to eliminate most or all flaws in the production process so that products of uniform quality always emerge. But a service company has no production process to perfect, no mechanical plateau to achieve. It delivers a service, and all it can do each day is try to deliver it better than it did yesterday. McDonald decided that his company would compete against its own past efforts and against the efforts of other utilities.

Yet, McDonald was uncertain whether a full-out quality program could ever work at a service company. But in 1984, Kansai Electric, one of Japan's largest utility companies, won the Deming Prize, and all doubts vanished. Here was a company that had achieved what Florida Power was only stumbling toward—and whose methods were applicable to its needs. For McDonald, it was nothing less than a breakthrough. "When we really got rolling was when Kansai allowed our top people to come over there and open up their records," McDonald recalls. "Before that, it was only my faith. Then it became a certainty."

Hudiburg, who led a group of managers to Japan in late 1984, was astonished at the progress Kansai had made just during the period it prepared for the Deming competition. For example, Kansai once had more scrams—emergency shutdowns of nuclear reactors—than Florida Power had. Now it had fewer. And Kansai had managed to find solutions that eluded the American utility. Hudiburg had once struggled with a chronic problem of the utility industry—errors by meter readers. Florida Power's meter readers made one error for every 2,000 meter reads. Kansai's had reduced the error rate to one in every 150,000 reads. How? The Japanese found that most of the mistakes were being made on dial meters, so they replaced them with digital meters.

"That's when I could see what was possible," Hudiburg says. "Until then, I thought the process had limited potential." In Japan, Hudiburg and his colleagues studied improvements not only at Kansai but at other companies and conferred with some of the country's leading quality experts (some of whom became regular consultants for

Florida Power). Hudiburg returned to Florida with a faith as strong as McDonald's. The experience, he says, was like getting "struck by lightning on the road to Damascus."

McDonald had been fighting brush wars over quality management through the early '80s; now he had enough ammunition to win. Hudiburg brought in specialists to set up a full training program for workers who were joining teams. Courses covered such areas as statistical analysis, advanced problem-solving and decision-making techniques, communications skills and group dynamics. These were the tools the teams would require if they were to analyze the problems that arose in their work and seek measurable solutions. Quality teams continued to form throughout the company. By the end of 1984, there were 689 teams, and by the end of the following year, there were 1,302.

Given the scope of the undertaking, mishaps in the early stages were inevitable. McDonald recalls the revolt of the middle managers. "We just about split our pants early on," he says. "We spent all this time and money on training and all of a sudden it became apparent that we were getting significant resistance from middle management." The reason? McDonald and Hudiburg were getting top management and workers fired up with training, but they were ignoring middle managers entirely. The result was that the managers didn't know what to do with the good ideas percolating out of the teams, worried about turf and resisted change—when change was the idea. Soon, middle managers joined the training regimen, and the enterprise continued to expand.

Today, Florida Power has about 1,900 quality teams—comprising most of the work force. Each team works to solve specific problems that stand in the way of company objectives—for example, reducing employee injuries. "What is the main cause of injuries to meter readers?" one team asked. After analyzing injury reports, the team found the culprit to be dog bites. The solution: Enter canine information on the company computer. Now when a meter reader calls up an address on his hand-held computer to check a customer's name and electricity use, he also gets a mean-dog alert.

To keep vigilance at a fever pitch, management set up a series of competitions to reward the teams that were most effective in achieving their goals. The company's highest recognition for exceptional work is the President's Cup, which is awarded once a year. Last year's winner was the team of seven linemen who gave the cable pullers the product they wanted. The reward was a week's trip to Japan's prestigious National Quality Control Conference in Tokyo. It was the first time the conference had invited an American team to attend.

Visit Hudiburg's plainly furnished office at Florida Power's headquarters in Miami and you quickly learn why C. Jackson Grayson, head of the American Productivity and Quality Center in Houston, calls the

CEO a "fanatic" about quality. After a few minutes of conversation, Hudiburg suddenly opens a loose-leaf binder and says, "Have you seen those charts?" He turns to a page containing Florida Power's list of the 16 top electric utilities in the country. Each company is ranked by such standards as price increases, NRC violations, employee injuries and customer complaints. Hudiburg says that in 1987, his company ranked 11th. Last year it ranked fourth. Every company is improving, he says, but Florida Power is improving faster than anyone else. He wants his company to be the best by 1992. "If we continue to make the progress we are making," he says, "we could get there in '91, maybe even '90 if we really push."

Covering Hudiburg's walls, like memento mori, are framed stock certificates of failed companies, most of them utilities. His tie clasp is a miniature version of the so-called Deming wheel—a circle divided into four quadrants, each containing a letter of the alphabet: P,D,C,A. The letters stand for the four elements of Deming's quality process: Plan, Do, Check, Act. "Americans are good at planning and doing," says Hudiburg. "But they're not so good at checking and acting." To keep up the faith, he makes several trips a year to Japan to monitor improvements in quality programs at Kansai and elsewhere.

Critics complain that Hudiburg has been a bit crass in pursuit of the Deming Prize. One of the critics is Philip Crosby, who says much of the attention Florida Power is receiving is the result of unseemly self-promotion and "breast-beating." A lot of companies are making progress in quality; they just don't talk about it as much.

The critics miss the point, says Hudiburg. Quality is a long quest strewn with obstacles, and a major one is employee skepticism. A manager must use any tactic he can to motivate workers. The primary purpose of pursuing the Deming is to get employees on their toes and to accelerate improvements. "It would be hard to get people moving as quickly as we are without some stimulant," he says.

In challenging for the Deming, Florida Power faces a staggering array of criteria to be met. The utility's application covers 1,000 pages of documentation in 10 bound booklets. When the Deming examiners fly in from Japan this summer to conduct audits, they will be free to question any worker they want. Employees must be able to supply the data to support their answers within three minutes. The company's point man on the Deming is Wayne Brunetti, an executive vice president. "It's overwhelming," he says. "You realize there is always more to do." To get Florida Power ready, Brunetti has had to expand his normal 50- to 60-hour week to 80 hours.

What are the utility's chances of winning? The odds are in Florida Power's favor simply because it was allowed to compete, says Junji Noguchi, executive director of the Japanese Union of Scientists and Engineers, which administers the award. "Two years ago, 10 companies were permitted to apply and nine won the prize," he says. "Last year, six applied and five won."

Skeptics about the quality program can still be found—Hudiburg estimates they make up 10 to 15 percent of Florida Power's work force. "But the data are so overwhelming, no one can come out directly against it anymore." McDonald is less restrained in his assessment. "For managers," he says, "this is the best tool to get your job accomplished that management science has created."

The results have certainly been impressive. Customer complaints to the Florida Public Service Commission have dropped by almost a third since 1984. Last year customers were without power an average of only 48 minutes, down 52 minutes from 1982. NRC violations last year dropped to 40, from 58 in 1986.

The benefits are also showing up on the bottom line. By investing $100 million to update and repower a couple of generating units during the past two years, Florida Power has added capacity equivalent to a new 700-megawatt generating unit, which costs almost $1 billion. Hudiburg has decided that construction of a new plant can wait until 1993.

Such moves are helping to keep residential rates moderate. Most of Florida Power's 3 million customers are in south Florida, where utilities have no access to cheap hydro or coal power. Yet rates are just 5 percent above the national average, says Dan Rudakas, an analyst at Duff & Phelps in Chicago. In addition, Florida Power is adding 130,000 customers a year, an increase that would drive most utilities to seek regular rate increases. The company hasn't requested a general rate increase since mid-1984.

McDonald and Hudiburg warn that quality isn't free—improvements take hard work and fierce dedication. "Any large company is going to have to devote years to it," Hudiburg says. Some Florida Power managers took early retirement to avoid the added demands of the new quality program. At company social functions, employees' spouses buttonhole the two executives to complain about the late work hours.

Undaunted, Hudiburg is looking to the future. He wants to use the quality program to prepare for a changing industry. Utility transmission lines may someday be deregulated, he says, putting Florida Power in the same position as the telephone companies. Already, more and more industrial customers are building their own cogeneration plants. And expectations are changing. Ten years ago, Kent Sterett says, a short power blip would never be noticed by residential customers. No more. Now, a failure causes customers to chase around their homes resetting blinking clocks, VCRs and microwaves. In the face of increasing competition, says Hudiburg, a quality program is the best way to hold on to those customers. Florida Power & Light intends to have the Deming Prize to prove it.

HOW VELCRO GOT HOOKED ON QUALITY

Instead of inspecting quality into its fasteners, the company learned to manufacture quality into the product

K. THEODOR KRANTZ

The phone call came out of the blue one morning in August 1985. It was from our Detroit sales manager, who told me that General Motors was dropping us from its highest supplier quality rating to the next to lowest level, four (on a one to five scale). We had 90 days to set up and start a program of total quality control at our sole U.S. plant, in Manchester, New Hampshire, or face the loss of not only an important customer but also our most promising growth market.

The blow was especially hard because we were feeling pretty good about our quality control. About a year earlier we had sent our QC man to school to learn statistical process control and had brought in a consultant to talk to management for half a day and do some training with the quality control staff. Essentially we had done this the way you approach projects, like launching a new product or putting in a safety program in a certain area: you set up the project and choose a project team, then you delegate the work.

We had a reputation in the marketplace for products of the highest quality. True, a year earlier we had also made a toothless attempt to modernize Velcro's quality program. The effort had been delegated to the quality assurance manager, and it had ended stillborn. Nevertheless, the phone call came as a real shock.

To get an idea of what we had to do, we needed to talk to GM. So five Velcro managers flew out to Detroit and met for a couple of hours with the buyer who had given the news to our sales manager, her boss, and two GM quality control people. They told us that our products—which included tape for binding car seat parts together and for binding fabric to the roof—were fine and we were meeting their delivery schedules. But they said our process was unacceptable; we were *inspecting* quality into the product, we were not *manufacturing* quality into the product.

They were dissatisfied with the fact that we were throwing away 5% or 6% or 8% of tape, depending on the product. They wanted quality maintained up and down the line to prevent such waste. And they said that to have the head QC person report to the head of manufacturing was unacceptable. They wanted him to report to me.

We flew back East, feeling thoroughly chastened. It was no consolation to realize that all three U.S. auto producers were feeling great pressure to upgrade their quality, cut costs, and reduce the number of suppliers. We were not alone in getting the heat from GM.

We had 90 days to clean up our act, and in that time we had heavy education requirements. We had to get all 500 Manchester employees through a quality course of varying degrees of intensity, we had to work up a fairly exhaustive quality manual, and we had to start the rudiments of a statistical process control program in the plant. I had a bias against consultants, but we were out of time. We hired a local group of consultants that specializes in quality control.

The consultants started an education program for hourly and salaried employees, with emphasis on problem-solving techniques. We installed statistical process control and started keeping detailed records. We set up a steering committee consisting of the heads of sales, finance, personnel, marketing, manufacturing, R&D, quality, and MIS, as well as me. It met—and still meets—mainly to monitor progress of improvement teams, relying in part on the data from the SPC system.

The consultants were very helpful in pushing and pushing us. We needed an outside agent to make us see we weren't progressing as well as we in management thought we were.

I can recall the aggravation I felt in steering committee meetings when a consultant would relay concerns voiced by hourly employees that were surprises to us. The consultants knew more about problems in the plant than we did.

(There are many good reasons, by the way, why smaller businesses shy away from hiring consultants. For one thing, they may seem expensive in relation to the value they claim to offer. They may be unfamiliar with the business, so they take too much time getting up to speed. And they can disrupt the organization. But they are valuable for the expertise they bring, the cross-fertilization of ideas they spread, the benefits they can bring in a devil's advocate role, and—as evidence in Velcro's case—the compression of time they can achieve.)

At the end of 90 days, we showed the General Motors people a PERT chart to indicate how far we had come. They said we seemed to be on the right track. They would be back in six months, they said, to inspect us.

Naturally, we were pleased at this reprieve, but we really had only scratched the quality surface. It takes a lot more than 90 days for, say, the loom operator on the third shift really to believe in quality and act on that belief. It was a long time before we got quality instilled throughout the organization, before people were making changes for Velcro instead of GM. But it has happened, as these figures on waste reduction as a percentage of total manufacturing expenses, by fiscal year, testify:

1987, 50% reduction from 1986
1988, 45% reduction from 1987

We got our house in relatively good order and soon were back in GM's good graces. We expected to move up to a two rating, but by that time the company had changed its supplier quality program to Targets of Excellence. Even as our quality improved, the standard against which we are measured was moving as well. All the auto companies have upgraded their programs—Chrysler has its Quality Excellence and Pentastar programs, and Ford has Q1 and Total Quality Excellence—and what was acceptable three years ago is no longer good enough. As we participated in all three programs, we had concerns that we would face conflicting requirements.

PERVASIVE COMMITMENT

The General Motors people were right in acknowledging that our quality watch was OK. Actually, the strength of our quality program was a major reason why we had survived a severe decline in prices some years before—due to a capacity overhang in the tape industry caused by gearing up to meet demand for shoes—and the reason why we had gained a foothold with the Big Three automakers. But the General Motors people were also right in their claim that our program was faulty because we inspected quality into the product instead of manufacturing it.

We had QC people at a few points in the process, for example, at the point where the tape was rolled up for shipment to customers. Quality determination coming at the end of the production process had to be relayed back up the line, and such feedback is often incomplete, unreliable, and certainly untimely. Besides, we were throwing out a certain amount of product because it was defective or didn't meet specifications. We were wasting all the value we had added in the production process, like dyeing, coating, and slitting. Moreover, when we found a problem at the end of the process, it might have run for several days before being spotted. Needless to say, if you're on JIT, you can't handle problems in this manner and still meet schedules.

In Velcro's case, if a weave defect cropped up, by the time it was noticed thousands of yards of material might have been made. What a waste! We weren't being quality-effective, and we weren't being cost-effective either.

On top of that, there were internal problems. The consultants had picked up on these in conversations with hourly workers in the plant. Changes had been coming thick and fast. First there had been heavy demand for footwear, which we couldn't meet. Then there had been a dramatic squeeze on margins from the import competition, making a shorter time frame in the manufacturing process necessary to improve service. The super emphasis on quality was one more change layered on top of the others.

At the start of the new drive to instill a quality ethic throughout the Velcro organization, I had envisioned a high degree of contagiousness for this "disease." The rationales were clear and simple. How could anyone argue with the well thought-out logic of W. Edwards Deming and other proponents?

- Do it right the first time.
- Employees are happier and more satisfied making good parts than making bad ones.
- Quality should be an important purchasing criterion.
- People must be trained properly.
- Teamwork is vital to success.

But even if there hadn't been bewilderment and discontent out in the plant, the major changes that management was seeking would have contributed enough "vaccine" to block progress of the disease. The solution was to involve everybody from the top down and show them that the organization's survival depended on improvement. The message from General Motors went a long way toward demonstrating that reality.

When you look at the manuals that both GM and Ford have put out in the last year, it's clear that their focus is not so much on the product but on continuous improvement. And the improvements sought are not just on the production line or the shop floor but also in the financial department, in the marketing department, in the sales department, and so on. When you're a supplier to these companies, they want to see your cost control programs and your cost reduction programs because they realize they're all tied together. That's how the Japanese have reached the position they enjoy in the automotive business.

It may be a cliche to say that you have to involve everybody in management, including the CEO—but it's true. Only if hourly and salaried employees see that top management is totally committed to quality will quality command a high priority with them. One way they see it is in meetings of the steering committee every two weeks to hear employees talk about their continuous improvement projects. I make it a point to sit in on every meeting, and if I'm out of town, the meeting is postponed. Moreover, I'm a member of one of the teams working on quality improvements.

So the rank and file has good reason to believe that a commitment to quality comes at the highest level. That's a big step, but it's only a step. An even bigger step is getting the hourly workers to understand that continuous improvement not only benefits them but also needs them. Opening up the channels and getting them to communicate is vital because, as Deming and Joseph M. Juran said, the people on the floor know the process better than their boss or anybody up the line. Many of the best ideas for building a better quality product are in their heads, waiting to spring out.

As our QC director is fond of pointing out, communication is the glue that holds the quality effort together. The company newsletter usually has a lead article featuring quality or some of our continuous improvement teams. Weekly meetings with a handful of employees, me, and key staff members feature the same topic. Quarterly talks to all employees discuss progress in this area. The point is that the smaller size of a company makes communication to the organization easier (but still not easy!), and it is vital that the CEO exploit this advantage.

ADMINISTRATIVE ROADBLOCKS

At the time we came under pressure from General Motors, we had 23 quality control people in the plant. (Now we have 12.) To the machine operators, quality was their responsibility—that is, someone else's. The quality control people were stationed at certain points, and they would inspect on a sample basis and say whether the particular run was good or bad. What was bad was thrown out. Nobody changed the process; there was no pressure on anybody to make a change. Many manufacturing people were extremely reluctant to take charge of quality; that was for the end of the line, when somebody else sorts out the errors.

To assume that the production employees were causing the waste would have been a mistake, and to beat on them about it without giving them the tools to deal with the problem would have been a bigger mistake. They would only have been afraid to report it. That's the fear element Deming talks about. The waste is going out in a dumpster during the third shift, and management thinks it's running at minimal waste until it takes inventory. We knew we had to invest in operator training, in more attention paid to operators, in machine repair and redesign, and in measurement and reporting techniques that tracked results, focused on responsibilities, and established up-and-down communication.

Part of the reason for the lack of pressure for change was the supervisors. We'd hear comments like "My boss won't let me shut the machine down. We make junk on my shift, but he doesn't care. He just says we've got to get x yards of material out. I show him the material, and he says, 'Run it anyway.'" The supervisors were a big barrier to making the operators responsible for quality.

The SPC system we installed went a long way toward pinpointing where in the production process we needed improvement. The charting mechanism of SPC also put pressure on the people on the line who had difficulty with the idea that quality and quantity aren't mutually exclusive expectations. The operators used to protest, "I see what you're saying, but I know that when I speed up the machine it makes more mistakes." Gradually we pulled the quality control people out of stations early in the process, then we pulled them out of points later in the process. The number of mistakes declined.

Ad hoc teams, which we call "continuous improvement" teams, not QC—to emphasize the fact that we can always do it better—were another powerful mechanism. We have had some 120 teams over the past three years and now have about 50. (Half of these are in the administrative area; I'll get to those in due course.) At first the teams were led by supervisors, but now hourly employees are sometimes at the head. We've had some spectacular savings in spare-parts consumption from a team led by an hourly employee.

To increase awareness, manufacturing started a material review board consisting of a rotating group of salaried and hourly people. Each day, they look at substandard material from each unit's production, discuss the causes of the defects, and decide on the disposition of the material. This helps to close the loop on awareness of problems, ensuring feedback to the responsible department and encouraging corrective action.

We haven't entirely overcome the difficulty of getting the supervisors to buy into the new way of doing things. The problem has deep roots. At Velcro, as at a lot of mature companies, many of these individuals were trained during an era when the boss was king. Supervisors who hark back to this era often view participatory problem solving as a threat to their authority. On top of that, hourly employees may grasp innovations like SPC more readily than their supervisors do, which tends to produce a defensive attitude regarding the procedures.

Our approach has focused on building successful examples, especially among the younger supervisors who are often more receptive to new ideas. Once we had some "carriers" in these ranks, we could get a quality "infection" spread among many of their peers, whom they saw every day. One of these carriers is a supervisor in the coating area. Early in the days when we trained operators to be their own QC persons, he was one of them. After his promotion to supervisor, he came up with a procedure to reduce the sample size and improve the measurement of coating. His example helped people realize that the new era wasn't all that threatening. He wasn't a graduate engineer; he had no more education than they did.

We try to get the supervisors to understand that the people who work under them are in many respects as good as they are. They have certain skills that can be used and built up. We try to show the supervisors that building up the rank and file doesn't weaken their position. On the contrary, when a production unit meets its goals or makes an improvement, they look good. Eventually, many supervisors come to accept the tenet of Deming's and Juran's that the people on the floor know the process better than their boss or anybody up the line.

Even so, some supervisors never get the idea. We have had to terminate people who had been with Velcro a long time but who, after considerable effort on their part, hadn't gotten the message. They had become a roadblock for other people.

SPREADING THE GOSPEL

In a manufacturing company, it's natural for everybody to think of the manufacturing side when the word "quality" comes up. Marketing and sales holler about the quality of the product, but the quality of *what* they do never comes under question. When they understand we're all in this together, we can get them involved.

That's why about half of our quality improvement teams are in departments other than manufacturing. One of the teams in finance is trying to improve the accuracy of the payroll. A tenet of quality is that you have inside customers as well as outside customers, and you have to satisfy both. When the paychecks are not correct, your inside customers get very upset, particularly the inevitable few who think the company is taking advantage of them. It's a very important morale issue. Moreover, responding to complaints and reissuing paychecks cost money.

Another team in finance has reduced the number of copies of purchase orders from six to three and number of copies of invoices from six to four (the goal being two). The sales operation has a team evaluating the quality of its service. Sales managers are interviewing customers on the phone to ascertain how well we're meeting their needs. The cost of quality in sales is to an extent quantifiable, such as time spent in dealing with a customer's complaint and lost business.

Because the heads of the line and staff functions all serve on the steering committee, it is another way of spreading the word about quality throughout the organization. Function managers who cannot attend the biweekly meetings send deputies, thus ensuring continuity. Moreover, employees giving presentations about their continuous improvement projects usually sit through the others scheduled for that day. So they get a wider view too.

It's not easy to maintain a high level of interest in a program like ours, so a periodic stimulus is needed. The accompanying chart sketches the benefits to Velcro of occasional shots in the arm. The first, of course, was the General Motors threat. The second was a bench-marking effort, a trip to a prospective customer that was also a GM supplier. This visit gave us new ideas and also confirmed the value of SPC charting. The third shot in the arm came when our QC head left and we hired a replacement. The former was good, and we feared a period of drifting. But under the new person, the program really took off. For yet another stimulus, we may bring the consultants back for a time.

THERE'S NO FINISH LINE

In the search for quality, there's no such thing as good enough; there's never a finish line. Moreover, the finish line sometimes seems farther away than ever. We have discovered that in our current year in the campaign against waste. When we realized significant waste reduction (as a proportion of total production expenses) in fiscal 1987 and 1988, we had skimmed the cream. Now it's much harder to make improvements, and we have been unable to lower the figure in our current year.

Still, Velcro has come a long way since the days when it enjoyed patent protection and didn't have to worry much about its customers. We gave the product to them when we wanted and in the form we wanted, because they couldn't get it anywhere else. Now Velcro is a customer-driven company where quality is in the eye of the customer. Whether a production run is acceptable is something the customer ultimately decides.

Sometimes quality is the customer's perception; it's not an absolute. It's all relative, depending on the customer's requirements. In the shoe industry, hook-and-loop on a pair of kid's sneakers isn't especially important since the goods barely last three months, if that. But with a $600 knee brace, the quality of the hook-and-loop closure is very important.

For the textile customer, appearances are important; whereas in the medical business, the concern is cleanliness. The automakers want durability, reliability, and capability. With government, the specifications are all-important. Car manufacturers want uniform performance, but they wouldn't care if the weave on the Velcro tape's backing is not uniform. But on the knee brace, where appearance is important, the weave has to be right.

Since quality is relative, the supplier must be sensitive to the customer's particular requirements. They may involve a varying mix of dimension, performance, cosmetic characteristics, or chemical elements. Here is an essential element of quality that doesn't necessarily show up in the SPC charts. But it's part of the goal of customer satisfaction that creates barriers to competition.

THE MOTORLA STORY

Motorola Inc. is the 1988 winner of the Malcolm Baldrige National Quality Award

BILL SMITH

To know a company's people is to know the company. The task of creating a "quality culture" is much easier within a company that already has an existing culture based on people values: A national quality award may be presented to a company, but it is the people within the company who, by their dedication to customer satisfaction, cause the company to be recognized as a quality leader. Loyalty to the company and to fellow workers, as well as respect for the individual, are essential ingredients to any quality winner, be it the Deming Prize or the Malcolm Baldrige National Quality Award.

Motorola is a public stock corporation, but the traditions established by Paul Galvin are carried on by his son Bob, the current Chairman of the Board. As in many Japanese companies, there is a great spirit of loyalty to the company.

Many of Motorola's present employees are the sons and daughters of the original Motorola work force. A large number of families have more than one member working within the company. This feeling of the Motorola family is visibly evident at celebrations such as the anniversary or retirement of long service employees, or on the day of an employee's birthday, when his associates bring a cake from home to celebrate the occasion.

Bob Galvin recalled attending a retirement party held several years ago, where the retiree told him that he and his family had met the night before, and counted a total of 5ㄴ relatives who were either currently working for Motorola, or had worked for the company in the past.

Motorolans greet each other by first name and unless visitors are present, the dress code is informal; that is, men do not wear suit jackets. It is not uncommon for an engineering department to declare a "jeans" day, especially if the day will be devoted to cleaning up the laboratory. After working hours, especially in the summer, many change into sports attire to play with their department's softball, volley ball, or other team on the fields of the "campus."

Much has been written about the practice of life-time employment in Japanese companies. At Motorola, an employee becomes a member of the Motorola Service Club after ten years of service. A member of the Service Club may not be released from the company without the concurrence of Bob Galvin, the Chairman.

In 1981, Motorola established, as one of its Top Ten Corporate Goals, the improvement of quality by ten times by 1986. The first reaction by some of the managers was that of skepticism. "We don't know how to achieve such an ambitious goal," they said. The response from the corporate management was, "We agree that it seems to be an impossible goal, but in the process of working toward that goal, we will find new ways to run our business at significantly improved quality levels. Each of these new ways will ultimately lead us to the ten times improvement."

And so, during the five years of the program, new methods were implemented. Some methods resulted in evolutionary improvement, but others resulted in step function improvements. The renewed emphasis on a "reach out" quality goal enabled Motorola to achieve its objective.

The most difficult problem which faced Motorola during this period was the fact that each organizational unit was free to define its own quality metrics. Within Motorola, a very decentralized company of many different businesses, it was a generally held belief that each business was truly different, and so it made sense that each knew the best way to measure quality for its business.

Because of the different way each business measured its quality level, it was nearly impossible for top management, in the normal course of conducting periodic operations reviews, to assess whether the improvement made by one division was equivalent to the improvement made by another. In fact, it was difficult for the manager of an operation to rate his quality level compared to that of another operation, because the measurements were in different terms. However, significant improvements were made regardless of the metric used.

During the second half of 1985, with one-and-one-half years to go in this five year program, the Communications Sector established a single metric for quality, Total Defects per Unit. This dramatically changed the ease with which management could measure and compare the quality improvement rates of all divisions. For the first time it was easy to evaluate the other divisions. They all spoke the same language.

THE QUALITY IMPROVEMENT PROCESS, 1987 - 1992 "FOUR YEAR ONE-HUNDRED TIMES" QUALITY IMPROVEMENT

Management of the Quality Improvement Process during this period is based on Motorola's practice of "Management by Measurement."

This style of management says that by establishing measurements which are correlated to the desired end result, and regularly reviewing the actual measurements, the organization will focus on those actions necessary to achieve the required improvement.

By 1986, after the Communications Sector adopted the uniform metric, Total Defects per Unit, the goal for defect reduction was uniformly applied to all operations. The required percent reduction was the same, regardless of the absolute level. The improvement rate achieved by the sector was much greater than had been achieved in the "five year ten times" program, and so the measurement was adopted by the entire corporation.

In January 1987, Motorola restated its corporate quality goal to be:

- *Improve 10 Times by 1989*
- *Improve 100 Times by 1991*
- *Achieve Six Sigma Capability by 1992*

This goal applied to all areas of the business, not just product quality.

The use of the common metric, Defects per Unit, at last provided a common denominator in all quality discussions. It provided a common terminology and methodology in driving the quality improvement process. The definition was the same throughout the company. A defect was anything which caused customer dissatisfaction, whether specified or not. A unit was any unit of work—a circuit board assembly, a page of a technical manual, a line of software code, an hour of labor, a wire transfer of funds, or whatever output your organization produced.

WINNERS—THE MALCOLM BALDRIGE NATIONAL QUALITY AWARD

Although it does not have the many years of tradition associated with the Deming Prize, the ultimate goals of the Malcolm Baldrige National Quality Award are the same as for the Deming Prize. There are several differences between the two, however.

The Deming Prize process appears to be much more formal, including several years of "apprenticeship" in preparing for final consideration as a winner. Many years may elapse between the original application and the awarding of the Deming Prize. The Baldrige Award has no such waiting period. In both cases, the company must establish and maintain an effective quality improvement process, and in either case this is a process which takes years to accomplish.

When one visits different Deming Prize winners, and views the flow charts and plans which govern the quality improvement process, one perceives a great deal of similarity, even to the format of the documentation of the processes. This is perhaps due to the use of consultants from JUSE, whose standards are uniformly applied to all applicants. This degree of standardization is not yet apparent in the Baldrige process, although it may evolve as the award process matures. Currently, there is no standard requirement for format of the documented process, although the application criteria are fairly specific on intent, execution and results. As time progresses, some changes may occur in both processes. Each will recognize some advantage to using a technique employed by the other. Since the quality improvement process itself is never ending, we can assume these changes will be adopted as customer expectations increase.

When Motorola applied for the Malcolm Baldrige Award in 1988, like other applicants, it was required to submit a written application, not to exceed 75 single pages, covering seven major subject areas. In the case of a large diversified company, such as Motorola, a supplement, not to exceed 50 pages, may be used to provide information on each of the essentially different businesses within the company.

Motorola did, in fact, submit a basic application which answered all seven subject areas on a company-wide basis.

Four supplements were also submitted for the communications, cellular telephone, semiconductor and automotive businesses.

All applications are numerically scored by a board of examiners. The board of examiners is comprised of more than 100 quality experts selected from industry, professional and trade organizations, and universities. Those selected must meet the highest standards of qualification and peer recognition. Examiners take part in a preparation course based upon the examination items, the scoring criteria, and the examination process.

Each application is scored by at least four members of the board of examiners. A maximum score is 1,000.

High-scoring applicants are selected for site visits to be made by one or more teams of examiners. The primary objective of the site visits is to verify the information provided in the written application and to clarify issues and questions raised during review of the application. The site visit may result in lowering the original score, leaving it unchanged, or in rare instances, increasing the score.

A complete written evaluation report, along with the examiners' recommendation is then forwarded to the board of judges.

Highlights of the Motorola quality improvement process are outlined in the seven following paragraphs, as they relate to the seven major subject areas. Naturally, all of the tools for quality improvement have been common knowledge for many years. The key to a successful quality improvement process is not in the tools themselves, but rather in the pervasive use of those tools within the everyday conduct of business.

The success of Motorola can be attributed to a clear understanding by management, from the chairman on down, that if Total Customer Satisfaction can be attained, the rest of the business takes care of itself. Most operational issues become crises, only as a result of some failure to totally satisfy the internal or external customer. Concurrent with this understanding which has caused the integration of quality strategy into the day to day operations of the business, is a common measurement which directly correlates to customer satisfaction.

LEADERSHIP

At Motorola, the quality culture is pervasive. The CEO formally restated our company objectives, beliefs, goals and key initiatives in 1987, and quality remained as a central theme. Total Customer Satisfaction is Motorola's fundamental objective. It is the overriding responsibility of everyone in the company, and the focus of all of our efforts.

The CEO also reaffirmed two key beliefs that have been part of the Motorola culture since the company began in 1928: Uncompromising Integrity, and Constant Respect for People. The CEO has identified three key goals for the corporation:

1. *Increased Global Market Share.*

2. *Best in Class in terms of people, technology, marketing product, manufacturing and service.*

3. *Superior Financial Results.*

To achieve these goals and provide Total Customer Satisfaction, Motorola concentrates on five key operational initiatives.

The first of these is *Six Sigma Quality.* We intend that all products and services are to be at the Six Sigma level by 1992. This means designing products that will accept reasonable variation in component parts, and developing manufacturing processes that will produce minimum variation in the final output product. It also means analyzing all the services we provide, breaking them down into their component parts, and designing systems that will achieve Six Sigma performance. We are taking statistical technologies and making them a part of each and every employee's job, regardless of assignment. Measuring this begins by recording the defects found in every function of our business, then relating them to a product or process by the number of opportunities to fabricate the product or carry out the process. We have converted our yield language to parts per million (ppm), and the Six Sigma goal is 3.4 ppm defect levels across the company. Despite the wide variety of products and services, the corporate goal is the same: Six Sigma by 1992.

Our second key initiative, *Total Cycle Time Reduction,* is closely related to Six Sigma Quality. We define cycle time as the elapsed time from the moment a customer places an order for an existing product to the time we deliver it. In the case of a new product, it is from the time we conceive of the product to the time it ships. We examine the total system, including design, manufacturing, marketing and administration.

The third initiative, *Product and Manufacturing Leadership,* also emphasizes the need for product development and manufacturing disciplines to work together in an integrated world.

Our fourth initiative, *Profit Improvement,* is a long-term, customer-driven approach that shows us where to commit our resources to give customers what they need, thus improving long-term profits. It recognizes that investing in quality today will produce growth in the future.

The final initiative is *Participative Management Within,* and *Cooperation Between Organizations.* This approach is designed to achieve more synergy, greater efficiency and improved quality.

Management demonstrates its leadership in the quality initiative in many ways. The CEO chairs the operating and policy committees in twice a quarter, all day meetings. The chief quality officer of the corporation opens the meetings with an update on key initiatives of the Quality Program. This includes results of management visits to customers, results of Quality System Reviews (QSR's) of major parts of the company, cost of poor quality reports, supplier-Motorola activity, and a review of quality breakthroughs and shortfalls. This is followed by a report by a major business manager on the current status of his/her particular quality initiative. This covers progress against plans, successes, failures, and what he projects to do to close the gap on deficient results, all pointed at achieving Six Sigma capability by 1992. Discussion follows among the leaders concerning all of the above agenda items.

In 1986, Bob Galvin began a more formal program of customer visits. These visits traditionally had been less systematic and covered only specific topics. Under the new program, members of top management talk to customers at various levels of their business. They ask two basic questions: What do you like about Motorola, and what don't you like? After each visit, a detailed report with specific recommendations is submitted. The visits have become so important that they have been made permanent, and extended to involve all officers. The visits have resulted in the reformulation of our basic goals and objectives mentioned earlier.

Our focus on very specific numeric goals, i.e., 10X, 100X, and Six Sigma capability is unique in this country. Quality System Reviews are not a new technology, but we believe very few companies have utilized this system, and it has been successful.

Cycle Time Management is a growing integral part of our programs, and in conjunction with Six Sigma, represents a very powerful and effective thrust.

Our recognition of quality excellence includes the CEO Quality Award, bestowed on an individual, a team, an operation, or higher level deserving organization by the CEO. This program is administered by the chief quality officer. The award consists of a plaque and each individual also receives a uniquely designed pin. We have applied the principles of Six Sigma Quality to non-manufacturing activities. This gives us a unique ability to benchmark the quality of services. For example, the Communications Sector Engineering Publications Department, using these techniques, reduced defects per equipment manual by a factor of 49 to 1, resulting in a cost savings per manual of 38%.

INFORMATION AND ANALYSIS

In our Six Sigma Quality program, the key elements of data are the defects found, compared to the number of opportunities to make defects in the product or process. Throughout Motorola, we have changed our data systems to record defects, opportunities, and the means, variation and limits of both product and process. We direct corrective action through use of Pareto charts, histograms, scatter charts, Ishikawa diagrams, etc.

Analytical techniques begin with the product design cycle, when circuits are analyzed for limit conditions and for Six Sigma distribution of characteristics. Components are evaluated based on internal or supplier data to verify that they will meet the quality and reliability criteria. We make stress and accelerated life tests throughout the engineering design cycle to identify the weak links and to improve product performance by designing in corrections. The environmental stress is always taken well beyond the engineering specifications for the product being designed.

Defect per unit goals are established during the design phase of the product and verified through early prototype and pilot runs.

Shipping takes place only when the budget is achieved for the defects per unit, and the unit successfully passes an accelerated life test.

Achieving an improvement rate of ten times in two years cannot be done by conventional corrective actions on current products. Such corrective actions must be taken, but they can only yield an evolutionary improvement rate.

Thus, the cornerstone of our strategy for dramatic improvement is one that requires each new product to be introduced at a defect per unit level that is typically one-fourth to one-fifth of the product it will replace, or significantly less than similar products in current production.

During the manufacturing phase of products, each step of the process is monitored for its quality performance in defects per million opportunities. Each manufacturing process step is evaluated as either one that can be improved consistent with our goals or as one that must be phased out. For those steps that can be improved, we establish SPC control charts, identify problems and use Pareto charts and histograms to facilitate the needed improvement. As interim goals are reached, tougher goals are set to keep the improvements flowing.

All equipment divisions prepare a management report (the 5-up chart) that shows five graphs of quality performance through the year. The charts show the defects per unit, final quality audit results, out of box quality as delivered to the customers via product performance reports, product warranty and cost of quality for the product or division. Motorola's Six Sigma Quality program is a unique approach to achieving Total Quality Control (TQC) or Company-Wide Quality Control (CWQC). The Six Sigma Quality program addresses quality in all aspects of the business: products and services, manufacturing and non-manufacturing, administration and operations. Our Six Sigma Quality program combines the following key ingredients:

1. *A superordinate goal of "Total Customer Satisfaction"*
2. *Common, uniform quality metrics for all areas of the business*
3. *Identical improvement rate goals for all areas of the business, based on uniform metrics*
4. *Goal-directed incentives for both management and employees*
5. *Coordinated training in "why" and "how" to achieve the goal*

STRATEGIC PLANNING

Our goals for both near and long-term improvement all stem from our objective of Total Customer Satisfaction. Our current level for expected results was first delineated in real terms in August 1981. After management elevated one of its senior business managers to become Motorola director of quality, it then set about to define the company's new goal going forward.

The need for an acceleration of our improvement process had become readily apparent from benchmarking efforts made throughout the company, as well as a realistic projection of where we thought customer expectations would be in five years.

In August 1981, the operating and policy committees approved our five-year goal to achieve a ten-times improvement in all our efforts on behalf of the customer. These committees represent the highest level of Motorola management. This quality program was effective and successful. As a result, the operating and policy committees tightened the goals in December 1986.

The new goals called for quality improvements of 10X in two years, 100X in four years, and achievement of Six Sigma capability in just five years in everything we do. This is one of Motorola's central operational initiatives. We feel these quantitative goals are necessary to achieve Total Customer Satisfaction.

Guided by this broad road map of where we would like to be, each business of the corporation incorporates its strategic thinking and plans into its Long Range Plan (LRP). At least once a year the company examines its strategic direction, and all facets of the business, such as new product programs, finances, technology, and quality, on a five-year, or LRP basis. The first year of such a plan is normally the Annual Plan. Thus, we plan and manage our quality improvement objectives just as we would new product introduction, technology and any other part of the company's activity.

Coupled to these basic quality business goals are goal-directed incentives for both management and employees. These are the Motorola Executive Incentive Plan (MEIP) and the Participative Management Program (PMP).

Finally, a large training and education university-like function (Motorola Training and Education Center, MTEC) provides training on quality at all levels, with specific emphasis on providing all employees the knowledge and skills necessary to achieve our quality goals.

We have quantitatively benchmarked best-in-class companies worldwide, and as a result of these efforts, have driven many of our products and processes to best-in-class levels. Examples include soldering, surface-mounted chip component placement, and cycle time in the production of pagers and cellular mobile radiotelephones. This process allows us to constantly strive to be the best-in-class in all aspects with true measurements for our goal setting and results.

HUMAN RESOURCES

The mission of Motorola's training function is to provide the right training to the right people at the right time. One measure of the success of our training program is our having received the American Society for Training and Development's annual award for excellence. Other measures of success can be seen in the scope and internal evaluation of our training.

On the average, we provide one million hours of training per year to our employees. In 1987, we spent $44 million on training. This represented 2.4% of the corporate payroll. Forty percent of the training is devoted to quality improvement processes, principles, technology, and objectives.

During the past three years, over 150 hours of quality-related training have been developed, and are being delivered to assembly operators, technicians, engineers, support groups, and the management of these functions. "Course maps" help employees and their managers select programs which respond to individual needs as well as the key corporate initiative of Six Sigma Quality.

Three important parts of our quality training are MTEC training, product/process-specific training, and special management training. Motorola's corporate training function (MTEC) has been able to demonstrate a significant increase in the number of quality-related training programs they have delivered to our employees corporate-wide:

In 1985, 37% of MTEC training was devoted to quality; in 1986, 43% was devoted to quality; in 1987, 73% of the total MTEC training was devoted to quality.

Training programs in Statistical Process Control, Design for Manufacturability, and Understanding Six Sigma are helping us reach our ambitious goal of 100-fold improvement in four years. These courses provide a set of problem-solving strategies and tools for continuous improvement toward perfection in everything we do. The classes developed by MTEC also provide the framework around which product/process-specific training is added.

To support our commitment to Total Customer Satisfaction through quality in all that we do, we have developed the Motorola Management Institute (MMI). This intensive two-week program in world-class design, manufacturing and quality issues is intended for manufacturing, design and operational managers at both senior and support levels. Participants build in their professional expertise to enhance their leadership, vision, and decision-making skills.

MMI topics include customer-centered culture and marketing for world-class manufacturing and quality, designing for manfacturability, information systems, cycle time management, technology, and supply and change management. Leading experts present the latest information and facilitate the exchange of ideas.

Last year's Senior Executive Program focused on the critical corporate objective of Total Customer Satisfaction. The program involved all 240 officers of the corporation, as well as key customer contact people, such as senior sales representatives and sales/service managers.

In 1970, Motorola formed the Science Advisory Board Associates (SABA). As the organization charter describes it, SABA is dedicated to identifying and rewarding exceptional creative engineering talent and contribution. Approximately 300 Motorola engineers have been honored as associates. In 1988, we inducted 24 candidates, including two quality professionals. We had previously inducted six people from Quality Departments over the prior three years.

The crown jewel of recognition awards at Motorola is the Chief Executive Office Quality Award. This prestigious award is presented, with appropriate ceremony, by the corporation's chairman or chief executive officer or chief operating officer to an individual or group for significant contributions to quality. This award is highly publicized throughout the corporation and is mentioned in Motorola's Annual Report. We've granted 40 such awards, involving 5,100 employees, since the inception of the program in 1984.

In 1987, a Chief Executive Office Award was given to product teams within the Government Electronics Group for providing over 900 space communication systems to the U.S. Government over the past ten years. None of this equipment has experienced a failure. All of the color photographs of the planets sent from Voyager and other deep space probes were sent to earth via Motorola communications equipment.

QUALITY ASSURANCE OF PRODUCTS AND SERVICES

Motorola utilizes various methods to obtain inputs from it customers. The methods vary with the type of input which is being sought, and generally fall within one of the following categories:

Voice of the Customer

Listening to the "Voice of the Customer," the process of assessing the customer's perception of the total quality of Motorola as a supplier, is accomplished by visits to customers by the chairman, CEO, and other high level executives within the company. During these visits, customers are made to feel at ease in discussing any area of the business relationship, whatsoever, be it product or service. The results of these one-on-one meetings create a top-down driving force within the organization toward the achievement of Total Customer Satisfaction.

Generic Product/Service Requirements

Many new product ideas begin with a unique blend of new technology from the research laboratories, together with customer needs that have been waiting for solutions. There are a number of examples of how Motorola and its customers have combined efforts to bring about a new solution in the marketplace. Some of these are mentioned here: IBM and Motorola combined efforts to specify, develop and install a sophisticated nationwide radio data network to revolutionize the field maintenance and repair of computer systems.

Motorola's subsidiary, ComputerX, has pioneered cell control and interactive network systems for manufacturing automation, based on the strong needs of the manufacturing community (MAP Protocol).

Motorola and Codex worked together with major international airlines in the definition of broad-based data communications networks and the special requirements of the airline industry.

The Bandit pager program of the Paging Division is notable, not only for its fully automated manufacturing capability, but for the extension of that automated system to include the order entry process, which in the future will be directly accessible to the customer.

Specific Product/Service Requirements

In the Communications Sector customer requirements for new products are captured in a contract book generated at the beginning of the development effort. The contract contains all features and requirements that the sales organization deems necessary to satisfy customer requirements. In some cases, such as portable two-way radio, blind market surveys are conducted to determine performance, size, weight, cost, and other features preferred by the majority of customers in the marketplace.

The new AIEG Detroit Application and System Engineering Center is an example of Motorola's dedication to enhancement of customer inputs to new product designs. It is an example of Motorola's commitment to the concept of early supplier involvement. Dedicated almost exclusively to engine and vehicle testing on customer systems, it has been welcomed by the customer as a way to jointly specify system related issues which have so far defied formal specification, and to proactively develop solutions to potential problems in future designs.

Application Specific Integrated Circuits (ASICs) are integrated circuits that perform unique functions within a customer's electronic product. SPS has made significant strides in providing design tools which are directly accessible to customers, enabling them to perform the otherwise complicated task of designing complex functional devices for a special need. So-called cell libraries are provided by Motorola for use on many of the existing work stations currently in broad use in design laboratories. The next generation of tools, the silicon compiler, will advance the customer's ability to create a device whose function is explicitly defined by the customer to fill a particular need.

RESULTS FROM QUALITY ASSURANCE OF PRODUCTS AND SERVICES

Today Motorola stands alone as the only non-Japanese supplier of pagers to Nippon Telegraph and Telephone (NTT). Motorola first earned the right to be a prime supplier in this prestigious Japanese market though the introduction of our highly reliable RC13 pager in 1982. This product was released at a proven reliability level 40% better than the standards then in existence in Japan for communication equipment.

Through a program of dedicated design improvements and philosophy of never settling for second best from ourse' /es or our suppliers, the quality of Motorola paging products, as measured by

NTT, has improved sevenfold since this initial product entry. Today, after having shipped more than a half million pagers to Japan, Motorola can be proud of product MTBF (mean time between failures) figures which typically exceed 130 years.

The Motorola Paging Division continues to look toward this Japanese market challenge as a catalyst in our pursuit of product excellence and a symbol of our global competitiveness.

CUSTOMER SATISFACTION

Our customers recognize us as a leader in quality. *Electronic Business* magazine recently asked 600 companies for information on quality awards they had received in the last two years. The magazine singled out Motorola as receiving close to 50 awards and certified supplier citations. This was the highest number submitted. The number doubled between 1986 and 1987, and the momentum continues.

One basis measure of customer satisfaction is repeat business. Motorola has repeatedly been awarded contracts for the Defense Department's Very High Speed Integrated Circuit (VHSIC) research program, which originated in 1979 and continues today.

Motorola, unlike almost any other *Fortune* 100 company, uses all of its executive officers from both the corporate and sector/group levels to go out, interview and interface with our customers on specific customer satisfaction items. These officers talk with multiple levels of the customer's organization. The results of these interviews are brought back, analyzed and disseminated throughout all of Motorola. Results are reviewed at corporate operating committee meetings, and follow-up customer meetings continue until issues are resolved and Total Customer Satisfaction is achieved.

TOOLS FOR THE MANAGER

From *Quest For Quality: How One Company Put Theory to Work*

ROGER L. HALE, DOUGLAS R. HOELSCHER, AND RONALD E. KOWAL

Management support and enthusiasm are the keys to maintaining a quality emphasis. If a company's managers care, employees will care. But change is hard. If managers are to support a program of change, they must stand to gain from that program.

Tennant Company's quality process has made management jobs more secure and personally enriching, and it has provided opportunities for financial reward. Managers know this now, but in the beginning no one knew how the quality process would affect his or her job. And no one knew if it was here to stay or even if the company's CEO was solidly behind the effort.

The first step in gathering management support is to communicate top management's long-term commitment to the quality process. We launched a number of activities aimed at doing just that. These included staging the first ZD Day, publicizing throughout the company the quality pledges signed by our executives, and forming a Quality Team made up of representatives from all departments.

The next step is to explain to managers and supervisors what the process entails and to define their roles. At Tennant Company, members of our first Quality Team led managers and supervisors through a review of Phil Crosby's 14 steps to quality, and they outlined five ways in which the process must be supported:

- *Knowledge*—Managers and supervisors must know enough about the program to explain it to their employees.
- *Attitude*—They must be positive about the program.
- *Example*—They should set an example of doing the job right the first time.
- *Training*—Managers and supervisors must make sure their employees know what is expected of them and have the skills or training needed to do the job.
- *Recognition*—They should acknowledge employees for jobs well done.

In explaining Crosby's 14 steps to quality, we were also offering managers and supervisors a reason to buy into the process—job security. Because we had a history of profit sharing, good benefits, and promoting from within, our people already understood the connection between the health of Tennant Company and their job security. With Crosby's 14 steps, they now had a way to contribute to the company and their own well-being.

We also provided managers the opportunity to directly benefit from supporting the quality emphasis by changing their compensation program. Traditionally, part of the compensation package for salaried employees was based on achieving certain annual goals. We now asked our salaried people to make one of those goals quality related.

Ultimately, there was another, more intangible advantage for managers and supervisors who supported the quality process, but it was one they had to learn from experience. The process has made some jobs easier and the working environment more pleasant. As one supervisor said, "Quality is not just the quality in a piece of equipment; it is the quality of how you treat each other. Now we go after the reasons why something went wrong, not after people. Just eliminating finger pointing makes my job easier. And I feel more secure and confident knowing that no one is going to point a finger at me. I depend on my people to produce good quality parts. And they depend on me to find a solution if there is a problem that prevents them from doing their jobs right."

This kind of interdependence can drastically reduce the pressure managers personally feel to do everything themselves. But interdependence is possible only when managers and supervisors transfer some of their power to their people, so that those people can truly become responsible for the work they do.

Occasionally, a transfer of responsibility results in the elimination of some management jobs. When employees do their jobs right the first time, the need for people in inspection and rework is cut dramatically. In addition, employees need less supervision as they take greater control over their jobs and become more responsible for the work they produce.

At Tennant Company, some jobs were eliminated because of changes brought about by the quality process. Many of these changes were absorbed through attrition and retirement. Rather than rehire, we moved people around. Other changes were addressed by retraining and career counseling.

Offering retraining and career counseling not only looks at the issue of job elimination; it also opens opportunities in the company and reduces job burnout. And this helps keep good people who want to change jobs but don't want to change companies.

The quality process challenges a company to create an interdependent and responsible work environment. The responsibility for doing this lies with the manager, and to operate effectively, managers need the tools outlined in the body of this chapter.

COMMUNICATION

Communication is knowing how to elicit clear, concise feedback from people, knowing how to set goals and communicate them to employees, and knowing how to acknowledge the accomplishments employees make every day.

If we had been asked to name some of the biggest problems we had when we began our quality process, communication would not have been mentioned. We thought communication within Tennant Company was excellent.

Once a month, a general meeting involving every employee was held in each department. We would talk about what was happening in the company, in the department, in other departments, and how we were doing financially. We knew of few other companies that communicated in this way.

In addition, we had the traditional communication tool, the company newsletter, to keep us informed of corporate news, policy changes, and promotions, anniversaries, and birthdays.

There is nothing wrong with these communication activities, which are still an ongoing part of the culture at Tennant Company. But they were not truly part of a communication process, and engaging in them did not automatically mean we were good communicators.

Communication, our first Quality Team told us, involves knowing how to elicit clear, concise responses from people; knowing how to set goals and communicate them to employees; and knowing how to acknowledge the accomplishments and efforts employees make every day. In all of these areas, the team said, Tennant Company managers were not communicating.

Managerial skills can rise to the level demanded by the 101 quality process only when these communication skills are employed. And these skills can be acquired only with the most basic communication skill of all—listening.

Although listening is the most fundamental communication skill, it is also the one most often taken for granted. Listening is hard work. It requires us not only to hear, but also to interpret and evaluate. Only then can we respond accurately and complete the communication cycle. When the cycle is complete, we have a common ground for understanding.

Many resources are available for learning how to listen. Tennant Company turned to the company whose name we associated with listening—Sperry Corporation (now Unisys). Sperry provided us with materials they had been using in their listening courses, and they referred us to their consultant, Lyman Steil. A former professor at the University of Minnesota, Steil currently heads his own consulting firm, Communication Development Inc.

Two of our trainers attended Steil's course on listening. They and another employee then designed an in-house course, using information they had obtained from Steil, Sperry, and several other sources.

The first people to attend the five-part course were executives and managers from manufacturing. Eventually, every manager and supervisor in the company attended, either voluntarily or by request of their boss.

Some of these graduates then asked the trainers to present a condensed version of the course to their line people during the time set aside for departmental meetings. The full course involves four sessions, each two-and-one-half hours long and covering a specific topic or exercise as follows:

• Why we need to listen

• How to listen actively by paraphrasing the message and relaying it back to the sender

• Resolving conflict with good listening techniques

• Role playing

• Videotaping role playing for later critique

The second part of our communication program, "Working Together," is about how we express ourselves to one another. This five-part course covers the following topics:

• Understanding yourself

• Understanding others

• Styles of communication

• Mapping issues (including identifying issues, contracting to work together, identifying intentions, and generating solutions)

• Building self-esteem

As with the listening course, we went outside the company to set up the program. Our primary consultant was Sherod Miller, president of Denver-based Interpersonal Communications Programs Inc., and one of the authors of the workbook "Working Together."

All our managers and supervisors received in-house verbal communication training. Some line people also received the training at the request of their department managers.

The listening and verbal skills courses helped us realize what our individual responsibility is in the communication process. We know listening is important. It takes energy, and personal bias can get in the way of how accurately we receive a message. We know it is our responsibility to ask for more information when we need it, and to ask for clarification if a message seems vague. The courses had another very important effect: They fostered employee involvement in small groups and in the quality process because they convinced people that the contributions could make a difference.

In a company our size, it takes about two years to train all the managers and supervisors. It is, therefore, important to make the programs available continuously. So far, we have not found it necessary to offer refresher courses in listening and verbal communication. But some of the principles we learned from these courses have been built into other training programs in group process skills and performance appraisals.

TRAINING FOR THE LONG HAUL
Training is an integral part of the quality process and is as ongoing as the process itself. Basic problem solving requires training; advanced problem solving requires training. Preventing problems requires training.

Tennant Company's training program provides people with the tools they need to do the job right the first time. Our traditional approach to training, which was confined to on-the-job instruction and selected management seminars, could not answer the demands of the quality process.

The quality process requires that employees know how to communicate, how to set goals, how to measure progress, how to solve problems, and how to work together in groups.

These five how-to categories form the backbone of our training program and are discussed individually in other sections of this chapter. Other courses, such as value analysis and time management, fill out the training schedule.

When we began the quality process, we had no long-range training program outlined. We did not have a full-time trainer. For the most part, the program evolved as the process challenged us to master new skills and as our people became better able to identify their own training needs. When we started, we knew that managers and supervisors, who were expected to carry the process forward, would need to be schooled in the fundamentals. By the end of 1983, they had taken classes in developing quality measurements, setting quality goals, applying costs to quality measurements, and recognizing and supporting the achievements of employees.

Managers and supervisors, in turn, began telling us what training would be useful for their people. Many of them, for example, requested communication training and made time available for it during departmental meetings.

Based on their comments, which we solicited through a needs-assessment survey, we were encouraged to continue our basic courses in communication and problem solving. Some of the most frequent requests were for courses in decision making, performance appraisal, interviewing, and career development.

Everyone at Tennant Company is eligible for some type of training on company time. We ask all our employees to elect job-specific courses and to discuss training needs with their supervisors. Supervisors may also request that some courses be mandatory.

To make sure employees are aware of the training courses available to them, we print and distribute training calendars. The calendars, updated every six months, list when and where the courses are held, whether they are companywide or department-specific, and who can attend. Subjects include everything from time management, to one-time courses in response to specific management needs, to technical courses such as torque training and blueprint reading.

If you think training is expensive, consider the price of ignorance.

The courses are taught by our employee training administrator, outside consultants, and a large pool of internal part-time trainers with expertise in special areas. Many of the courses are designed internally, some are adapted from generic material, and others are purchased from outside suppliers.

When we began our quality process, we found that 85 percent of the total cost of quality was failure cost associated with not doing things right the first time. Another 12 to 13 percent was spent in appraisal, or inspection. Only 2 to 3 percent went to prevention, which primarily involved training. Because of our quality emphasis, those ratios have changed: By 1987, 17 percent of the cost of quality was attributed to failure, 39 percent to appraisal, and 44 percent to prevention.

Training takes time. Our supervisors and managers have all taken at least five training courses. About 90 percent of our line workers have been involved in at least one training program.

With a Minneapolis work force of nearly 1,000 employees, training hours add up. In 1987, trainers spent 650 hours in classroom instruction. Fewer classes were offered in 1988, but each year more than 1,000 students receive on-the-job instruction.

Though we can not attach bottom-line figures to the benefits the training at Tennant Company has provided, we do know it has paid off in reduced errors on the job. And we also know the truth of the slogan that is prominently displayed in the offices of two managers: "If you think training is expensive, consider the price of ignorance."

PINPOINTING PROBLEMS AND IDENTIFYING CAUSES
Employees need to be involved not only in detecting problems but in solving them.

Unlike nearly every other aspect of the quality process at Tennant Company, our Error Cause Identification (ECI) program is becoming obsolete. That makes us happy, because it means two things: We have drastically reduced our errors, and we have dramatically improved our ability to communicate directly with each other.

We use the ECI program to pinpoint problems that prevent people from doing their jobs right the first time. The process begins when employees fill out a form listing snags that prevent them from doing their assigned jobs. Without this information, the quality process cannot proceed.

Trying to solve the problems employees listed led us to form small groups. The problems were too numerous and varied for just a few people to handle. Because we asked employees to get involved not only in detecting problems but also in solving them, our people began to understand that they really could make a difference in how Tennant Company operated.

NUMBER OF ECIs SUBMITTED

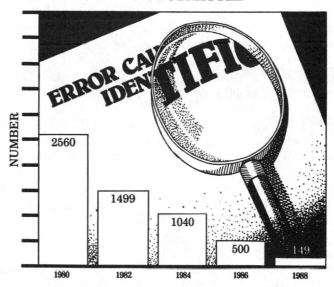

At first, we made the ECI forms available only to employees at one facility. Based on the enthusiastic reception there, we introduced them to the manufacturing department and then to the rest of the company.

The early forms were complicated, with elaborate codes to fill in and questions to answer. But employees grabbed the opportunity to explain obstacles they encountered on the job, noting everything from inadequate equipment to inscrutable or mismatched blueprints.

The first year we took the ECI program companywide, the forms hit us with the speed and force of a mountain snowstorm. Our evaluators, those employees designated to resolve the problems, were buried under a mountain of 3,400 forms. The evaluators painstakingly reviewed them, making sure the right people became involved in seeking solutions.

Because there were too few evaluators reviewing too many forms, which were often hard to decipher, we feared the ECI program would create more problems than it would solve. Employees became increasingly frustrated as weeks and some times months went by before anyone acknowledged or addressed their problems.

To eliminate the backlog, we increased the number of evaluators and simplified the form. We asked evaluators to meet one-on-one with the people who had initiated the forms so they could understand each problem more precisely. If the initiators were satisfied that the evaluators understood the problems, they signed the form and the evaluators went to work on solutions. If initiators were not satisfied, they could ask their managers or supervisors to intervene.

One-on-one talks between initiators and coordinators produced two results: (1) initiators knew that their problems had been acknowledged and understood; and (2) evaluators had more time to spend solving problems rather than sending the ECI forms back to the initiators for clarification.

We are now completing 90 percent of all ECIs within 30 days. ECIs that are unsolved after 60 days go to a management committee for review.

ECI forms are available in our plants and offices throughout the country. They are sent to three coordinators in Minneapolis who keep track of the paperwork and follow up on forms that evaluators find hard to handle.

Early in the program, the coordinators, who have other job responsibilities, spent nearly all their time with the ECIs. Now they each spend about four hours a week on ECIs.

The best indicator of our success in promoting one-on-one communication about problems is the decreasing number of ECI forms submitted by employees. The number of ECIs has dropped from a peak of 3,400 in 1981 to about 149 in 1988. This doesn't mean we only have 149 problems in the company. It does mean we're learning how to work together to solve the problems we have without filling out forms. We hope to eliminate the ECI system within the next few years as people develop trust in the informal system.

THE FASTENER COMMITTEES

Tennant Company customers include some of the largest manufacturing companies in the country, among them carmakers. In 1978, the following incident with one of the biggest carmakers began a long quest for quality led by Daryl Gabrielson, designer of floor scrubbers.

The auto maker had just purchased the largest scrubber Tennant Company makes. But all was not well. Daryl's boss came to him with a request: "How would you like to go to Detroit? The customer has some questions about the design of our squeegee linkage. Maybe you could help."

Daryl wasn't alarmed. He had just redesigned the squeegee, and it probably needed adjusting to the customer's floor.

But he quickly found that more than a minor adjustment was needed in Detroit. He was greeted in the auto maker's maintenance department: "If you don't put this thing together right now, you can take it back to Minneapolis."

When the scrubber was delivered to the customer's dock, bolts and nuts were loose everywhere. Even worse, this wasn't the first time this had happened. Daryl had heard complaints from service trainers who helped local service and salespeople uncrate and install new machines. They were often told to bring their tool kits to put the machine together before it could be used.

Long before his trip to Detroit, Daryl had been trying to develop a standard for fasteners. The design groups for each of Tennant Company's three major products wanted different sizes, types, makes, and quality of nuts and bolts. Although the situation was an organizational nightmare, even the design chief and the keeper of our standards weren't convinced of the need for consistency. However, the Detroit problem was impossible to ignore.

We wish we could say that once the problem was recognized, it was solved immediately. But even in a company paying great attention to quality, problems sometimes are not easily solved. In fact, it took eight years. Without Daryl, we might still have problems keeping our machines together.

After Daryl's Detroit report, Fastener Committee 1 was organized. This committee looked into standardizing some of the fasteners and studied how we clamp two pieces of metal together. Their findings: Yes, we have a problem with fasteners.

Four months later, in March 1979, Fastener Committee 2 was formed. All its members were new—except Daryl. They looked at the clamping issue left over from committee 1, and checked into buying some new tools. After much research, they recommended switching from grade 2 to grade 5 hardware. It was a drastic step, fraught with implications: Where was all the grade 2 hardware? How would we collect it? How would we convince the assemblers it wasn't the right quality for our application? After all, they'd been using grade 2 for years.

To our surprise, the assemblers were ready for a change. They'd been frustrated by fastener heads breaking off, and they were tired of drilling out bolts.

At the same time, our tool supplier recommended we use torque tool equipment. Heads broken from bolts were a sign of overtightening. The torque tool would shut off when the correct tightness was achieved. The assemblers wouldn't have to guess when to shut off the pneumatic air tools, the supplier said.

Well, the assemblers didn't appreciate the insinuation that they had been guessing. Some of them had been assembling machines for 10 years. The torque equipment recommendation was tabled, and Fastener Committee 2 continued investigating what it would take to upgrade fastener hardware.

In January 1980, Fastener Committee 3 got under way. Once again, all the members were new—except Daryl. This committee decided to concentrate on a onetime hardware changeover. But they found that you can't just change from one grade to another without affecting other types of hardware. They recommended hardened flat washers, grade 5 nuts, flat socket head screws, and elimination of spring lock washers.

Two years later, in April 1982, Fastener Committee 4 was organized. All the members were new—except Daryl. The supplier had given the company a quote of $92,000 to change to torque control tools. The company wasn't ready for that, but it was ready to implement the recommendations of committees 2 and 3. Tennant Company assemblers switched to grade 5 hardware, obtained hardened Bat washers, and eliminated spring lock washers.

The committee was on a roll. It reviewed our current product models looking for improper hardware. They changed and updated methods and put together a pictorial instruction book for all 75 assemblers to show how to put the machines together.

By this time, Daryl had an ally. Dave Sorenson, an industrial engineer, had joined him in his fight for standard fasteners. Dave had served on Committee 4 and he was in too far to get out.

Daryl and Dave set up control charts to monitor (with newly purchased testing equipment) the reliability of the tools being used by the assembly line. They completed a Fastener Standards Book. Hardware was reduced from 1,200 varieties to 900. From now on, design teams had to have approval from Daryl before ordering any new hardware. He was also to be included in new-product team meetings to discuss questions about clamping bolts to joints and to make recommendations about other hardware.

In November 1983, the last committee—Fastener Committee 5— was formed. Members included the vice president of engineering and manufacturing, the new test equipment auditor, the final inspection supervisor, the company's technical trainer and Daryl and Dave. For the next three years, team members worked together like a finely tuned orchestra. They set their goal: no loose fasteners by December 1985. With the support of the vice president on the team, they recommended purchase of the new torque control equipment—even though the cost estimate had gone from $92,000 to more than $200,000. The trainer developed a three-part course required of every employee who had anything to do with fasteners. Between January and August 1984, 230 manufacturing and engineering employees were trained. Each one received a torque control book—the basic manual.

In January 1985, the 230 employees who had received torque training were given a one-hour update session. Still, Committee 5 was not sure that everyone was using the new tools. They knew that many of the old-style pneumatic tools were tucked away, and some were being used. One afternoon, just before quitting time, the committee members rolled carts onto the assembly floor and collected the last of the pneumatic guns. They found them hidden in shoes and desks, fastened under work benches with magnets, hidden under rags. Some of their owners yelled and cursed. Others said the team members wouldn't be able to sleep nights because of what they'd done. Still, the committee was determined. By the end of the year, the group achieved its goal. The torque equipment worked, and there were no loose fasteners.

By 1986, the last committee could turn its work over to assembly supervisors and employees. From that long experience, we learned that any improvement in quality takes time, and that an overall commitment to quality achieves results. Without the quality emphasis, the teamwork, and small group training, the torque program would never have survived.

Throughout this six-year journey, Daryl, Dave, and the technical trainer have become torque experts in the industry. If you ask Daryl how to get rid of loose fasteners, he'll reply, "You start with a trip to Detroit."

SMALL GROUPS SOLVE PROBLEMS
The primary medium for solving problems at Tennant Company is the small group.

The dominant pronoun at Tennant Company is *we*. Small groups account for some of our most significant quality gains, such as the elimination of hydraulic leaks and the increase in shipments made on the day orders are received.

Solving problems in small groups is the antithesis of finger pointing, either outward or inward. Instead of blaming, group members learn to empathize with people in different departments and seek common ground for solutions.

Since 1980, approximately two-thirds of our work force has participated in small groups. One major factor in their success is that many are vertically integrated. This means they are composed not only of people who have first-hand knowledge of the problems, but also of people who can remove the obstacles to a solution. These are our "champions."

We didn't learn to include all levels of management in small groups from reading a book, and we hadn't observed this practice in traditional Japanese quality circles. We found it out along the way. Group participation is going to dwindle if solutions are continually thwarted because members of the group can't cross departmental lines, approve budget expenditures, or clear the way with top management.

This doesn't mean we require every group to have such a member. For example, if one small group is working on a limited problem and the solution needs only a supervisor's approval, that's fine. But small groups know they can recruit someone to eliminate barriers if necessary.

Another important element that has made small groups and many other aspects of our quality process successful is training. Small group members need technical and interpersonal training.

The technical training we used for small group skills was adapted from the Japanese Union of Scientists and Engineers (JUSE) manuals (the "red book" and the "blue hook"). Our basic study course provides group members with these seven tools:

- brainstorming
- cause-and-effect diagrams
- Pareto diagrams
- histograms
- check sheets
- graphs
- management presentations

This study course is under the direction of our manager of quality and reliability. Group members use company time to take the course, which requires at least 10 hours to complete.

Our advanced study course trains participants in statistical process control techniques. It covers statistical process control (SPC) concepts such as:

- the normal curve
- standard deviation
- process capability
- control charting for variables
- control charting for attributes
- scatter diagrams

By the end of 1990, every employee in purchasing, manufacturing, and engineering will have completed the SPC course. Because each class uses the SPC techniques on a real-life project, SPC has already been used in a number of manufacturing groups.

Small-group members can also take a course in group process skills, taught by our human resource trainer. This course first became available in 1984 in response to a needs-assessment survey. People said they needed to understand group dynamics and how to work together as a team.

Tennant Company's two-day group process skills course incorporates many of the fundamentals of listening skills and verbal communication. In one of its most useful lessons, the course encourages members to express their feelings and air their gripes, even if they seem somewhat unrelated to the problem at hand. Once members have a chance to vent their feelings, they are better able and more willing to concentrate on solving specific problems.

The group skills course also teaches us to diagnose why the group gets off track and how to redirect its course by confronting the "blocking dynamic," which can be caused by poor communication, lack of cooperation, or not having the people needed to solve the problem.

We believe that another factor in group success is flexibility. We do not insist that our groups follow traditional quality circle guidelines in which groups are always ongoing and the supervisor is always the team captain. In fact, we encourage groups to limit their work to a specific problem. We do this, one manager explained, "because quality circles can go on forever, and people end up meeting just for the sake of meeting. We want people to work together to solve a specific problem, then disband once that's done. In addition, traditional quality circles usually have the same members year after year. So the group loses its pizzazz."

At Tennant Company, we rotate membership in ongoing groups, such as the Quality Team and the ZD Day Planning Committee. Membership rotation not only broadens employee participation in groups, but brings a fresh viewpoint to the previous group's activities. New members can build on those activities, changing them when they need to.

There is also a great deal of flexibility in how groups form at Tennant Company. For example, anyone, from a line person to a manager, may decide to form a group. Or, the impetus can come from the quality department, because it collects and analyzes data from all departments, and its managers have a panoramic view of the problems and the problem solvers.

The quality department also helps managers introduce the concept of small groups by providing training and attending some meetings. This is what happened at Tennant Trend, Inc., a subsidiary that makes small, commercial floor-cleaning products.

Tennant Trend, Inc., management recruited members for the subsidiary's first problem-solving small group and provided them with a directive: "Find out what our biggest problem is." The group pinpointed back orders as the problem to attack and made it a goal to reduce back orders from 44 percent of all orders to 0 percent.

Approximately 18 months after the group's solutions were introduced, back orders dropped to 10 percent, the average shipment time of back orders decreased from 45 days to 30 days, and Tennant Trend, Inc., had saved at least $20,000. Since then, Tennant Trend, Inc., has continued to achieve improved performance in pursuit of its goal to eliminate backorders. In 1988, backorders were reduced to 5 percent. As of November 1989, backorders had been further reduced to 3 percent. The average shipment time to fill a backorder decreased from 11 days in 1988 to 9.5 days in 1989, resulting in a savings of $9,000.

By working together, group members from each department (material control, production, purchasing, and customer service) achieved a better understanding of how their department's work affects others.

Though we place as few constraints on groups as possible, we do have one rule that always applies: Groups must include people who will be directly affected by the group's work. This is probably why we have so many interdepartmental groups at Tennant Company. For example, in new product design, group members will include people from various engineering departments (design, test, industrial engineering, and quality engineering), and people from marketing, production control, production, material handling, and purchasing.

Working in small groups helps us recognize how our actions affect other people. It also reduces problems down the line, because we coordinate our activities up front. In essence, groups help us understand that we have customers inside, as well as outside, the company.

Many of our managers and supervisors, especially in manufacturing and engineering, took the lead in encouraging the formation of small groups. They let employees know that management was serious about the program and that their participation was important. As soon as word spread about the success some of these groups were having, new groups began to form spontaneously.

But small groups aren't going to be successful automatically. Management has a responsibility to support them by making sure every group gets the members it needs. We don't draft people, but we do ask for people from the various types of jobs. Management also makes sure the group gets the training it needs and has the time to meet (usually one hour a week on company time). Management must also broadly approve of, if not direct, the goal set by the group. And, as we mentioned before, management must be willing to be part of the group if the group requests it.

We have found that the optimum group size, especially for groups that form to solve a specific problem, is from 8 to 10 people. If the groups are much larger, it is difficult for everyone to speak during the one-hour meeting.

The optimum group size is eight to ten people. Groups must include people who will be directly affected by the group's work.

Finally, an element as essential to group success as it is to individual success is recognition. Recognition can be given in a variety of ways. At Tennant Company, we recognize group achievements in the company newsletter; we offer cash awards to groups that come up with ways to save the company money; we present awards to groups for outstanding achievement. We also invite groups to set up display booths at ZD Day. At ZD Day III, half of Tennant Company 80 operational groups took us up on this invitation. Based on the interest those displays produced among our employees, 60 groups displayed their achievements in 1987.

SETTING GOALS AND MEASURING PROGRESS
People work better when they can define what "win" means on the job.

Americans like to know who's winning. Whether the game is baseball, bowling, or tennis, and whether we're watching or playing, we want to know the score. Our experience at Tennant Company with setting goals and taking measurements taught us that the same is true in the workplace.

People work better when they can define what winning on the job means. To keep score, people need to have goals and the skills and tools that allow them to measure their progress. Faith is not enough in the quality business.

Our experience with goal setting was limited. Traditionally we asked only our managerial people to set goals, but we never gave them any standard guidelines to follow. We routinely took measurements in our manufacturing department. In other areas, people measured things we thought were important but which, we learned when we began listening to employees, contributed little to our understanding of how to do the job better.

All that had to change. For the quality process to work, goal setting had to become a companywide activity, not an infrequent exercise. And the people who led the activity—the managers and supervisors—had to set goals with some consistent skill.

The best way to proceed is slowly, setting highly achievable goals at first and then gradually adding more difficult, complex goals. In 1980, we asked our managers and supervisors to set a goal for their groups or departments. Most set vague goals like, "I want to do better." That was fine as a warm-up; at least everyone had a goal.

A year later, we asked the managers and supervisors how they performed. Most didn't know, because their goals were vague and they didn't know how to measure their progress. At that point, we began a training program for all managers and supervisors.

Our purpose was to train managers and supervisors to identify and track problems that interfered with doing the job right the first time. Our major quality measurements began to take shape from the information we gathered during that process. We also taught our people how to apply costs to the quality measurements they were developing.

Next, we had to put those measurements in the context of goals.

The manager of employment and development devised an in-house course to teach managers and supervisors how to set goals, how to get employees to participate in setting goals, and how to make goals meaningful. For a goal to be meaningful, it must be measurable, realistic, and attainable. It also has to be visible, so everyone knows what is expected. Many managers, for example, put their department's monthly, quarterly, or annual goals in chart form and posted the charts where all employees could see them.

We began distributing literature about goal setting. One of the best pieces was a pamphlet called "Guide to Successful Goal Setting," published by Management by Objectives Inc. The 37 steps outlined in the pamphlet are brief and to the point. They cover everything from the nature of goals to the expected results.

After the training was completed and managers and supervisors began to feel more confident about setting and measuring goals, they began to enlarge their scope, moving from department and group goals to quality and productivity goals. This evolutionary process took about four years. By starting with small, limited, achievable goals, people gradually gained the confidence to set bigger, more challenging ones.

The managers and supervisors, in turn, asked their people to set individual or group goals, depending on the nature of each person's job. Though we did not give line people formal training in setting goals, managers and supervisors did assist them. Goal setting became a standard practice throughout the company, and the goals were as varied as the jobs of the people who set them.

For example, the goals set and achieved by an area service representative helped him win an Award of Excellence. He set three annual goals:

- to have 90 percent billable hours
- to sell at least 60 replacement brushes
- to contribute toward the sale of at least three machines

Tennant Company expects service representatives to spend most of their time serving customers. This representative quantified that expectation into a goal he could measure and achieve. The second two goals reflect his own initiative.

For example, the representative says he had sold brushes before but had not kept track of how many. Sixty brushes seemed like a realistic goal. And by giving customers the best possible service and passing leads to salespeople, he knew he could contribute to machine sales.

This example is important because the representative set his own goals. No one else could have set goals that better used the representative's skills to make the greatest contribution to Tennant Company. We have found this to be true many times, whether the job belongs to a service representative, a clerk, or a line worker. When people work with a supervisor to set their own goals, they have a great incentive to achieve them because they're the ones who created them.

We've come a long way from the days when all we measured was the manufacturing department's output. Every department in the company now has goals and ways to measure progress. And there are as many types of goals as there are jobs in the company, from production to service to office procedures. Even seemingly minor tasks such as returning phone calls and responding to Telex messages can be measured, and performance improved by setting goals.

Setting and tracking goals unites work groups by giving them a sense of purpose and a course of action. Our Oakland Service/San Francisco Sales Group came up with seven major one-year goals, including increasing sales of various products, increasing service reps' billable hours, and decreasing the number of unsatisfactory machine demonstrations due to machine failures.

By year's end, the Oakland/San Francisco group had attained two goals and exceeded two others.

At Tennant Company, we made goals in all our product designs. These goals tell the designers and everyone else concerned, including the people who manufacture the product and the people who sell it, what they can expect in terms of completion dates, warranty expense, and defects detected in the final test.

We've also been able to set goals and measure progress in traditionally hard-to-quantify areas such as marketing. For example, our international marketing department, which coordinates international sales activities, has set a goal of three-day turnaround for handling orders, quotes, and complaints.

Goals and measurements are road signs on the quality journey.

That's not always easy to achieve when you're dealing with calls and correspondence worldwide. But by tracking their turnaround time, department members became aware of the steps necessary to meet schedules, such as keeping a sufficient amount of printed material on hand and referring field people to their own manuals or brochures for answers to their questions.

Goals are road signs on the quality journey. They also provide an opportunity to recognize our own achievements and those of our co-workers. Small groups or departments, for example, often hold informal celebrations when they reach the goals they set. Frequently, they're written up in our company newsletter. This kind of recognition gives us confidence in our ability to do our jobs right.

RECOGNITION: KEEPING FEEDBACK IN THE FOREFRONT
Awards establish an ideal and encourage specific behavior that conforms to the ideal; positive feedback motivates employees to do their best each day.

Recognition, as we've said, is one of the most powerful tools for involving employees in a quality emphasis. The recognition program that evolved at Tennant Company over the past six years has two key elements: formal awards and informal recognition. Recognition is more a process than a program, and it now occurs every day at the company.

Awards and informal recognition complement one another. Awards establish an ideal and encourage specific behavior that conforms to the ideal; positive feedback motivates employees to do their best each day. It is a medium for recognizing a broad number of people without invoking the win/lose attitude that awards almost inevitably generate.

We learned these lessons during our quality journey. We didn't realize the value of positive feedback until we were three or four years into the quality process. Like most companies, we thought about recognition in terms of awards. So in the beginning we focused on designing an awards program to acknowledge people's contributions to quality. At the same time, we informally researched the recognition programs of other companies; however, we found little to emulate because we wanted our awards to recognize quality alone.

We did, however, observe one characteristic that we wanted to avoid: having a management group or an executive select the award recipients. We felt that this would make the awards seem biased to the employees.

Eventually, we established three rules.

1. Our program would be peer driven. An employee could nominate anyone of equal or lesser rank, but not anyone he or she reported to directly.

2. Recipients would be selected by a committee of employees of different rank and from different departments in the company.

3. We would establish a set of criteria for selecting recipients and print these criteria on the nomination forms. We created these guidelines, almost inadvertently, by asking ourselves what type of behavior we wanted to encourage. We came up with five behaviors that became guidelines for judging individual achievement nominations:

• Continuous superior performance in doing work right the first time over a minimum of one year

• A cooperative, positive approach to problem solving

• Taking the initiative in corrective action to solve problems (identifying errors, determining the cause of errors, correcting errors, or preventing errors)

• Setting quality goals and demonstrating high-level effort to attain goals

• Communications and other actions that support the quality process

As small groups sprang up at Tennant Company, we also decided to include group awards in our program. A group can be as small as two people or as large as a department. There are three group awards criteria:

1. Continuous superior performance in doing work right the first time

2. Taking the initiative in corrective action to solve problems

3. Setting quality goals and demonstrating high-level efforts to attain goals

The review process for individual and group award nominees is similar. As the nominations are received, the awards committee sends out questionnaires to people who are in contact with the nominees. The questionnaires help assess the individual or group's performance based on the awards criteria.

From these assessments, the committee assigns a value of one to five points for each criterion, then multiplies the total by the weighted value of each criterion. For example, the first and second individual award criteria are equal in value and higher than the other three criteria.

Individual awards are given annually to no more than 2 percent of the work force. Of that 2 percent, about one-third receive the Award of Excellence, a 10-carat gold ring with diamond chips around a stylized Q. The others receive Special Recognition Awards, 10-carat gold pins shaped like the Tennant Company Quality emblem. In addition, all recipients are given plaques.

The Group Excellence Awards are presented twice a year to no more than six groups each time. Each group member receives a gold pin, and the whole group shares the plaque.

We selected jewelry and plaques as award items because they best fit our requirements of making the awards visible and valuable symbols of the quality emphasis.

Our executives present the awards at formal banquets, one for individuals and one for groups. Recipients can bring a guest. We also acknowledge winners by writing about them in the company newsletter, posting bulletin board announcements, and engraving their names on a wall plaque in the reception area. In total, we spend about $50,000 a year on our formal awards program.

Although it is well suited to recognizing outstanding performers, this program has its limitations. The awards program takes place only once or twice a year, and its narrow scope underscores the significance of the awards. Because of its design, it leaves out a broad percentage of the work force.

The Koala T. Bear Award was designed to broaden recognition to more employees. We adopted the namesake of the award, a small, stuffed koala bear, as the mascot of our quality emphasis. The bear also occasionally appears in a cartoon in the employee newsletter.

The award is given monthly to employees who consistently meet their job standards and display a positive attitude. In addition to these essential criteria, nominees are reviewed on the basis of their special efforts in one of three areas: output, quality, and efficiency.

Like the formal awards program, this one is peer-driven, so employees cannot nominate an immediate supervisor. A committee of people from different ranks and different departments makes the final selections.

The committee for the Koala T. Bear Award asks people who benefit from the nominees' work to evaluate the nominations, and the number of winners is unrestricted. As few as two employees, or as many as 20, may qualify for the award in any given month.

The award, a certificate and a stuffed koala bear wearing a Tennant Company Quality T-shirt, is presented at work by a member of the committee. The presentation begins with the appearance of a committee member who dresses up in a bear costume. Other committee members gather around to honor the recipient.

Even Koala T. Bear did not solve one nagging question: How could Tennant Company recognize employees daily for their efforts? In a survey, Tennant Company executives were asked by the president to rate the company on the eight hallmarks of outstanding companies named by the authors of *In Search of Excellence*. They rated Tennant Company low in one of those categories—employee recognition.

In Search of Excellence advocates the use of positive reinforcement. Our executives felt we slipped in providing reinforcement, and a subsequent survey of 200 employees selected at random supported this view.

To correct this imbalance, we formed a Positive Feedback Committee in 1984 to make recognition a larger part of our corporate culture. As one committee member put it, "We want people to enjoy coming to work, to think that work is fun as well as something to do. Positive feedback is related to making people feel good about their jobs and wanting to do a good job." In short, recognition is a powerful motivator.

The committee created a positive reinforcement awareness campaign. They provided managers and supervisors with note pads printed with the slogan "That-a-Way" so notes can be written to employees for a job well done. The campaign also included posters and buttons urging everyone to give positive reinforcement, not just to think about how often they get it.

The team produced videos in which employees role-played the do's and don'ts of positive reinforcement. For example, reinforcement should not contain a mixed message: "You're producing more parts, but unfortunately you're making more errors." After that kind of message, people will remember only negative comments. Whether it's positive or negative, feedback should be sincere, appropriate, and timely.

Recognition can be directed to groups as well as individuals. Small, informal celebrations are a good way to let groups of people know they are performing well. One manager, for example, brings coffee and doughnuts when his people reach their production quotas for the quarter. Others may bring in pizza for lunch. Such gatherings are inexpensive enough to be funded from petty cash, but they have a powerful effect in giving a group a sense of accomplishment. Many people feel this is an effective way of having an informal celebration.

The committee's efforts to improve positive reinforcement began to have an effect. In 1985 and 1987, a survey of the same 200 employees revealed that they believed Tennant Company was doing a better job of recognizing employee effort. This good news encouraged the committee to stay together for another year to work on ways to keep the issue of feedback in the forefront.

To meet this objective, the committee wrote and distributed a positive feedback mission statement that contains five key objectives:
- to enjoy working together
- to look for positives
- to understand and appreciate each other
- to build each other's self-esteem
- to handle negative situations in a positive way

The team also planned a long-range campaign to make more videos and to distribute packets of positive reinforcement information to managers and supervisors. Now, rather than the team holding meetings on positive feedback topics, managers and supervisors will conduct them in their own departments.

As one employee explained, "Positive reinforcement makes people want to try harder. If you recognize them for something they tried, whether it was successful or not, at least you're supporting them for having tried. If you recognize them for having made the effort, you're going to get more."

APPENDIX

1991 EXAMINATION CATEGORIES AND ITEMS

Malcolm Baldrige National Quality Award

1991 EXAMINATION

The **Leadership** category examines how senior executives create and sustain clear and visible quality values along with a management system to guide all activities of the company toward quality excellence. Also examined are the senior executives' and the company's quality leadership in the external community and how the company integrates its public responsibilities with its quality values and practices.

1.1 Senior Executive Leadership (40 pts.)

Describe the senior executives' leadership, personal involvement, and visibility in developing and maintaining an environment for quality excellence.

AREAS TO ADDRESS

a. senior executives' leadership, personal involvement, and visibility in quality-related activities of the company: (1) goal setting; (2) planning; (3) reviewing company quality performance; (4) communicating with employees; and (5) recognizing employee contributions. Other activities may include participating in teams, learning about the quality of domestic and international competitors, and meeting with customers and suppliers.

b. senior executives' approach to building quality values into the leadership process of the company

c. senior executives' leadership and communication of quality excellence to groups outside the company. Groups may include national, state, community, trade, business, professional, education, health care, standards, and government organizations.

Notes:
(1) The term "senior executives" refers to the highest-ranking official of the organization applying for the Award and those reporting directly to that official.
(2) The type and extent of the activities of senior executives within and outside the company could depend upon company size, resources, and other business factors (see Business Factors, pages 22-23).

1.2 Quality Values (15 pts.)

Describe the company's quality values, how they are projected in a consistent manner, and how adoption of the values throughout the company is determined and reinforced.

AREAS TO ADDRESS

a. brief summary of the content of policy, mission, or guidelines that demonstrate the company's quality values

b. company's communications activities to project the quality values throughout the company. Briefly describe what is communicated and the means and frequency of communications.

c. how the company determines and evaluates how well the quality values have been adopted throughout the company, such as through surveys, interviews, or other means, and how employee adoption is reinforced

1.3 Management for Quality (25 pts.)

Describe how the quality values are integrated into day-to-day leadership, management, and supervision of all company units.

AREAS TO ADDRESS

a. key approaches for involving, and encouraging leadership in, all levels of management and supervision in quality; principal roles and responsibilities at each level

b. key approaches for promoting cooperation among managers and supervisors across different levels and different functions of the company

c. types, frequency, and content of reviews of company and of unit quality performance; types of actions taken to assist units not performing according to plans or goals

d. key indicators the company uses to evaluate the effectiveness of its approaches to integrating quality values into day-to-day management and how the evaluation is used to improve its approaches

Note: *Key indicators refer to principal measures of some characteristics of quality or effectiveness.*

1.4 Public Responsibility
(20 pts.)

Describe how the company extends its quality leadership to the external community and includes its responsibilities to the public for health, safety, environmental protection, and ethical business practice in its quality policies and improvement activities.

AREAS TO ADDRESS

a. how the company promotes quality awareness and sharing with external groups. Groups may include national, state, community, trade, business, professional, education, health care, standards, and government organizations.

b. how the company encourages employee leadership and involvement in quality activities of organizations mentioned above

c. how the company includes its public responsibilities such as business ethics, public health and safety, environmental protection, and waste management into its quality policies and practices. For each area relevant and important to the company's business, briefly summarize: (1) principal quality improvement goals and how they are set: (2) principal improvement methods; (3) principal indicators used to monitor quality; and (4) how and how often progress is reviewed.

Notes:

(1) Health and safety of employees are not covered in this Item. These are addressed in Item 4.5.

(2) See Business Factors, pages 22-23.

2.0 Information and Analysis *(70 pts.)*

The *Information and Analysis* category examines the scope, validity, use, and management of data and information that underlie the company's overall quality management system. Also examined is the adequacy of the data, information, and analysis to support a responsive, prevention-based approach to quality and customer satisfaction built upon "management by fact."

2.1 Scope and Management of Quality Data and Information *(20 pts.)*

Describe the company's base of data and information used for planning, day-to-day management, and evaluation of quality, and how data and information reliability, timeliness, and access are assured.

AREAS TO ADDRESS

a. (1) criteria for selecting data to be included in the quality-related data and information base; and (2) scope and types of data: customer-related; internal operations and processes; employee-related; safety, health, and regulatory; quality performance; supplier quality; and other

b. processes and techniques the company uses to ensure reliability, consistency, standardization, review, timely update, and rapid access throughout the company. If applicable, describe approach to ensuring software quality.

c. how the company evaluates and improves the scope and quality of its data and information and how it shortens the cycle from data gathering to access

Notes:

(1) The purpose of this Item is to permit the applicant to demonstrate the breadth and depth of the data assembled as part of its total quality management system. Applicants should give brief descriptions of the types of data under major headings such as "employees" and subheadings such as "education and training," "teams," and "recognition." Under each subheading, give a brief description of the data and information. Actual data should not be reported in this Item. Such data are requested in other Examination Items.

(2) Information on the scope and management of competitive and benchmark data is requested in Item 2.2.

2.2 Competitive Comparisons and Benchmarks *(30 pts.)*

Describe the company's approach to selecting quality-related competitive comparisons and world-class benchmarks to support quality planning, evaluation, and improvement.

AREAS TO ADDRESS

a. criteria and rationale the company uses for seeking competitive comparisons and benchmarks: (1) relationship to company goals and priorities for improvement of product and service quality and/or company operations; (2) with whom to compare — within and outside the company's industry

b. current scope of competitive and benchmark data: (1) product and service quality; (2) customer satisfaction and other customer data; (3) supplier performance; (4) employee data; (5) internal operations, business processes, and support services; and (6) other. For each type: (a) list sources of comparisons and benchmarks, including company and independent testing or evaluation; and (b) how each type of data is used.

c. how the company evaluates and improves the scope, sources, and uses of competitive and benchmark data

2.3 Analysis of Quality Data and Information *(20 pts.)*

Describe how data and information are analyzed to support the company's overall quality objectives.

AREAS TO ADDRESS

a. how data described in 2.1 and 2.2, separately and in combination, are analyzed to support: (1) company planning and priorities; (2) company-level review of quality performance; (3) improvement of internal operations, business processes, and support services; (4) determination of product and service features and levels of quality performance that best predict improvement in customer satisfaction; and (5) quality improvement projections based upon potential use of alternative strategies or technologies

b. how the company evaluates and improves its analytical capabilities and shortens the cycle of analysis and access to analytical results

Note: *This Item focuses primarily on analysis for company-level evaluation and decision making. Some other Items request information based on analysis of specific sets of data for special purposes such as human resource practices and complaint management.*

3.0 Strategic Quality Planning (60 pts.)

The *Strategic Quality Planning* category examines the company's planning process for achieving or retaining quality leadership and how the company integrates quality improvement planning into overall business planning. Also examined are the company's short-term and longer-term plans to achieve and/or sustain a quality leadership position.

3.1 Strategic Quality Planning Process
(35 pts.)

Describe the company's strategic quality planning process for short-term (1-2 years) and longer-term (3 years or more) quality leadership and customer satisfaction.

AREAS TO ADDRESS

a. how goals for quality leadership are set using: (1) current and future quality requirements for leadership in the company's target markets; and (2) company's current quality levels and trends versus competitors' in these markets

b. principal types of data, information, and analysis used in developing plans and evaluating feasibility based upon goals: (1) customer requirements; (2) process capabilities; (3) competitive and benchmark data; and (4) supplier capabilities; outline how these data are used in developing plans

c. how strategic plans and goals are implemented and reviewed: (1) how specific plans, goals, and performance indicators are deployed to all work units and suppliers; and (2) how resources are committed for key requirements such as capital expenditures and training; and (3) how performance relative to plans and goals is reviewed and acted upon

d. how the goal-setting and strategic planning processes are evaluated and improved

---

Notes:

(1) Strategic quality plans address in detail how the company will pursue market leadership through providing superior quality products and services and through improving the effectiveness of all operations of the company.

(2) Item 3.1 focuses on the processes of goal setting and strategic planning. Item 3.2 focuses on actual goals and plans.

3.2 Quality Goals and Plans *(25 pts.)*

Summarize the company's goals and strategies. Outline principal quality plans for the short term (1-2 years) and longer term (3 years or more).

AREAS TO ADDRESS

a. major quality goals and principal strategies for achieving these goals

b. principal short-term plans: (1) summary of key requirements and performance indicators deployed to work units and suppliers; and (2) resources committed to accomplish the key requirements

c. principal longer-term plans: brief summary of major requirements, and how they will be met

d. two- to five-year projection of significant changes in the company's most important quality levels. Describe how these levels may be expected to compare with those of key competitors over this time period.

Note: *The company's most important quality levels are those for the key product and service quality features. Projections are estimates of future quality levels based upon implementation of the plans described in Item 3.2.*

The **Human Resource Utilization** category examines the effectiveness of the company's efforts to develop and realize the full potential of the work force, including management, and to maintain an environment conducive to full participation, quality leadership, and personal and organizational growth.

4.1 Human Resource Management (20 pts.)

Describe how the company's overall human resource management effort supports its quality objectives.

AREAS TO ADDRESS

a. how human resource plans are derived from the quality goals, strategies, and plans outlined in 3.2: (1) short term (1-2 years); and (2) longer term (3 years or more). Address major specific requirements such as training, development, hiring, involvement, empowerment, and recognition.

b. key quality goals and improvement methods for human resource management practices such as hiring and career development

c. how the company analyzes and uses its overall employee-related data to evaluate and improve the effectiveness of all categories and all types of employees

Notes:

(1) Human resource plans and improvement activities might include one or more of the following: mechanisms for promoting cooperation such as internal customer/supplier techniques or other internal partnerships; initiatives to promote labor-management cooperation such as partnerships with unions; creation or modifications in recognition systems; mechanisms for increasing or broadening employee responsibilities; and education and training initiatives. They might also include developing partnerships with educational institutions to develop employees and to help ensure the future supply of well-prepared employees.

(2) "Types of employees" takes into account factors such as employment status, bargaining unit membership, and demographic makeup.

4.2 Employee Involvement (40 pts.)

Describe the means available for all employees to contribute effectively to meeting the company's quality objectives; summarize trends and current levels of involvement.

AREAS TO ADDRESS

a. management practices and specific mechanisms, such as teams or suggestion systems, the company uses to promote employee contributions to quality objectives, individually and in groups. Summarize how and when the company gives feedback.

b. company actions to increase employee authority to act (empowerment), responsibility, and innovation. Summarize principal goals for all categories of employees.

c. key indicators the company uses to evaluate the extent and effectiveness of involvement by all categories and types of employees and how the indicators are used to improve employee involvement

d. trends and current levels of involvement by all categories of employees. Use the most important indicator(s) of effective employee involvement for each category of employee.

Note: *Different involvement goals and indicators may be set for different categories of employees, depending upon company needs and upon the types of responsibilities of each employee category.*

4.3 Quality Education and Training (40 pts.)

Describe how the company decides what quality education and training is needed by employees and how it utilizes the knowledge and skills acquired; summarize the types of quality education and training received by employees in all employee categories.

AREAS TO ADDRESS

a. (1) how the company assesses needs for the types and amounts of quality education and training received by all categories of employees (Describe how the needs assessment addresses work unit requirements to include or have access to skills in problem analysis and problem solving to meet their quality objectives.); (2) methods for the delivery of quality education and training; and (3) how the company ensures on-the-job reinforcement of knowledge and skills

b. summary and trends in quality education and training received by employees. The summary and trends should address: (1) quality orientation of new employees; (2) percent of employees receiving quality education and training in each employee category annually; (3) average hours of quality education and training annually per employee; (4) percent of employees who have received quality education and training; and (5) percent of employees who have received education and training in statistical and other quantitative problem-solving methods.

c. key methods and indicators the company uses to evaluate and improve the effectiveness of its quality education and training. Describe how the indicators are used to improve the quality education and training of all categories and types of employees.

Note: *Quality education and training addresses the knowledge and skills employees need to meet the quality objectives associated with their responsibilities. This may include basic quality awareness, problem solving, meeting customer requirements, and other quality-related aspects of skills.*

4.4 Employee Recognition and Performance Measurement (25 pts.)

Describe how the company's recognition and performance measurement processes support quality objectives; summarize trends in recognition.

AREAS TO ADDRESS

a. how recognition, reward, and performance measurement for individuals and groups, including managers, supports the company's quality objectives; (1) how quality relative to other business considerations such as schedules and financial results is reinforced; and (2) how employees are involved in the development and improvement of performance measurements

b. trends in recognition and reward of individuals and groups, by employee category, for contributions to quality

c. key indicators the company uses to evaluate and improve its recognition, reward, and performance measurement processes

4.5 Employee Well-Being and Morale *(25 pts.)*

Describe how the company maintains a work environment conducive to the well-being and growth of all employees; summarize trends and levels in key indicators of well-being and morale.

AREAS TO ADDRESS

a. how well-being and morale factors such as health, safety, satisfaction, and ergonomics are included in quality improvement activities. Summarize principal improvement goals and methods for each factor relevant and important to the company's work environment. For accidents and work-related health problems, describe how underlying causes are determined and how adverse conditions are prevented.

b. mobility, flexibility, and retraining in job assignments to support employee development and/or to accommodate changes in technology, improved productivity, or changes in work processes

c. special services, facilities and opportunities the company makes available to employees. These might include one or more of the following: counseling, assistance, recreational or cultural, and non-work-related education.

d. how employee satisfaction is determined and interpreted for use in quality improvement

e. trends and levels in key indicators of well-being and morale such as safety, absenteeism, turnover, attrition rate for customer-contact personnel, satisfaction, grievances, strikes, and worker compensation. Explain important adverse results, if any, and how problems were resolved or current status. Compare the current levels of the most significant indicators with those of industry averages and industry leaders.

5.0 Quality Assurance of Products and Services *(140 pts.)*

The *Quality Assurance of Products and Services* category examines the systematic approaches used by the company for assuring quality of goods and services based primarily upon process design and control, including control of procured materials, parts, and services. Also examined is the integration of process control with continuous quality improvement.

5.1 Design and Introduction of Quality Products and Services *(35 pts.)*

Describe how new and/or improved products and services are designed and introduced and how processes are designed to meet key product and service quality requirements.

AREAS TO ADDRESS

a. how designs of products, services, and processes are developed so that: (1) customer requirements are translated into design requirements; (2) all quality requirements are addressed early in the overall design process by all appropriate company units; (3) designs are coordinated and integrated to include all phases of production and delivery; and (4) a process control plan is developed that involves selecting and setting key process characteristics for production and delivery of products and services and how these characteristics are to be measured and controlled

b. how designs are reviewed and validated taking into account key factors: (1) product and service performance; (2) process capability and future requirements; and (3) supplier capability and future requirements

c. how the company evaluates and improves the effectiveness of its designs and design processes and how it shortens the design-to-introduction cycle

Notes:

(1) Design and introduction may include modification and variants of existing products and services and/or new products and services emerging from research and development.

(2) Service and manufacturing businesses should interpret product and service requirements to include all product- and service-related requirements at all stages of production, delivery, and use. See also Item 7.1, Note (3).

(3) Depending on their type of business, applicants need to consider many factors in product and service design such as health, safety, long-term performance, measurement capability, process capability, maintainability, and supplier capability. Applicant responses should reflect the key requirements of the products and services they deliver.

5.2 Process Quality Control *(20 pts.)*

Describe how the processes used to produce the company's products and services are controlled.

AREAS TO ADDRESS

a. how the company assures that processes are controlled within limits set in process design. Include information on: (1) types and frequencies of measurements; and (2) what is measured, such as process, product, and service characteristics.

b. for out-of-control occurrences, describe: (1) how root causes are determined; (2) how corrections are made so that future occurrences are prevented; and (3) how corrections are verified

c. how the company evaluates the quality of the measurements used in process quality control and assures measurement quality control

---

Notes:

(1) For manufacturing and service companies with measurement requirements, it is necessary to demonstrate that measurement accuracy and precision meet process, service, and product requirements (measurement quality assurance). For physical, chemical, and engineering measurements, indicate approaches for ensuring that measurements are traceable to national standards through calibrations, reference materials, or other means.

(2) Verification of corrections and verification of improvements in 5.2b, 5.3c, and 5.4b should include comparison with expected or predicted results.

5.3 Continuous Improvement of Processes *(20 pts.)*

Describe how processes used to produce products and services are continuously improved.

AREAS TO ADDRESS

a. principal types of data and information the company uses to determine needs and opportunities for improvement in processes: (1) data from day-to-day process control; (2) field data such as customer data, data on product and service performance, and data on competitors' performance; (3) evaluation of all process steps; (4) process benchmark data; and (5) data of other types such as from process research and development and evaluation of new technology or alternative processes

b. how the company evaluates potential changes in processes to select from among alternatives

c. how the company integrates process improvement with day-to-day process quality control: (1) resetting process characteristics; (2) verification of improvements; and (3) ensuring effective use by all appropriate company units

---

Note: *The focus of this Item is on improvement of the primary processes used to produce the company's products and services, not on maintaining them or on correcting out-of-control occurrences, which is the focus of Item 5.2.*

5.4 Quality Assessment *(15 pts.)*

Describe how the company assesses the quality of its systems, processes, practices, products, and services.

AREAS TO ADDRESS

a. approaches the company uses to assess the quality of its systems, processes, practices, products, and services such as process reviews or audits. Include the types and frequencies of assessments, what is assessed, who conducts the assessments, and how the validity of assessment tools is assured.

b. how assessment findings are used to improve systems, processes, practices, training, or supplier requirements. Include how the company verifies that improvements are effective.

5.5 Documentation *(10 pts.)*

Describe documentation and other modes of knowledge preservation and knowledge transfer to support quality assurance, quality assessment, and quality improvement.

AREAS TO ADDRESS

a. (1) principal quality-related purposes of documents such as for recording procedures and practices and for retaining key records; and (2) uses of documents such as in standardization, orientation of new employees, training, maintaining records for legal purposes, or for quality-related tracking of products, processes, and services

b. how the company improves its documentation system: (1) to simplify and harmonize documents; (2) to keep pace with changes in practice, technology, and systems; (3) to ensure rapid access wherever needed; and (4) to dispose of obsolete documents

Note: *Documents may be written or computerized.*

5.6 Business Process and Support Service Quality *(20 pts.)*

Summarize process quality, quality assessment, and quality improvement activities for business processes and support services.

AREAS TO ADDRESS

a. summary of process quality control and quality assessment activities for key business processes and support services: (1) how principal process quality requirements are set using customer requirements or the requirements of other company units served ("internal customers"); (2) how and how often process quality is measured; and (3) types and frequencies of quality assessments and who conducts them

b. summary of quality improvement activities for key business processes and support services: (1) principal quality improvement goals and how they are set; (2) principal process evaluation and improvement activities, including how processes are simplified and response time shortened; (3) principal indicators used to measure quality; and (4) how and how often progress is reviewed

Notes:

(1) Business processes and support services might include activities and operations involving finance and accounting, software services, sales, marketing, information services, purchasing, personnel, legal services, plant and facilities management, research and development, and secretarial and other administrative services.

(2) The purpose of this Item is to permit applicants to highlight separately the quality assurance, quality assessment, and quality improvement activities for functions that support the primary processes through which products and services are produced and delivered. Together, Items 5.1, 5.2, 5.3, 5.4, 5.5, 5.6, and 5.7 should cover all operations, processes, and activities of all work units. However, the selection of support services and business processes for inclusion in Item 5.6 depends on the type of business and quality system and should be made by the applicant.

5.7 Supplier Quality *(20 pts.)*

Describe how the quality of materials, components, and services furnished by other businesses is assured, assessed, and improved.

AREAS TO ADDRESS

a. approaches used to define and communicate the company's specific quality requirements to suppliers. Include: (1) the principal quality requirements for the company's most important suppliers; and (2) the principal quality indicators the company uses to communicate and monitor supplier quality.

b. methods used to assure that the company's quality requirements are met by suppliers. Methods may include audits, process reviews, receiving inspection, certification, and testing.

c. strategy and current actions to improve the quality and responsiveness of suppliers. These may include partnerships, training, incentives and recognition, and supplier selection.

Note: *The term "supplier" as used here refers to other company providers of goods and services. The use of these goods and services may occur at any stage in the production, delivery, and use of the company's products and services. Thus, suppliers include businesses such as distributors, dealers, and franchises as well as those that provide materials and components.*

The *Quality Results* category examines quality levels and quality improvement based upon objective measures derived from analysis of customer requirements and expectations and from analysis of business operations. Also examined are current quality levels in relation to those of competing firms.

6.1 Product and Service Quality Results (90 pts.)

Summarize trends in quality improvement and current quality levels for key product and service features; compare the company's current quality levels with those of competitors and world leaders.

AREAS TO ADDRESS

a. trends and current levels for all key measures of product and service quality

b. current quality level comparisons with principal competitors in the company's key markets, industry averages, industry leaders, and world leaders. Briefly explain bases for comparison such as: (1) independent surveys, studies, or laboratory testing; (2) benchmarks; and (3) company evaluations and testing. Describe how objectivity and validity of comparisons are assured.

Notes:

(1) Key product and service measures are measures relative to the set of all important features of the company's products and services. These measures, taken together, best represent the <u>most important factors that predict customer satisfaction and quality in customer use</u>. Examples include measures of accuracy, reliability, timeliness, performance, behavior, delivery, after-sales services, documentation, and appearance. These measures are "internal" measures. Customer satisfaction or other customer data should not be included in responses to this Item.

(2) Results reported in Item 6.1 should reflect the key product and service features determined in Item 7.1, and be fully consistent with the key quality requirements for products and services described in the Overview (see page 36).

6.2 Business Process, Operational, and Support Service Quality Results (50 pts.)

Summarize trends in quality improvement and current quality levels for business processes, operations, and support services.

AREAS TO ADDRESS

a. trends and current levels for the most important measures of the quality and effectiveness of business processes, operations, and support services

b. comparison with industry averages, industry leaders, and world leaders

Notes:

(1) Key measures for business processes, operations, and support services are the set of principal measurable characteristics that represent quality and effectiveness in company operations in meeting requirements of customers and of other company units. Examples include measures of accuracy, timeliness, and effectiveness. Measures include error rates, defect rates, lead times, cycle times, and use of manpower, materials, energy, and capital as reflected in indicators such as repeat services, utilization rates, and waste.

(2) The results reported in Item 6.2 derive from quality improvement activities described in Category 5 and Item 1.4, if appropriate. Responses should reflect relevance to the company's principal quality objectives and should also demonstrate the breadth of improvement results throughout all operations and work units.

6.3 Supplier Quality Results (40 pts.)

Summarize trends and levels in quality of suppliers and services furnished by other companies; compare the company's supplier quality with that of competitors and with key benchmarks.

AREAS TO ADDRESS

a. trends and current levels for the most important indicators of supplier quality

b. comparison of the company's supplier quality with that of competitors and/or with benchmarks. Such comparisons could include industry averages, industry leaders, world leaders, principal competitors in the company's key markets, and appropriate benchmarks. Describe the basis for comparisons.

Note: *The results reported in Item 6.3 derive from quality improvement activities described in Item 5.7. Results should be broken down by major groupings of suppliers and reported using the principal quality indicators described in Item 5.7.*

The *Customer Satisfaction* category examines the company's knowledge of the customer, overall customer service systems, responsiveness, and its ability to meet requirements and expectations. Also examined are current levels and trends in customer satisfaction.

7.1 Determining Customer Requirements and Expectations *(30 pts.)*

Describe how the company determines current and future customer requirements and expectations.

AREAS TO ADDRESS

a. how the company determines current and future requirements and expectations of customers. Include information on: (1) how market segments and customer groups are determined and how customers of competitors and other potential customers are considered; (2) the process for collecting information and data. This should include what information is sought, frequencies of surveys, interviews or other contacts, and how objectivity is assured; and (3) how other information and data are cross-compared to support determination of customer requirements and expectations. Such information and data might include performance information on the company's products and services, complaints, gains and losses of customers, customer satisfaction, and competitors' performance.

b. process for determining product and service features and the relative importance of these features to customers and/or customer groups

c. how the company evaluates and improves its processes for determining customer requirements and expectations as well as the key product and service features

Notes:

(1) Products and services may be sold to end users by intermediaries such as retail stores or dealers. Thus, determining customer groups should take into account both the end users and the intermediaries.

(2) Product and service features refer to all important characteristics of products and services experienced by the customers throughout the overall purchase and ownership experiences. This includes any factors that bear upon customer preference or customer view of quality — for example, those features that enhance them or differentiate them from competing offerings.

(3) An applicant may choose to describe its offerings, part of its offerings, or certain of its activities as products or services irrespective of the SIC classification of the company. Such descriptions should then be consistent throughout the Application Report.

7.2 Customer Relationship Management (50 pts.)

Describe how the company provides effective management of its relationships with its customers and uses information gained from customers to improve products and services as well as its customer relationship management practices.

AREAS TO ADDRESS

a. means for ensuring easy access for customers to seek assistance and to comment. Describe types of contact, such as telephone, personal, and written, and how the company maintains easy access for each type of contact.

b. follow-up with customers on products and services to determine satisfaction with recent transactions and to seek data and information for improvement

c. how the following are addressed for customer-contact personnel: (1) selection factors for customer-contact jobs; (2) career path; (3) special training to include: knowledge of products and services, listening to customers, soliciting comment from customers, how to anticipate and handle special problems or failures, and skills in customer retention; (4) empowerment and decision making; (5) attitude and morale determination; (6) recognition and reward; and (7) attrition

d. how the company provides technology and logistics support for customer-contact personnel to enable them to provide reliable and responsive services

e. how the company analyzes key customer-related data and information to assess costs and market consequences for policy development, planning, and resource allocation

f. principal factors the company uses to evaluate its customer relationship management, such as response accuracy, timeliness, and customer satisfaction with contacts. Describe how the factors or indicators are used to improve training, technology, or customer-oriented management practices.

Notes:

(1) Other key aspects of customer relationship management are addressed in Items 7.3, 7.4, and 7.5.

(2) Item 7.2c addresses important human resource management requirements specifically for customer-contact personnel. This is included in Item 7.2 for special emphasis and coherence.

7.3 Customer Service Standards (20 pts.)

Describe the company's standards governing the direct contact between its employees and customers and how these standards are set and modified.

AREAS TO ADDRESS

a. how well-defined service standards to meet customer requirements are set. List and briefly describe the company's most important customer service standards.

b. how standards requirements and key standards information are deployed to company units that support customer-contact personnel. Briefly describe how the company ensures that the support provided by these company units is effective and timely.

c. how service standards are tracked, evaluated, and improved. Describe the role of customer-contact personnel in evaluating and improving standards.

Note: *Service standards are objectively measurable levels of performance that define quality for the overall service or for a part of a service. Examples include measures of response time, problem resolution time, accuracy, and completeness.*

7.4 Commitment to Customers *(15 pts.)*

Describe the company's commitments to customers on its explicit and implicit promises underlying its products and services.

AREAS TO ADDRESS

a. types of commitments the company makes to promote trust and confidence in its products, services, and relationships. Include how the company ensures that these commitments: (1) address the principal concerns of customers; (2) are free from conditions that might weaken customer confidence; and (3) are understandable.

b. how improvements in the quality of the company's products and services over the past three years have been translated into stronger commitments. Compare commitments with those of competing companies.

Note: *Commitments may include product and service guarantees, product warranties, and other understandings with the customer, expressed or implied.*

7.5 Complaint Resolution for Quality Improvement *(25 pts.)*

Describe how the company handles complaints, resolves them, and uses complaint information for quality improvement and for prevention of recurrence of problems.

AREAS TO ADDRESS

a. how the company ensures that formal and informal complaints and feedback given to different company units are aggregated for overall evaluation and use wherever appropriate throughout the company

b. how the company ensures that complaints are resolved promptly and effectively. Include: (1) trends and levels in indicators of response time; and (2) trends in percent of complaints resolved on first contact with customer-contact personnel.

c. how complaints are analyzed to determine underlying causes and how the findings are translated into improvements. This translation may lead to improvements such as in processes, service standards, training of customer-contact personnel, and information to customers to help them make more effective use of products and/or services.

d. key indicators and methods the company uses to evaluate and improve its complaint-related processes. Describe how indicators and methods address effectiveness, response time improvement, and translation of findings into improvements.

Notes:

(1) A major purpose of aggregation of complaint information is to ensure overall evaluation for policy development, planning, training, and resource allocation. However, this does not imply that complaint resolution and quality improvement should await aggregation or that resolution and improvement are necessarily centralized within a company.

(2) Trends and current levels in complaints are requested in Item 7.7.

7.6 Determining Customer Satisfaction *(20 pts.)*

Describe the company's methods for determining customer satisfaction, how satisfaction information is used in quality improvement, and how methods for determining customer satisfaction are improved.

AREAS TO ADDRESS

a. how the company determines customer satisfaction for customer groups. Address: (1) brief description of market segments and customer groups; and (2) the process for determining customer satisfaction for customer groups. Include what information is sought, frequency of surveys, interviews or other contacts, and how objectivity is assured. Describe how the company sets the customer satisfaction measurement scale to adequately capture key information that accurately reflects customer preference.

b. how customer satisfaction relative to competitors is determined

c. how customer satisfaction data are analyzed and compared with other customer satisfaction indicators such as complaints and gains and losses of customers. Describe how such comparisons are used to improve customer satisfaction determination.

d. how the company evaluates and improves its overall methods and measurement scales used in determining customer satisfaction and customer satisfaction relative to competitors

Notes:

(1) Information sought in determining customer satisfaction may include specific product and service features and the relative importance of these features to customers, thus supplementing information sought in determining customer requirements and expectations.

(2) The customer satisfaction measurement scale may include both numerical designators and the descriptors assigned to them. An effective scale is one that provides the company with accurate information about specific product and service features and about the customers' likely market behaviors.

7.7 Customer Satisfaction Results *(70 pts.)*

Summarize trends in the company's customer satisfaction and in indicators of adverse customer response.

AREAS TO ADDRESS

a. trends and current levels in indicators of customer satisfaction for products and services. Segment these results by customer groups, as appropriate.

b. trends and current levels in major adverse indicators. Adverse indicators include complaints, claims, refunds, recalls, returns, repeat services, litigation, replacements, downgrades, repairs, warranty costs, and warranty work. If the company has received any sanctions under regulation or contract over the past three years, include such information in this Item. Briefly describe how sanctions were resolved or current status.

7.8 Customer Satisfaction Comparison *(70 pts.)*

Compare the company's customer satisfaction results and recognition with those of competitors that provide similar products and services.

AREAS TO ADDRESS

a. comparison of customer satisfaction results. Such comparisons should be made with principal competitors in the company's key markets, industry averages, industry leaders, and world leaders.

b. surveys, competitive awards, recognition, and ratings by independent organizations, including customers. Briefly describe surveys, awards, recognition, and ratings. Include how quality and quality attributes are considered as factors in the evaluations of these independent organizations.

c. trends in gaining or losing customers and in customer and customer account retention. Briefly summarize gains and losses of customers, including those gained from or lost to competitors. Address customer groups or market segments, as appropriate.

d. trends in gaining and losing market share relative to major competitors, domestic and foreign. Briefly explain significant changes in terms of quality comparisons and quality trends.

ABOUT THE AUTHORS

C. Philip Alexander is president of Ann Arbor Consulting Associates, Inc., specializing in quality and human systems development. He holds graduate degrees in engineering and business from Case Western Reserve University and the University of California-Berkeley. He is a senior member of ASQC.

Charles E. Bobbitt, Jr., is plastics laboratory manager, supplier quality engineering, Motorola, Inc., Phoenix, AZ.

Edward J. Broeker is director of quality assurance for Nekoosa Packaging's three paper mills and 20 corrugated box plants. He holds a bachelor degree in education from Northwestern University.

Don Clausing is the Bernard M. Gordon Adjunct Professor of Engineering Innovation and Practice at MIT. He has edited Genichi Taguchi's works in English and is a leading exponent of his views. Mr. Clausing is formerly with Xerox.

Roland A. Dumas, Ph.D. is an independent researcher, writer and consultant in total quality management. He is affiliated with the Japan-based Kaizen Institute and the Achieve Group in Canada. Mr. Dumas serves on the Malcolm Baldrige National Quality Award Board of Examiners.

Roger L. Hale is president and chief executive officer of Tennant Company, Minneapolis.

John Hillkirk reports on business for *USA Today*.

Douglas R. Hoelscher is vice president of engineering/manufacturing/purchasing, Tennant Company, Minneapolis.

Lawrence Holpp is a senior consultant at Development Dimensions International, Pittsburgh.

Masaaki Imai has helped more than 200 non-Japanese joint-venture companies adopt Japanese management approaches. He is chairman and founder of the Tokyo-based Cambridge Corporation, an international management consulting and executive recruiting firm.

Gary Jacobson reports on business for *The Dallas Morning News*.

Ronald E. Kowal is director of manufacturing/purchasing, Tennant Company, Minneapolis.

K. Theodor Krantz spent 20 years in manufacturing with American Standard, CertainTeed, and Saint Gobain, the French building products maker. In 1983, he became chief financial officer of Velcro Industries N.V., a Netherlands Antilles company. A year later, he became president of its subsidiary, Velcro USA.

Joseph Oberle is staff editor of *TRAINING* magazine.

Bill Smith is senior quality assurance manager, Communications Sector, Motorola, Inc.

Genichi Taguchi is executive director of the American Supplier Institute and director of the Japan Industrial Technology Transfer Association. He is author of *The System of Experimental Design* (ASI Press, 1987). In 1989 Mr. Taguchi received MITI's Purple Ribbon Award from the emperor of Japan for his contribution to Japanese industrial standards.

Barbara J. Young is program director of Kodak Express at Kodak Australiasia Ltd. in Australia. She holds a M.S. degree in statistics from the University of Wyoming and is an ASQC certified quality engineer.

REQUIRED READING FOR HUMAN RESOURCES PROFESSIONALS

MAIL ORDERS TO:

LAKEWOOD BOOKS
50 South Ninth Street, Minneapolis, MN 55402
800-328-4329 or **612-333-0471**
to charge your order, or for quantity discounts.

Please send me the following publications:

Qty.	Title	$ Amount
_____	Adult Learning In Your Classroom. $19.95.	_____
_____	Creative Training Techniques Handbook. By Bob Pike. $45.95.	_____
_____	Designing and Delivering Cost-Effective Training—And Measuring the Results. $39.95.	_____
_____	Effective Training Delivery. $19.95.	_____
_____	Evaluating Training. $19.95.	_____
_____	Instructing for Results. By Fredric Margolis and Chip R. Bell. $19.95.	_____
_____	Performance Technology. $19.95.	_____
_____	Service Wisdom: Creating and Maintaining the Customer Service Edge. By Ron Zemke and Chip R. Bell. $19.95.	_____
_____	Training Terms. $19.95.	_____
_____	Understanding Training: Perspectives and Practices. By Fredric Margolis and Chip R. Bell. $19.95.	_____
_____	What Works at Work: Lessons From the Masters. By George Dixon. $29.95.	_____
_____	Creative Training Techniques Newsletter. 12 issues/yr. $89 U.S.; $99 Canada; $109 Other Foreign.	_____
_____	The Service Edge Newsletter. 12 issues/yr. $98 U.S.; $108 Canada; $118 Other Foreign.	_____
_____	Total Quality Newsletter. 12 issues/yr. $128 U.S.; $138 Canada; $148 Other Foreign.	_____
_____	Training Directors' Forum Newsletter. 12 issues/yr. $118 U.S.; $128 Canada; $138 Other Foreign.	_____

SUBTOTAL	**Subtotal:**	_____
In Canada add 7% GST# 123705485 *(applies to all products)*	**Add GST:**	_____
In MN add 7% sales tax; in WI add 5% sales tax *(does not apply to newsletters)*	**Add Tax:**	_____
Add $4 for first book; $3 each additional book for shipping & handling.	**Add S&H:**	_____
TOTAL	**Total Amount Enclosed:**	_____

☐ Check or money order is enclosed. Check payable to Lakewood Publications. (U.S. Funds)

☐ Please charge: ☐ VISA ☐ MasterCard ☐ American Express

Card # _____ Exp. _____/_____ Signature _____
(Required for Credit Card use)

NAME _____

TITLE _____

COMPANY _____

ADDRESS _____

CITY _____ STATE _____ ZIP _____

PHONE (_____)_____

H363

ORDER FORM MISSING?
Call 800-328-4329
or 612-333-0471
and ask for an up-to-date catalog of
Lakewood books and publications for
managers and human resources professionals.

Mail Your Order Form
and Payment Today To:

Lakewood Books
50 South Ninth Street
Minneapolis, MN 55402